THE FLAVORS OF
SICILY

THE FLAVORS OF
SICILY

BY ANNA TASCA LANZA
FOREWORD BY CAROL FIELD
PHOTOGRAPHS BY ALESSANDRO LEONE

CLARKSON POTTER/PUBLISHERS
NEW YORK

ALSO BY ANNA TASCA LANZA

The Heart of Sicily

DESIGN BY
Donna Agajanian

FRONTISPIECE: *Zibibbo grapes on the vine.*

Text copyright © 1996 by Anna Tasca Lanza

Photos copyright © 1996 by Alessandro Leone

Published by Clarkson N. Potter, Inc./Publishers, 201 East 50th Street,
New York, New York 10022. Member of the Crown Publishing Group.

Random House, Inc. New York, Toronto, London, Sydney, Auckland

CLARKSON N. POTTER, POTTER, and colophon are trademarks of
Clarkson N. Potter, Inc.

Printed in the U.S.A.

Library of Congress Cataloging-in-Publication Data

Lanza, Anna Tasca.

The flavors of Sicily : stories, traditions, and recipes for warm-
weather cooking / Anna Tasca Lanza. — 1st ed.

Includes index.

1. Cookery, Italian—Sicilian style. 2. Food habits—Italy-Sicily.

I. Title.

TX723.2.S55L34   1996   96-1149

641.59458—dc20   CIP

ISBN 0-517-70079-4

10   9   8   7   6   5   4   3   2   1

First Edition

FOR
FABRIZIA AND LUCA
RUGGERO AND VIRGINIA
WHO ARE MY LIFE

ACKNOWLEDGMENTS

No book is a solo venture, and I would like to thank all the people who helped me with this one. Judith Weber, my agent, believed in me and encouraged me from the beginning. Her hard work and her affection are very precious to me. She is a born diplomat. Roy Finamore, my editor, has, as always, drawn on his not inconsiderable talents to make this a very handsome book and to guide it home. His faith in me has touched me deeply.

Above all, I would like to thank Susan Derecskey, my alter ego, who helped me write this book, as she did with *The Heart of Sicily*, reading my mind with uncanny precision. I won't ever forget our games of "Ping-Pong," when the faxes were going back and forth so fast it seemed we were across a table instead of across an ocean. Thank you, Susan, for all you have done for me.

I would like, too, to thank all my other friends in America and in Europe who have taken an interest in my work and who have helped me in countless ways, big and little. Their enthusiasm and support have strengthened my resolve to continue to document the folkways of my native land. A special thank-you to all those who have come to visit and cook with me at Regaleali and who have shared their knowledge and cooking wisdom with me.

I also owe a debt to the people of Sicily, who have aided me in my research with generosity and a spirit of adventure.

And, of course, a big thank-you to my family—to my parents, whose love follows me wherever I go, whatever I do; to my sisters and my brother and their children, who have been so loving and helpful; to my daughter and son-in-law and the grandchildren, who brought the joy of youth back into my life. I especially want to thank Vences, my husband, for not objecting to having a fax machine in the living room.

ABOVE: *Ladles for cheese making hang in the caseificio.*

ABOVE: *Bread sculpted into a cluster of grapes for San Giuseppe's day.*

CONTENTS

THE RECIPES

FOREWORD
by Carol Field

When Anna Tasca Lanza wrote her first book, *The Heart of Sicily*, she took us inside the family estate at Regaleali to meet her extraordinary parents, their *monzù*, or chef, Mario Lo Menzo, the shepherds and gardeners and bread bakers, and brought up deep insights into the food and culture that have been part of her family's life for decades. Now Anna ventures beyond the gates of Regaleali as a wise, wry, and passionate guide to a Sicily known only to insiders. Come along, she says, in her strong authoritative voice, to eat and celebrate some of Sicily's great festivities and then join me, my sisters and my brothers-in-law, my nieces and nephews, and my friends on our informal holidays.

Anna's itinerary links the extraordinary flavors of the products of earth and sea with her childhood memories of food, with Sicilian folklore and regional tradition. She introduces us to the deep tastes of fruits and vegetables nourished by the strong Sicilian sun. She wants us to know how many kinds of lemons and oranges grow and what they taste like and how to cook with them; she encourages us to suck the sweetness from apricots as tiny as grapes and as sugary as honey, to taste sorb apples and snuffbox peaches with their ambrosial juices, and to let our tongues linger over the flavor of jam made from amazingly aromatic Zibibbo grapes. She takes us to Pantelleria, where caper plants grow in the volcanic soil and their buds are preserved in crystals of sea salt. She is determined that we taste sea urchins and their golden roe as she has since ambulatory fishermen arrived in her parents' garden with baskets of their spiny catch.

Nothing daunts the intrepid Anna. Not the skepticism of her family and helpers when she embarks on experiments to make foods as they were made in the past, nor the awesome task of spreading the hand-squeezed juice of four thousand pounds of tomatoes on tables and waiting one week to produce two hundred pounds of a bright, sweet-tasting sun-dried tomato paste. No wonder it is legendary! Watching Anna in her kitchen, where she is always in action, and following her on her rounds of little-known Sicilian island towns, it becomes clear that she has a vocation and a true passion for preserving the tastes and traditions of Sicilian food as a way of preserving the culture.

I can personally attest to her fascination because I've been lucky enough to spend time with Anna. Before I ever went to Regaleali, I'd been to Sicily in the course of doing research on festivals and great moments in the agricultural calendar when food is brought forth in astonishing plenty. And I had seen bakers making some of the great number of indigenous breads. But Sicily through Anna Tasca Lanza's eyes is an experience apart—just as walking across the carpet of wild chamomile in the courtyard of her house, smelling the fragrance released as we arrive at her front door, is a powerful sensory introduction to her passion for Sicilian plants, agriculture, and tradition.

Yes, I love being at Regaleali with her wonderful parents, but I also love it when Anna gets behind the wheel of her car and we go off together to nearby inland villages set in the profoundly satisfying landscape with its softly swelling hills and rich grasses that appear almost blue in some lights. Sometimes we race along, but mostly we amble, so we don't miss the remarkable countryside. She waves her hand in a broad sweeping gesture to point out swathes of red sulla, French honeysuckle, which is still used as forage for animals, and her voice rises, encouraging me to look closely at the fields of scarlet and magenta sweet peas to see if I can spot hives seeded there by beekeepers. (Later we will taste the remarkable honey that results.) She pulls off at the side of the road, encouraging me to pick some sambuco, the umbrella-shaped flower whose tiny white blossoms are sometimes used to flavor breads and desserts. When I put a single stalk in my room, the entire space is perfumed as if by an enormous bouquet. We've gone together to neighboring villages where she stops to shop or trade recipes or gather information while chatting with whole family groups clustered together on the front step while they shell peas or fava beans.

Yes, this is Anna's informal Sicily, where we are as likely to be hearing about the incomparable Sicilian balm, *mostardo di mosto*, a grape gelatina studded with nuts, as we are to be tasting Easter lamb roasted with red wine or spaghettini with artichokes or peach granita or *fuoco*, a homemade hot pepper sauce. It isn't just that she has delicious and inviting simple country food and recipes—although she certainly does—but she sets all these true tastes and ingredients of Sicily in the context of the people, the artisans, the beautiful islands that give them life and wraps them in the embrace of a culture of enduring fascination.

INTRODUCTION

When my first book, *The Heart of Sicily*, was published, I thought I would never write another. I had said everything I wanted to say, I'd made new friends, had a good time. But then I began thinking about all the things I hadn't said. I had hardly touched on old customs and traditions beyond the borders of Regaleali, the Tasca estate and winery, and I also wanted to tell about new discoveries that I'd made after I finished *Heart*. My curiosity and my determination to record as many aspects of daily life as I could, at least in the domain of food, kept calling me back.

Gradually, I began to focus on the sun, a powerful natural force in Sicily, which blesses everything that grows there with intense flavor and which shapes the daily life and beliefs of the people. I began to see how the flavors and festivals of Sicily were intertwined. I began to appreciate how dependent they were on the passage of the sun, which shines on the island relentlessly, beating down on it almost every day of the year but especially from mid-March through September.

The abundant fertility of Sicily and, of course, its strategic position as the largest island in the Mediterranean, lying athwart all the shipping routes and situated off the coast of Africa like a stepping-stone to Europe, made it a crossroads of conquest since ancient times. Artifacts dating back to the Phoenicians have been found on the island of Motia, near Marsala. Traces of the early Greeks endure, both objects, like amphorae and clepsydrae of the type used by the Minoans, and foods. The Greeks, in their drive westward in the time of Graecia Magna, brought the olive, to this day a key element of Sicilian domestic economy. Malvasia, a very sweet wine for which dried and freshly picked grapes are crushed together, is made today in Salina in the Eolian Islands in the same way as it was in ancient Greece. Cheese is still made as Homer described it in *The Odyssey*.

Under the Romans, Sicily grew wheat, hard durum wheat that could be stored against times of famine, and for centuries Sicily was known as "the granary of Rome." During a certain period, it was fashionable for a Roman family to have a Sicilian cook, and many Sicilian dishes were recorded in the Latin literature. Mamertino, a Sicilian wine, became famous under the Romans; it is said that Julius Caesar toasted with it. The wine is still produced around Messina and sold locally; it is now used mainly for making sweet desserts.

The Latins were followed in around 800 by the Arabs, who ruled for about three hundred years. The Arabs had a profound influence on all areas of Sicilian life. Where food was concerned, they spread the practice of gardening by encouraging small plots, as opposed to the Roman system of large estates suited to growing wheat. The Arabs introduced their highly developed methods of irrigation to Sicily as well as citrus, rice, and sugarcane. Consequently, the Sicilians had sugar long before the rest of Europe, and they used it to make extraordinary sweetmeats, including marzipan. The Sicilian way with sweets—and the notorious Sicilian sweet tooth—have deep Arab roots.

The Arabs also brought pasta, previously unknown, in the form of noodles. Wine making, however, ceased because of the prohibitions of the Koran, but the Arabs brought the Zibibbo grape to Sicily, a name which in their language means raisin but which for us means the very best table grape, big and juicy and full of heavenly flavor. We owe the association of pleasure with food to the Arabs as well.

From the culinary point of view, the next important invaders were the Spaniards, who introduced the foods of the New World to Sicily— tomatoes, peppers, squash, and beans, and, of less significance to Sicilians, potatoes and corn. It's almost impossible to think of Sicilian cuisine without tomatoes, peppers, and zucchini, but they are, in fact, relative newcomers.

After the end of Arab rule, wine making resumed. By the mid-nineteenth century, Sicilian wine was enjoying a certain fame in Europe, mainly Marsala. Because of the Napoleonic Wars, the English—who were particularly fond of fortified wines such as port and sherry—were cut off from Portugal and Spain. They found that the vineyards around Marsala resembled the Spanish *terroir*, and they developed a wine similar to sherry. Marsala wine is still very much in use in the Sicilian kitchen—and on the Sicilian table.

In the past, Sicilian table wines were appreciated for their intense color, strong body, and high alcohol content. They were very useful for blending. But over the past twenty years, a revolution has taken place in Sicilian wine making. The vineyards have been done over, new varieties planted, and modern methods of wine making introduced. The result has been fine wines that draw special nuances from the Sicilian soil and sun and can compete on the world market with the best Europe and California have to offer.

I am proud that the Tasca family, starting with my father and now with my brother and his sons carrying on the tradition, has been a leader in the modernization of the Sicilian wine industry. Our Chardonnay and Cabernet Sauvignon wines have won many top prizes in European competitions. Regaleali's latest wine is the Nozze di Diamante, a dessert wine, which my father made and presented to my mother on their sixtieth (diamond) wedding anniversary on June 3, 1995.

At the beginning of the twentieth century, Sicily went through a time of remarkable splendor, La Belle Epoque. The cuisine of the island was greatly influenced by social changes during this period. Wealthy families hired *monzù* chefs, who were trained in the tradition of French haute cuisine, to which they brought their own touches of Sicilian fantasy. It was a baronial cuisine—rich, lavish, and elaborate.

The cuisine of the common people could not have been more different—simple and poor, based mainly on foods they could cultivate: durum wheat flour for bread and pasta, fresh vegetables, and dried peas and beans. Meat appeared on the table rarely, mainly during religious festivals. The choice was lamb, rabbit, pigeon, or *gadduzzu* (*rooster* in dialect).

The two cuisines, however, shared an appreciation for a certain balance of ingredients and flavors that had evolved over the centuries. Pasta knew no social barriers. Simple pasta dishes—pasta with tomato sauce, pasta with anchovies and breadcrumbs, pasta with oil and garlic—appeared on the tables of aristocrats as well as peasants. Both classes loved sweets. Sicilians relish elaborate arrangements of shapes and colors in their food. Marzipan extravaganzas like the *trionfo di gola* (literally, the triumph of gluttony, a marzipan-covered cake) and the *grappola* (a cluster of marzipan grapes), and the baroque biscuits of Pantelleria and the Eolian Islands continue to excite the Sicilian imagination.

Sicilians love a celebration, with lots of food and many different dishes. From the groaning tables of San Giuseppe's day to the picnics of Pasquetta to the grand buffets for family and friends on Santa

Rosalia's day in Palermo or on Ferragosto everywhere on the island, Sicilians enjoy the sense of plenitude and display.

Sicilians love to cook, and they love to eat. The modern urban lifestyle is rapidly eroding many culinary traditions, but they are still strong in the countryside.

The country people of Sicily have been very generous to me, inviting me into their homes and sharing with me their cooking traditions and secrets. I hope I have repaid their trust and my heritage by recording in this book the past that remains alive today. It is my hope to tell that story to readers around the world, both to those Sicilians who left their native land to seek their fortune and to people everywhere who care about history as it was lived by everyman.

Anna Tasca Lanza
Regaleali

OVERLEAF: *Approaching Rinella on Salina in the Eolian Islands.*

MARZO

Framed by a window no bigger than a Bible, a brilliant moon lights the entire countryside. The smell of the flowers and trees coming into bloom is dizzying. All you can hear is the white owl, hooting and breathing hard. The cool breeze of the night makes you want to go on forever. This is how spring begins in Sicily.

We only recently started putting big windows in houses in the country. There used to be no heat, and small windows keep out the bite of the tramontana (north wind). In fact, when you drive from Palermo to Regaleali, the Tasca winery and agricultural estate where I have my cooking school and make my home, one of the first things that strikes you about Vallelunga, the nearest village, is that there are no windows in the walls that face north. It is as if some awful thing happened there that has to be kept hidden from view. But it is only the wind.

LEFT: *Fierce winds blow across the land, leaving some patches barren.*

SAN GIUSEPPE

Behind those walls and shuttered small windows, the celebrations and votive offerings the outside world knows nothing about take place. In Sicily, many people still make such offerings to the saints. Someone who had a car accident and survived or who suffered a mysterious illness and recovered, for example, might make a vow to remember publicly the saint to whom he prayed.

The saint most often honored in this way is San Giuseppe (Saint Joseph), whose feast day is March 19, very near the first day of spring. It is my father's name day, so we have always observed it in our own way at Regaleali. And I've always known, of course, about the fanciful breads and ornate bread altars that you find all over Sicily, even though we don't construct them ourselves.

BREAD ALTARS

Some of the most elaborate of these bread altars (called *cene di San Giuseppe* in Italian) can be found in the town of Salemi, about 50 miles (80 km) southwest of Palermo. The townspeople there really enter into the spirit of the custom, setting up mini altars in shop windows, right amid their displays of shoes or jewelry or other goods. Outstanding examples of the craft are collected and displayed in the local folk art museum.

Every year, starting about a week before the feast, altars are erected in homes, schools, and public places. The first time I saw these altars, they took my breath away. The official town altar is the most elaborate of them all. The men of Salemi construct open chapels of wood and metal scaffolding, which they cover with branches of myrtle and laurel and hang with lemons and oranges. They set up the altar inside and cover it with a white cloth. A picture of the Holy Family or the familiar portrait of San Giuseppe cradling the Christ Child in one arm and holding a lily in his other hand is hung over the altar.

Meanwhile, the women of Salemi have been busy baking breads for the altars. This *pane di decorazione*, a bread that is not meant to be eaten, is made of a special dough that the women mold and cut into shapes based on symbols traditionally associated with the Holy Family. Making these breads is considered an offering to the saint.

Working with nimble fingers, sharp knives, and pointy scissors, the women of Salemi create new breads every year. Human inventiveness and skill transform the basic shapes into objects of art. Some of the breads are almost childlike in their simplicity; others are truly baroque, with swirls and curlicues and delicate openwork. The bread is glazed, then baked until shiny.

The larger breads are arranged on the altar in their ordained places with a large star or flower representing Christ, the light and perfume of life, in the center. To one side are symbols of the Virgin—a branch of palm, representing peace, and a halo—to the other, symbols of Joseph—his staff sprouting a lily and his carpenter's tools. Certain symbolic foods are placed on the altar as well: dates, which nourished Mary during the flight from Egypt, and fava beans and sprouting corn—spring's first growth and a sign of the earth's renewal. Smaller symbolic breads are hung on the chapel framework along with the citrus fruit.

After the altars are blessed and viewed, the townspeople go home to sit down to huge banquets. The exact dishes vary somewhat from family to family, but pasta with olive oil, breadcrumbs, parsley, and sugar is sure to be on the table. Ever since the Arabs introduced the cultivation of sugar to Sicily, Sicilians have been seasoning their food with it— though usually not their pasta. This unique sugared pasta used to be served in individual bowls, to be eaten with the hands. Now it is served on a platter like any other pasta and eaten with a fork.

With each dish, there are shouts of *"Evviva San Giuseppe!"* (Long live Saint Joseph!) and a drumroll to drive away evil spirits. At the end of the meal, each person is given a big piece of a consecrated loaf to keep in the house until the next San Giuseppe's day. It is supposed to bring fertility and good fortune in the coming year.

LE VERGINEDDE

In other towns and villages in Sicily, the traditional meal "at the invitation of San Giuseppe" is offered by some families. Customs differ from place to place. In some villages, children are invited to the feast to play the roles of Jesus, Mary, and Joseph. In Vallelunga and Valledolmo, the villages nearest to Regaleali, it used to be *le verginedde*, maidens from the countryside, who were invited. These days this special meal is more of a social occasion, an opportunity for young people to get together.

Each *verginedde*'s place is set with a wineglass and a *Pane di San Giuseppe* (page 28), a loaf of bread usually formed in the shape of San Giuseppe's beard and covered with white poppy seeds (*Papaver somniferum*). (White poppy seeds are used rarely—only for certain saint's days like San Giuseppe—because cultivation is restricted to private use.) Two fruits and two vegetables—an orange and a citron, a fennel bulb and a head of romaine lettuce—are also at each place. The number of *verginedde* invited depends on the host's generosity. The first time I attended such a feast, there were twenty-five, though six to twelve is more common.

San Giuseppe's presence is signified by a statue or portrait with candles and flowers on either side. The table is laden with dishes of every description. There used to be no meat since the feast of San Giuseppe falls during Lent, but those rules have been relaxed in recent years.

In Valledolmo, where the villagers are known to flaunt their affluence, the tables are much more elaborately set than those in Vallelunga. They are tiered, with the trousseaux of the *verginedde* around the lowest tier and the desserts on the highest one.

It was at one of the homes in Vallelunga, though, that I first saw *Pesche delle Due Sicilie* (Pastry Peaches, page 32). They were made by a local woman, one of those passionate home bakers who like to duplicate pastries they've seen or tasted elsewhere. Since these have no official name but are sold in pastry shops in Naples, I decided to call them after the Kingdom of the Two Sicilies.

The peaches are elaborate but not difficult to make. They get their blush from alchermes, a crimson liqueur that is made with spices and scented with rose, jasmine, and iris. The sale of alchermes has been banned in the United States because it contains cochineal, a red dye prepared from dried insects. Frankly, I don't understand this: People have been drinking alchermes for centuries without ill effects. To get the same peach color, you will have to use something else.

I made another interesting discovery in Valledolmo: stuffed birds on the San Giuseppe tables. You might see a wild duck standing on the table with its beak in a bowl of *sfince* (cream puffs) or find a heron in a corner of the room "eating" a doughnut.

Migratory water birds fly over central Sicily on their way to and from their winter habitat—heading south in the week of I Morti in November, north in the week of San Giuseppe. Many people believe that the birds bring rain, perhaps because it does rain then.

One evening as I came out of Case Vecchie, my home, a very large bird was flying in circles overhead, squawking like mad. I found Carmelo Di Martino, the caretaker, standing in the middle of the courtyard with his *coppola* (cap) on topsy-turvy, with the lining toward the sky. I was flabbergasted. I certainly had never seen that before! In all seriousness, Carmelo explained to me that if you put your cap on upside down, the birds will go crazy, crying and trying to bite each other, until you put your cap back on the right way. Then they will form a V and fly away.

On San Giuseppe's day, the table literally groans under the weight of all the food. Many different dishes, especially fried foods, are prepared in advance and served cold.

Both savory and sweet dishes abound—delicacies like battered and fried vegetables, *Sfince di San Giuseppe* (Fried Cream Puffs, page 31) in honor of the saint, and baked ones, *Sfince Infornate* (page 35). You'll find fried dough rings known in dialect as *Cuddureddi* (page 29), the ever-present *Cannoli* (page 34), and a few cookies, like *Amaretti* (page 36).

Fresh fava beans and *Macco* (page 39), pureed dried fava beans, a dish that dates back to antiquity, are obligatory. Other cooked bean dishes include *Pasta e Lenticchie* (Pasta with Lentils, page 40) and *Pasta e Ceci* (Pasta with Chick Pea Puree, page 41). All of these dishes are eaten on this day at room temperature.

Pasta con le Sarde al Pomodoro (Pasta with Sardines and Tomato Sauce, page 42), with such classic Sicilian flavors as wild fennel, pine nuts, and currants, is served. In some homes the dish is prepared with a sweetened breadcrumb topping. *Baccalà* (salt cod) that's been floured and fried is usually on the table as well.

Egg dishes include hard-boiled eggs, some of them fried and some not, and *Frittata al Formaggio* (page 47), a sheep cheese omelet that tastes best when left to stand and eaten at room temperature. Fresh and dried fruits are on the table in abundance.

Prominently displayed are a big whipped cream cake and a bowl of *Biancomangiare* (Blancmange, page 37), a very sweet cornstarch pudding that is made with milk or *Latte di Mandorle* (Almond Milk, page 37). It may be covered with any or all of the following: chocolate flakes, pistachios, almonds, a sprinkle of cinnamon, and *zuccata*, a preserve made from summer squash. Both the cake and the pudding are inscribed "*VV S. Giuseppe*"—Long live San Giuseppe—in chocolate on top and decorated all over with pink and silver candy confetti and tiny paper flags.

Pitchers of water and wine are set out on the table. Water is poured into each glass first, and then the wine is poured in very carefully. Being lighter than water, it stays on top.

On the morning of San Giuseppe, the villagers go from house to house comparing tables. They find plenty of food to sample at each one—and plenty to gossip about. At midday, the village priest makes the rounds to bless the tables.

Then, at last, everyone can sit down to eat. The host serves and the person who made the vow to San Giuseppe sits at the head of the table, shouting from time to time, "*Evviva San Giuseppe!*" Everyone shouts back, "*Evviva San Giuseppe!*"

In poorer villages, like Sclafani Bagni, there are no ornate communal altars, just simple altars at home with a picture of the saint flanked by candles and flowers. Nor is there a sumptuous display of food on the table, only a plate with two green olives, two black olives, and one orange segment at each place. A few simple dishes are served: everyday dishes like *Pasta e Fagioli Fredda* (Cold Pasta and Beans, page 43), *Riso e Lenticchie* (Rice and Lentils, page 44), and spaghetti with tomato sauce and breadcrumbs. Next come some fried vegetables: usually cauliflower, wild fennel, and *il cardo del pastore* (the shepherd's cardoon).

This vegetable is a real country delicacy. It is said that the shepherds, who know where all the wild plants grow, invented it so they would have something to take to their relatives when they went home at Carnival, their annual holiday. Weeks ahead of time, a shepherd would pick shoots of wild artichoke and wrap them with asphodel leaves until they were completely covered. Then he would bury them in the ground—only he knew where. When the *cardi* were dug up later, the shoots would be blanched white. These *cardi del pastore* have a subtle, delicate flavor. They are boiled briefly and prepared as salad with olive oil and salt and pepper, but they are especially good when battered and fried—the way they are prepared for San Giuseppe's table.

Dessert at these modest feasts in the poorer villages consists of *sfince, cannoli*, and fried bread dough with honey, which is called *guasteddi fritte* (fried rolls) at Sclafani. At the end of the meal, each guest is given a loaf of bread that has been blessed.

It's all great fun, but if you ask why this food or that is on the table, or why some other food is not on the table, the answer is always the same: "*Ma!* My mother and grandmother did it like this."

Mary Taylor Simeti, who has been observing our folkways since she married a Sicilian and settled here more than thirty years ago, thinks these customs go back to pagan times, that they are ways to propitiate the gods of the land. The four fruits and vegetables obviously mark the passing of the seasons—the end of winter (the orange and the citron) and the beginning of spring (the fennel and lettuce). I think it's also significant that certain foods that once were forbidden during Lent are eaten to break the long fast, since San Giuseppe usually falls about midway between Ash Wednesday and Easter Sunday.

Indeed, those fruits and vegetables are particularly good in Sicily at this time of year. Romaine lettuce and fennel are wonderful together in *Insalata di Lattuga Nostrana e Finocchio* (page 46). Since citrus is still plentiful, I always put some in the salad.

As the days grow longer and the hens are laying again, we also use more eggs, as in *Frittata di Verdura Amara* (page 48), an omelet made with bitter greens. The wild greens that are gathered in the countryside after there is rain are the best.

THE RECIPES

PANE DI SAN GIUSEPPE
Bread for San Giuseppe's Day

For San Giuseppe's Day, Sicilians sprinkle this bread with rare white poppy seeds (*Papaver somniferum*), which are used only on special occasions. Hulled sesame seeds give a similar look but a quite different flavor. This is a simple yeast-risen bread.

THIS MAKES 4 LARGE OR 8 SMALL LOAVES.

> *10 cups (4½ lb/2 kg) semolina flour (see Note)*
> *2 envelopes (7 g each) active dry yeast*
> *4 to 4½ cups (about 1 l) warm water*
> *2 tablespoons table salt or 1 tablespoon sea salt*
> *1 egg, lightly beaten with 1 teaspoon water, for glaze*
> *¼ cup (35 g) hulled sesame seeds*

Grind the flour, 3 cups at a time, in a food processor until silky to the touch, about 5 minutes. Whisk the yeast into 3 cups (700 ml) of the water in a large mixing bowl if mixing by hand or in the bowl of a heavy-duty mixer. Let stand for 5 minutes.

Add all but 1 cup (200 g) of the flour and the salt. With a wooden spoon or the paddle attachment, mix the flour into the yeast and beat until a dough forms. Turn out onto a floured surface or switch to the dough hook and start kneading the dough. Gradually add as much of the remaining 1 to 1½ cups water as the dough can absorb. Knead the dough until it is smooth and elastic, 15 to 20 minutes by hand, about 5 minutes by machine followed by 10 minutes by hand. Add more of the remaining 1 cup flour if the dough gets too wet and unmanageable.

Let the dough rest for about 5 minutes. For large San Giuseppe beards, divide the dough into 4 parts and curve each piece into a shape resembling the letter U. For small beards, cut the dough into 8 parts and shape each piece into a U. Dust large cloths with semolina and place the loaves on them, about 3 inches (7,5 cm) apart. Cover and let rise until doubled in bulk, about 1½ hours.

Preheat the oven to 400° F. (200° C.). Dust several baking sheets with semolina flour.

Using kitchen shears, make 3 deep cuts in the outer edge of each loaf, one in the middle and one on each side. Place the loaves on the baking sheets. Paint the loaves with the egg glaze and sprinkle with the sesame seeds.

Bake the loaves until golden brown and firm to the touch, 20 to 30 minutes for small loaves, 40 to 50 minutes for large loaves. Test by rapping on the bottom; the loaf should sound hollow. Cool on a wire rack.

NOTE. *Italian semolina flour is rimacinata, milled twice; it is finer than the semolina flour available in the United States. For bread with a texture most like the Sicilian, grind the American flour for a few minutes in a food processor.*

CUDDUREDDI
Sicilian Doughnuts

These dough rings are light and airy, and not at all greasy if you keep the oil hot and don't crowd the pan.

THIS MAKES 12 RINGS.

Pâte à choux (page 31)
All-purpose flour, for rolling the pastry balls
Vegetable oil, for frying
Confectioners' sugar, for dusting

Prepare the pastry dough as directed. Pinch off a walnut-size piece and roll the dough in the flour. Flour your finger and stick it through the middle to make a ring. Continue until all of the dough is used.

Heat 3 to 4 inches (8 to 10 cm) oil in a deep saucepan or deep-fat fryer until hot (365° F./185° C. on a candy thermometer or when a piece of dough dropped in the oil sizzles and floats on top). Carefully slip in several rings, as many as fit comfortably; do not crowd the pan. Fry the rings, turning with tongs as they brown on one side, until puffed and golden brown, about 5 minutes. Remove and drain on brown paper or paper towels. You will have to do the frying in batches, letting the oil get hot again before starting each new batch. Sprinkle with confectioners' sugar. Serve warm or at room temperature.

SFINCE DI SAN GIUSEPPE
Fried Cream Puffs

For San Giuseppe's day, these puffs are filled with Ricotta Cream, but in Salina in the Eolian Islands, where they are made for any occasion, they are simply rolled in cinnamon sugar.

THIS MAKES 24 PUFFS, 1 1/2 INCHES (4 CM) IN DIAMETER.

PÂTE À CHOUX

1 cup (250 ml) water
3 1/2 tablespoons (50 g) unsalted butter, cut into pieces
Pinch of salt
1 cup (150 g) all-purpose flour
3 eggs, at room temperature

Vegetable oil, for frying
Crema di Ricotta (page 33)

Combine the water, butter, and salt in a saucepan and heat until the butter melts and the water boils rapidly. Add the flour, all at once, and remove the pan from the heat. Stir until the mixture comes away from the sides of the pan. Let cool. (To speed up the cooling, you can turn the dough onto a marble slab and knead it until it is cool to the touch.) Put the dough in a bowl and knead in the eggs, one at a time, lifting the dough to incorporate air and lighten it.

Heat 3 to 4 inches (8 to 10 cm) oil in a deep saucepan or deep-fat fryer until hot (365° F./185° C. on a candy thermometer or when a piece of dough dropped in the oil sizzles and floats on the top). Spoon out almond-size pieces of dough and carefully push them off the spoon with your finger into the hot oil. Fry several at a time, but do not crowd the pot; the puffs need room to turn as they swell. Cook, turning with a skimmer or tongs, until golden brown on all sides, about 3 minutes. The puffs will triple in size. Remove and drain on brown paper or paper towels. You will have to do the frying in batches, letting the oil get hot again before starting each new batch.

When cool enough to handle, cut into the top and fill with Ricotta Cream. Serve at room temperature.

LEFT: *The tiny wild orchid still grows in secret places in Sicily.*

PESCHE DELLE DUE SICILIE

Pastry Peaches

Getting thirty perfect walnut half shells is tedious work, but once you have them, you can use them over and over again.

THIS MAKES 15 PASTRY PEACHES.

PASTRY SHELLS

30 or more large walnut half shells

Vegetable oil

2 cups (300 g) all-purpose flour

¾ cup (150 g) sugar

½ teaspoon baking powder

Pinch of salt

5 tablespoons (70 g) butter, margarine, or lard, cold, cut into ½-inch dice

2 large eggs

¼ teaspoon vanilla extract

2 cups (500 ml) heavy whipping cream

2 cups (500 ml) alchermes (see Note)

2 cups (400 g) sugar, for coating

Coat each shell lightly with vegetable oil.

Mix together the flour, ½ cup of the sugar, and the baking powder. Make a well and mix in the butter, eggs, and vanilla, using your fingers or a pastry blender, until crumbly. Squeeze the dough into a ball, cover, and let rest for 30 minutes.

While the dough is resting, whip the cream with the remaining ¼ cup sugar to soft peaks. Refrigerate until ready to use.

Preheat the oven to 300° F. (150° C.). Line and grease a baking sheet.

Take a rounded tablespoonful of dough, make a ball in the palm of your hand, and push the shell into it, spreading the dough to cover the shell. The dough should be about ⅜ inch (1 cm) thick.

Place on the baking sheet and bake for 30 to 35 minutes, or until pale golden. Detach the pastry shells from the walnuts. Cool thoroughly on a rack.

Pour half the alchermes in a small bowl and place half the sugar for coating in a flat soup bowl. Dip each shell into the alchermes, then roll in the sugar. Fill each half with whipped cream and put 2 halves together, like kissing couples. Pour more alchermes and more sugar into the bowls as needed.

Put the pastry peaches in a pretty bowl and serve.

NOTE. *The sale of alchermes is banned in the United States. I would suggest grenadine syrup or Campari as a substitute.*

CREMA DI RICOTTA
Ricotta Cream

Our ricotta, from the boiled whey of sheep's milk, has a tangier flavor and less homogeneous texture than the cow's milk ricotta found elsewhere. Sheep's milk ricotta is sometimes available in Italian grocery stores or from Paula Lambert's Mozzarella Company (page 252). If you want to approximate the tangy flavor, gradually mix a tiny bit of ricotta salata, a white, briefly cured sheep's milk cheese available in specialty food stores, into the drained ricotta, tasting as you go.

Traditionally, ricotta cream has *zuccata*, or squash preserve, and tiny bits of chocolate in it. You can substitute candied citron for *zuccata*. You need to start the Ricotta Cream the day before you want to use it.

THIS MAKES ABOUT 2 CUPS RICOTTA CREAM.

2 cups (1 lb/450 g) sheep's milk or whole cow's milk ricotta
About ½ cup (100 g) superfine sugar
½ teaspoon salt
½ cup miniature chocolate chips

Line a strainer with a piece of rinsed cheesecloth and spoon the ricotta into it or dump the ricotta directly into a fine-mesh plastic strainer. Set the strainer over a bowl, cover, and let drain in the refrigerator for several hours or overnight.

Pass the ricotta through a food mill or beat it with an electric mixer to lighten it. Add the sugar and salt and continue beating until light and fluffy. Stir in the chocolate chips. Cover and refrigerate until ready to use.

CANNOLI
Cannoli

Once you have metal cannoli tubes, which are available in most kitchenware stores, these pastries are amazingly simple to prepare.
THIS MAKES 8 CANNOLI.

CANNOLI SHELLS
> *1 cup (150 g) all-purpose flour*
> *½ teaspoon sugar*
> *1 teaspoon unsweetened cocoa powder*
> *1 tablespoon unsalted butter*
> *1 to 2 tablespoons red or white wine, Marsala, or Malvasia*
> *1 egg white, beaten with 1 teaspoon water*
> *Vegetable oil, for frying*
>
> *2 tablespoons miniature chocolate chips*
> *2 tablespoons chopped candied fruit, such as oranges or cherries*
> *½ recipe Crema di Ricotta (page 33)*

To make the shells, mix together the flour, sugar, and cocoa powder. Cut in the butter until crumbly. Add just enough wine for the dough to come together. Press into a ball, cover with plastic wrap or wax paper, and refrigerate for 30 minutes.

Divide the dough in half. Return one half to the refrigerator, and roll out the other into a 16 × 5-inch (40 × 14-cm) strip about ⅛ inch (0,3 cm) thick. Cut out 4 large 5 × 3½-inch (12,5 × 8-cm) ovals. Place a cannoli tube lengthwise on each one and bring up the sides to overlap slightly on top; brush with egg wash to seal.

Pour 3 to 4 inches (8 to 10 cm) oil in a deep-fryer or saucepan and heat to 365° F. (185° C.) or until a bit of pastry dropped into the oil sizzles immediately. Fry the cannoli a few at a time, without crowding the pot, turning with tongs, until golden brown, about 10 minutes. Remove and drain on paper towels. Remove the tubes while still warm.

Form the remaining cannoli, reheat the oil, fry, and drain on paper towels. The shells can be stored in an airtight container for 1 week.

Shortly before serving, mix the chocolate chips and candied fruit into the Ricotta Cream. Use a pastry bag fitted with a large plain tip or a small spoon to fill each shell.

SFINCE INFORNATE
Baked Cream Puffs

Plates of these delicate whipped cream–filled puffs find their place on San Giuseppe's tables. Sometimes the dough is shaped into swans.

THIS MAKES 2 DOZEN 1½-INCH (4-CM) PUFFS.

Pâte à Choux (page 31)
1 cup (250 ml) heavy cream
¼ cup (50 g) sugar

Preheat the oven to 375° F. (190° C.). Lightly grease a baking sheet.

Prepare the pastry dough as directed. Use a pastry bag fitted with a ½-inch (1,2-cm) plain tip to pipe the dough onto the baking sheet or drop it in almond-size mounds, 2 inches (5 cm) apart.

Bake until well puffed and golden, 20 to 25 minutes. Cool on racks.

Whip the cream, adding the sugar a tablespoon at a time, until quite stiff. When the puffs are cool enough to handle, cut into the top part of each one and fill with whipped cream.

ABOVE: *Prickly pear plants are a common sight in the countryside. The fruit, be it red or yellow, is very refreshing peeled and chilled.*

AMARETTI
Almond Cookies

Sicilian almonds are extraordinarily flavorful and oily, unlike almonds from California and other places. Adding some almond extract, which we do not use, to the cookie dough helps make up the difference. We would also include a few bitter almonds, which are prohibited in the United States, in a recipe like this. Because they were lacking, Michele Scicolone, who baked these cookies with me at Regaleali, reduced the amount of sugar in the ones she made when she got back home.

THIS MAKES 2 1/2 DOZEN COOKIES.

2¼ cups (10 oz/300 g) blanched almonds
⅔ cup (130 g) sugar
Grated zest of 1 lemon
2 egg whites
Salt
½ teaspoon almond extract
½ teaspoon vanilla extract
30 whole unblanched almonds, pine nuts, or candied cherries

Preheat the oven to 350° F. (180° C.). Butter and flour a large baking sheet.

Working in batches, combine the blanched nuts with some of the sugar in a food processor. Process until finely ground. Transfer to a large bowl, add the rest of the sugar and the lemon zest, and combine well.

Beat the egg whites with a pinch of salt and the almond and vanilla extracts until stiff but not dry. Add the egg white mixture to the almond mixture and stir lightly, not to flatten the egg whites. Pinch off enough dough to form a 1-inch (2,5-cm) ball. Flatten the balls very slightly, and place them 1 inch (2,5 cm) apart on the baking sheet. Insert a whole almond or pine nut, pointed end up, or a candied cherry in the center of each cookie.

Bake until the cookies are lightly browned and have small cracks on the surface, 25 to 30 minutes. Let cool briefly on the pan, then transfer to wire racks to cool completely. Store in an airtight container.

VARIATION. For flatter cookies, add 1 egg white. Spoon onto baking sheets about 1½ inches (3 cm) apart. Bake at 300° F. (150° C.) until lightly browned, about 20 minutes.

BIANCOMANGIARE
Blancmange

Blancmange, while no longer fashionable in some parts of the world, is still a very popular Sicilian dessert, especially in the countryside. It appears on every holiday buffet table, from San Giuseppe in March, through Il Festino in July and Ferragosto in August. We make two kinds, one with regular milk and the other with *Latte di Mandorle* (almond milk). In medieval times, blancmange was scented with rose water. If you like that flavor, stir in three to four tablespoons when you remove the pudding from the heat.

THIS MAKES ENOUGH FOR 8 PEOPLE.

> ½ cup plus 2 tablespoons (75 g) cornstarch
> 4 cups (1 l) milk, or Latte di Mandorle (recipe follows)
> ½ to ¾ cup (100 to 150 g) sugar
> Chopped pistachios, slivered almonds, bittersweet chocolate
>   flakes, ground cinnamon, and candied squash or citron,
>   for garnish

Combine the cornstarch and milk or almond milk in a saucepan and whisk until there are no lumps. Whisk in the sugar, ¾ cup if using milk, ½ cup if using almond milk. Put on low heat. Whisk constantly until the mixture comes to a boil. Boil for 1 minute and remove from the heat.

Pour into a bowl or dessert glasses. Cover with plastic wrap, pressing it directly on the surface. The pudding will thicken as it stands. Let cool to room temperature, then refrigerate until ready to serve.

Garnish the blancmange with any or all of the suggested garnishes. Serve cold.

LATTE DI MANDORLE
Almond Milk

A glass of cold almond milk with ice cubes is a good old-fashioned thirst quencher. Luca, my son-in-law, who lives in Verona in the north, loves it. We also sometimes use almond milk for *Biancomangiare* (above).

When we make almond milk in Sicily, we add some bitter almonds, about one tenth of the amount of regular almonds, but their sale is forbidden in the United States. Using almond extract helps compensate for their absence; add it gradually, tasting after each addition since almonds vary in intensity of flavor. The fresher they are, the more juice and taste you will get out of them.

THIS MAKES 4 CUPS (1 L).

> 1½ pounds (675 g) blanched almonds
> 6 cups (1,5 l) water
> 2 teaspoons almond extract
> 1 tablespoon sugar

Coarsely chop the almonds in a food processor. With the motor running, add the water a little at a time. (You may have to do this in batches.) Transfer to a bowl and add as much of the almond extract as you need to get a strong almond flavor. Let stand for 2 or 3 hours.

Strain through a double layer of rinsed cheesecloth and squeeze out as much almond milk as possible. Add the sugar a little at a time until sweetened to your taste. Refrigerate and serve chilled. Almond milk will keep for 2 days in the refrigerator.

ABOVE: *Flowers of the fava bean, grown in Sicily since antiquity.*

MACCO
Dried Fava Bean Puree

Dried fava beans have an extraordinary flavor, reminiscent of chestnuts. Unfortunately, they can be difficult to find, especially the peeled ones that are called for in this recipe. Dried favas with peels are dark brown. If you cannot find favas without peels, simmer the others until they soften, about 45 minutes. Squeeze out the beans as you would squeeze roasted garlic, and continue to simmer until they melt to a soft puree.

THIS MAKES ENOUGH FOR 4 PEOPLE.

2 cups (10 oz/300 g) dried peeled fava beans (see Note)
1 medium-size red onion, coarsely chopped
1 cup (60 g) chopped wild fennel or ½ cup (30 g) chopped dill
1 teaspoon sun-dried tomato paste dissolved in ¼ cup water
Salt and freshly ground black pepper
¼ cup olive oil
2 cups (100 g) toasted bread cubes

Soak the fava beans overnight in cold water to cover. Drain and rinse the pot.

Return the beans to the pot with fresh water to cover. Add the onion, wild fennel, and dissolved tomato paste, and bring to a boil. Reduce the heat and simmer, partly covered, until the beans disintegrate into a soft puree, at least 1 hour.

Season to taste with salt and pepper, drizzle with olive oil on top, and let cool to room temperature. Serve in individual bowls with toasted bread cubes.

NOTE. *Dried peeled fava beans are beige or yellow; in fact the package is sometimes labeled yellow favas. They are available in grocery stores catering to an Italian, Iranian, or Near Eastern clientele.*

PASTA E LENTICCHIE
Pasta with Lentils

Sicilian lentils are darker, smaller, and heavier than American lentils, which can, of course, be used in this recipe. (They will take a bit longer to cook.) French Le Puy lentils are more like the Sicilian ones; they are available in specialty food shops.

THIS MAKES ENOUGH FOR 4 TO 6 PEOPLE.

2 cups (1 lb/450 g) French lentils
6 cups (1,5 l) water
1 large stalk celery, sliced
1 red onion, sliced
1 small carrot, diced
Salt
1 cup (100 g) ditali or other small hollow pasta
Freshly ground black pepper
¼ cup (60 ml) olive oil
2 tablespoons chopped flat-leaf parsley

Combine the lentils, water, celery, onion, carrot, and 1 teaspoon salt in a medium saucepan and bring to a boil. Reduce the heat, cover, and simmer until barely tender, about 25 minutes. Remove from the heat and let cool. Set aside until ready to finish the dish.

When ready to finish the dish, bring a pot of salted water to a boil. Add the pasta and cook until al dente. Drain and add to the lentils. Mix well and season with salt and pepper. Drizzle with the olive oil and sprinkle with the parsley. Serve at room temperature.

PASTA E CECI
Pasta with Chick Pea Puree

This dish is one of several made with dried legumes that are found on the San Giuseppe's tables. The chick peas are flavored with a little bouquet of rosemary and garlic as well as aromatic vegetables. Chard improves the flavor and appearance of the dish.

THIS MAKES ENOUGH FOR 6 PEOPLE.

2 cups (400 g) dried chick peas
4 sprigs of rosemary
2 cloves garlic
1 large stalk celery, sliced
1 red onion, sliced
1 small carrot, diced
Salt
Ground hot pepper
1 pound (450 g) chard or beet greens, cut into ³/₄-inch (2-cm)
  strips (about 8 cups)
1½ cups (150 g) broken-up spaghettini
¼ cup (60 ml) olive oil
2 tablespoons chopped flat-leaf parsley or chives

Soak the chick peas overnight in cold water to cover. Drain. Rinse the pot and put the chick peas back in it. Add water to cover by at least 2 inches. Tie the rosemary around the garlic and add this to the pot. Add the celery, onion, and carrot. Cover and simmer until the chick peas are nearly tender, 2 to 2½ hours. Check from time to time and add more water if the chick peas look dry. Remove and discard the rosemary and garlic.

Puree about three quarters of the chick peas. Return the puree to the pot. Season to taste with salt and ground hot pepper. Add the chard and cook until it wilts, about 5 minutes. Remove from the heat and let cool. Set aside until ready to finish the dish.

When ready to finish the dish, bring a pot of salted water to a boil. Add the pasta and cook until al dente. Drain and add to the chick peas. Ladle into individual soup bowls, drizzle with the olive oil, and sprinkle with the parsley and additional ground hot pepper. Serve at room temperature.

PASTA CON LE SARDE AL POMODORO

Pasta with Sardines and Tomato Sauce

Pasta con le Sarde is sometimes called the national dish of Sicily. Unlike the classic recipe, this modest version has no saffron; it also has less fennel and fewer sardines. The sweetened breadcrumb topping is special for San Giuseppe's day. The sardines must be just out of the water. If not, omit them and make *Pasta con le Sarde a Mare*, literally, pasta with the sardines at sea.

THIS MAKES ENOUGH FOR 6 PEOPLE.

½ pound (225 g) wild fennel (see Note)
1 onion, coarsely chopped
1 pound (450 g) fresh sardines, cleaned
2 salted anchovies, filleted and rinsed, or 4 canned anchovy fillets
½ cup (125 ml) olive oil
1 heaping tablespoon pine nuts
1 heaping tablespoon dried currants
4 cups (1 l) tomato sauce, preferably homemade (page 228)
Salt and freshly ground black pepper
¾ cup (90 g) fine dry breadcrumbs
2 tablespoons sugar
1 pound (450 g) perciatelli or spaghetti

Boil the wild fennel for 10 minutes, or until tender. Drain and finely chop. Set aside.

Combine the onion, sardines, anchovies, and olive oil in a large saucepan and sauté until the onion is golden, the sardines break up, and the anchovies dissolve, about 10 minutes.

Stir in the wild fennel, pine nuts, and currants and cook for 2 to 3 minutes. Reserve 3 tablespoons of tomato sauce for the topping and add the rest to the sardine mixture. Cover and simmer until the sauce does not separate, 25 to 30 minutes. Season to taste with salt and pepper. Set aside.

Toast the breadcrumbs in a large skillet. Remove from the heat and stir in the sugar and the reserved 3 tablespoons tomato sauce. Set aside.

When ready to serve, bring a large pot of salted water to a boil. Add the pasta and cook until al dente. Drain and mix with the sauce. Top with some of the breadcrumb mixture.

NOTE. *Wild fennel is hard to come by outside Sicily. It grows wild in some places in California and Louisiana and is cultivated by gardeners, especially Sicilian-Americans. If you are lucky enough to find or get a bunch, use some fresh and blanch and freeze the rest. Bronze fennel, which is somewhat easier to find, is very similar in flavor. If you have some, use that. Blanch it for 5 minutes, drain, and chop fine. Otherwise, substitute ½ cup finely chopped fresh dill or a combination of dill and other herbs.*

PASTA E FAGIOLI FREDDA
Cold Pasta and Beans

Like *Pasta e Ceci* (page 41) and *Macco* (page 39), this souplike dish looks better served in individual bowls than from a tureen.

THIS MAKES ENOUGH FOR 6 PEOPLE.

2 cups (12 oz/350 g) dried borlotti or cranberry beans
1 medium-size red onion
1 small carrot
2 stalks celery
Salt and freshly ground black pepper
1½ cups (150 g) broken-up spaghetti or any small pasta shape
¼ cup (60 ml) olive oil
2 tablespoons chopped flat-leaf parsley
Ground hot pepper

Soak the beans overnight in cold water to cover. Drain and rinse the pot.

Roughly chop the onion, carrot, and celery and combine with the beans. Add enough water to cover by 1 inch (2,5 cm). Cover and simmer until the beans are nearly tender, 1 to 2 hours or more, depending on how long the beans were in storage.

Puree about three quarters of the beans. Return the puree to the pot and season to taste with salt and pepper. Remove from the heat and let cool. Set aside until ready to finish the dish.

When ready to finish the dish, bring a pot of salted water to a boil. Add the pasta and cook until al dente. Drain and add to the beans. Ladle into individual soup bowls, drizzle with olive oil, and sprinkle with parsley and ground hot pepper. Serve at room temperature.

RISO E LENTICCHIE
Rice and Lentils

The San Giuseppe tables abound with grain and bean dishes. Sometimes the grain is wheat in the form of pasta, sometimes rice. The beans include chick peas, favas, and lentils—the trio known since antiquity—as well as shell beans, which came to us from the New World. As for *Pasta e Lenticchie* (page 40), French Le Puy lentils will make the dish more like the Sicilian original, though American brown lentils are fine.

THIS MAKES ENOUGH FOR 6 TO 8 PEOPLE.

> *2 cups (1 lb/450 g) French or American lentils*
> *6 cups (1,5 l) water*
> *1 large stalk celery, cut into ¼-inch (less than 1-cm) dice*
> *1 small carrot, cut into ¼-inch (less than 1-cm) dice*
> *1 red onion, chopped into ¼-inch (less than 1-cm) pieces*
> *Salt*
> *¾ cup (170 g) long-grain rice*
> *Freshly ground black pepper*
> *¼ cup (60 ml) olive oil*
> *3 tablespoons chopped flat-leaf parsley*

Combine the lentils, water, celery, carrot, onion, and 1 teaspoon salt in a medium saucepan. Add enough water to cover by 1 inch (2,5 cm) and bring to a boil. Reduce the heat, cover, and simmer until the lentils are barely tender, 25 to 30 minutes for the French, 35 to 40 for the American lentils. Remove from the heat and let cool. Set aside until ready to finish the dish.

When ready to finish the dish, cook the rice as directed on page 113. Drain the rice and combine with the lentils, mixing gently with a fork. Add salt and pepper to taste. Drizzle with the olive oil and sprinkle with the parsley. Serve at room temperature.

ABOVE: *An old-fashioned scrubber, good for wooden cheese vats.*

INSALATA DI LATTUGA NOSTRANA E FINOCCHIO

Romaine Lettuce Salad with Fennel

This salad combines flavors that come together in spring in Sicily—romaine, fennel, citrus, and mint, the first herb out of the ground. Growing seasons are different in other parts of the world, so try this salad when you find healthy-looking fennel bulbs, probably in the fall or winter. You can make the dressing with tangerine juice instead of orange juice.

THIS MAKES ENOUGH FOR 6 PEOPLE.

1 head romaine lettuce, leaves washed and dried
1 fennel bulb, trimmed
¼ cup (60 ml) orange juice
2 tablespoons wine vinegar
¼ cup (60 ml) olive oil
Salt
¼ cup (15 g) fresh mint leaves, torn, or 1 tablespoon fresh
  thyme leaves or chopped flat-leaf parsley

Stack the lettuce leaves and cut them crosswise into 1½-inch-wide (4-cm) ribbons. Place in a salad bowl.

Quarter the fennel and cut crosswise into ¾-inch-thick (2-cm) slices. Add the fennel to the lettuce in the bowl.

Make a dressing by combining the orange juice, vinegar, oil, and salt. Just before serving, pour over the salad and toss. Sprinkle with the mint and toss again.

FRITTATA AL FORMAGGIO
Cheese Frittata

We make this with our wonderful fresh cheeses. You can substitute gouda or goat's milk gouda. The taste won't be the same, but the frittata will be very good.

THIS MAKES ENOUGH FOR 12 PEOPLE AS AN APPETIZER.

6 eggs
½ cup (60 g) grated caciocavallo or parmesan
½ cup (125 ml) milk
Salt and freshly ground black pepper
Olive oil
1 pound (450 g) caciocavallo, gouda, or goat's milk gouda,
*   cut into twelve 1½-inch (4-cm) squares each about ⅜ inch*
*   (1 cm) thick*

Beat the eggs in a bowl and stir in the grated cheese, milk, and salt and pepper to taste. Lightly coat a 9-inch (23-cm) nonstick or well-seasoned skillet with olive oil. Set the pan over medium heat.

Pour the egg mixture into the pan, spreading it to the edges. When it begins to set, add the cheese squares. Let cook until lightly browned on the bottom, 6 to 8 minutes. (Lift the edge with a spatula to peek.)

Slip the frittata onto a pan lid or plate, lightly grease the pan again, put the pan on the lid, and invert. Cook until lightly browned, 4 to 5 minutes.

Slide onto a serving plate. Cut into wedges, and serve warm or at room temperature.

FRITTATA DI VERDURA AMARA
Frittata with Bitter Greens

You can also make this frittata with plain steamed greens, but it is tastier if you sauté them first.

THIS MAKES ENOUGH FOR 4 PEOPLE AS A SIDE DISH.

1 pound (450 g) mixed bitter greens, such as kale, mustard
  greens, chicory, beet greens, etc.
1 clove garlic, minced
4 tablespoons olive oil
Salt
Ground hot pepper
6 eggs
½ cup (60 g) grated caciocavallo or parmesan
½ cup (125 ml) milk

Wash and trim the greens and boil or steam them until tender, about 10 minutes. Squeeze out the water. Roughly chop the greens.

Combine the garlic, greens, and 3 tablespoons of the olive oil in a nonstick or well-seasoned heavy 8-inch (20-cm) skillet and sauté over medium heat for 3 to 4 minutes, tossing often. Season to taste with salt and hot pepper.

Beat the eggs in a bowl; add the cheese, milk, and salt and hot pepper to taste. Pour over the greens, spreading the eggs to the edges. Let cook until lightly browned on the bottom, 6 to 8 minutes. (Lift the edge with a spatula to peek.)

Slip the frittata onto a pan lid or plate, lightly grease the pan with the remaining 1 tablespoon olive oil, put the pan on the lid, and invert. Cook until lightly browned, 4 to 5 minutes. Slide the frittata onto a serving plate. Cut into wedges and serve at room temperature.

ABOVE: *Some caper buds are left to flower for caperberries (page 101).*

APRILE

From the end of March through April and May, the Sicilian countryside is green, unbelievably green, and covered with wildflowers. The vines spring into leaf, and the wheat is still like blades of grass. Only a few patches of the fuschia-colored sulla, or French honeysuckle, remain as nature's palette shifts to shades of purple and gold. Masses of tiny orange and purple flowers hug the earth and poke out of crevices in the stones like wallflowers.

Yellow broom, calendula and buttercups, daffodils, crocus and narcissus create a golden haze on the hillsides. The fields are covered with pink asphodel, and wild violet and mauve sweetpeas, pinks, and tiny wild geraniums, bushes of them, bloom wherever they find a peaceful spot. Borage is in bloom, as blue as the sky above. Deep-blue irises and grape hyacinth come up in their usual places in the garden; sometimes they crop up in odd corners too.

LEFT: *Orange peel is dried to have the flavor all year round.*

THE GREEN OF SICILY

In the vegetable gardens, the first of the fava beans, *le prime fave* we call them, are ready to be picked—sometimes as early as mid-March, sometimes only at the beginning of April as in the year when we had snow on the ground at the end of March. These crunchy young beans can be eaten raw or braised as in *Fave a Spezzatino* (Braised Fava Beans, page 62). Peas, which enjoy their brief season at the same time, can be cooked the same way, as can baby artichokes. These are also very good on thin spaghetti in *Pasta con i Carciofi* (Spaghettini with Baby Artichokes, page 63).

Leafy greens, wild as well as cultivated, flourish. Spinach and chard are seeded in rows in the gardens; wild greens, like *mazzareddi* and *cavolicelli di montagna*, called *cavoluzzi di vigne* in dialect—some bitter, some peppery, some bland—seed themselves in the fields and hillside pastures. Any of these leafy greens or a combination can be boiled and sautéed for a plate of *Verdura Saltata* (Braised Greens, page 66). Another very popular dish made with wild greens is *Pasta con i Mazzareddi e Ricotta* (Perciatelli with Wild Greens and Ricotta, page 64).

The Sicilian asparagus (*Ruscus hypoglossum*) is a low, compact evergreen hedge with very thin and short spears, not at all like the ferny plant of the asparagus known to continental Europe and North America (*Asparagus officinalis*). Wild ones also exist; they grow in secret places that only the country people know. Sometimes my father gets a present of them on San Giuseppe's day, enough to have some on pasta and some in salad.

One year, on the way back from a wildflower hike in the Madonie Mountains, my sister Costanza, some students, and I stopped in a charming trattoria in Polizzi. We had a rendezvous to meet Alice Waters and her husband there and to bring them back to Regaleali with us. Called l'Orto dei Cappuccini (The Capuchins' Garden), this little restaurant served good fresh country food. We had wild asparagus prepared three ways—first, asparagus in an omelet with very little egg; then little bunches of asparagus in a salad dressed with oil and lemon juice; and third, asparagus mixed with homemade tagliatelle. The wild asparagus were followed by wild mushrooms. What a Sicilian welcome for a California chef!

A vegetable that is very much appreciated in Sicily is fennel. It's eaten raw at the end of the meal, almost like a palate cleanser. Unlike the Romans, who dip their fennel into *pinzimonio*, a mixture of olive oil, salt, and pepper, Sicilians dip it straight into sea salt. Fennel is also very refreshing in salads, such as *Insalata di Lattuga Nostrana e Finocchio* (page 46). Another good salad with fennel is *insalata di finocchio e cedro* with citron. Since that fruit is almost impossible to find in its natural state in the United States (most of the crop is candied), it may be easier to make a salad of fennel and oranges. Dress it with a light vinaigrette and season it with fresh thyme leaves and a few black olives. Any kind of orange will do, but blood oranges add dramatic color and special flavor. At the height of the season, it's a treat to have *Finocchi al Forno* (Baked Fennel, page 67) under a cheese crust.

THE GOLD OF SICILY

Gold and green lemon groves punctuate the countryside in Sicily. When the trees are in bloom, the smell that wafts on the breeze is intoxicating, and the fruit retains some of that aroma. I think that's why filmmakers like to use the lemon to symbolize memory, as in *Cinema Paradiso*, which opens with a shot of a bowl of *lumie*. The *lumia* is one of the most aromatic and subtle of the lemons. The so-called sweet lemon, which is quite small, is also very delicate in flavor. There are thin- and thick-skinned varieties of the standard lemon as well. Citron is a different fruit. It has an unusually thick pith and not much flesh; it's important to get both parts in your mouth at once since the flesh is very sour.

Not surprisingly, lemon is a ubiquitous Sicilian flavor, appearing in just about every course, including vegetables, salads, and desserts. When the lemon juice seems too harsh, though, I substitute something mellower, like tangerine or orange. Another alternative is lime, which you might want to use in *Insalata di Pollo con Olive e Limone* (Chicken Salad with Green Olives and Lemons, page 68) if your lemons are very sour. This chicken salad also has an orange in it, as well as the salty green olives.

Another good chicken and citrus dish is *Pollo all'Arancia* (Orange Roasted Chicken, page 69), in which the chicken is basted with orange juice and white wine. This is a departure from the classic recipe in which a whole lemon is stuffed in the cavity and the bird is rubbed all over with salt and then roasted in a rather hot oven.

Oranges are with us all winter long, first the "blond" ones and then the blood oranges (*sanguinelli*). We are never without oranges in winter. In spring, blood oranges are commonplace in Sicily, starting at the end of February with the Tarocco and ending with the Moro, which is the smallest and the darkest variety. They are not at all fashionable the way they are in northern Europe and the United States. In fact, we juice them for breakfast; visitors to Regaleali are always surprised when they are handed a tall glass of that red orange juice. At the end of the season, I fill my refrigerators at Regaleali with blood oranges so I can have the juice all summer long.

Blood oranges are best raw, and I use them as much as I can alone or in salads, both sweet and savory. For *Gelatina di Sanguinelli* (page 70), a spectacular gelatin dessert, only a small portion of the juice is heated and then just long enough to dissolve the sugar.

Of the tangerines, the last—and the best—are the Marzuddi, which ripen in March and, at higher elevations, April. (*Mandarini dei Ciaculli* is the formal name, after the district outside Palermo where they first were grown.) They are very juicy with a thin skin and pits. My mother and I can eat four or five each at one sitting. Marzuddi are also used to make a gelatin dessert, substituting tangerine juice for the blood-orange juice in *Gelatina di Sanguinelli*. These are the ones I use for *Mandarinetto* (page 70), a golden tangerine cordial.

So many kinds of oranges and mandarin oranges, or tangerines, are grown in Sicily that it's impossible to name them all. To make matters worse—or better, as the case may be—growers are constantly introducing new varieties in an attempt to extend the citrus growing season. In the old days, it began with the first tangerines in late November and went on until the end of March or the beginning of April. To extend the citrus *flavoring* season, Sicilians have long dried the peel. This is easy enough to do: Peel the fruit in one long strip and hang it in a sunny spot. Keep the dried peels in a jar or tightly sealed plastic bag. Nowadays the juice is frozen commercially and end-of-season citrus is kept in cold storage to bridge the gap from April to October.

Compared to oranges, the loquat or Japanese plum, which we call *nespola*, seems to be one of those fruits that requires having a tree in your backyard to enjoy, though it does show up from time to time in specialty food shops. The loquat bruises easily, which means shippers don't want to handle it nor growers grow it even though it is such a wonderful fruit to eat. Sicilian loquats are about the size of a plum tomato, and there are two varieties, one more sweet and one more sour. Both are apricot in color with a firm flesh, tough skin, and from two to five large pits. Sometimes we pick them off the trees and eat them just like that in big bites, spitting out the skin and pits. Of course, it's more civilized to eat loquats in fruit salad, alone or with cherries. For that, the loquats should be cut in half, peeled, and pitted.

CORDIALS

Homemade cordials are very much a Sicilian tradition. We drink *Mandarinetto* and *Limoncino* (lemon cordial) iced. My father and brother like to drink grappa, but that's because it's made from our own grape pomace and tastes very good. Cordials are made at home, using the alcohol that is sold in Italian food stores for the purpose. (Strong vodka, 90 proof, is a perfect substitute.) Any citrus, or a combination, can be used in place of the tangerine in *Mandarinetto*; any kind of berry, in place of the wild strawberries in *Liquore di Fragoline* (page 96). *Nocino* (page 107), the potent walnut liqueur, can also be made at home without any special equipment. Cordials are made with herbs as well. In Sicily, as in the rest of Europe, the monks and nuns were masters of these herbal concoctions, the formulas for which they kept secret behind their high monastery walls.

THE NUNS' STORY

Sicily has a long history of convent sweets. Starting centuries ago, nuns made these elaborate confections, first to give as gifts and then to sell when the convents fell on hard times. The practice is rapidly dying out now because of changes in both the world within the convents and the world outside. Few young women are drawn to the cloistered life, and as the old nuns die, their secrets die with them. Recipes were transmitted from person to person, never written down.

The modern world seems impatient with tradition and shows little interest in recording it. Those who do care might be described as "several characters in search of the nuns' recipes" after *Six Characters in Search of an Author*, the play by Luigi Pirandello, one of Sicily's most famous writers. We keep seeking to reconstruct those old recipes, using notes, photos, and the memory of how the sweets looked and tasted.

At one point, three of us devotees—Mary Taylor Simeti, Giuliana Caramazza, whose hobby is reproducing convent sweets, and I—gathered at Regaleali to try to re-create some of the nuns' marzipan specialties for a magazine article. For this marzipan marathon, we started by making a batch of filling. We made a sugar syrup and then added chopped pistachios, almond flour, *zuccata* (squash preserves), citrus marmalades—we used tangerine, citron, and bitter orange, a little of each—and lots of cinnamon. Next we made a batch of *Pasta Reale* (page 71), marzipan or royal dough as we call it.

The magazine article was to come out in April, so our first creation was a Paschal Lamb, because there is no Easter in Sicily without the lamb. We did a medium-size one with a sweet smile and trusting eyes, the famous large one with curly fleece being beyond our skills.

Then we turned to three other classics: the *cuore*, a preserve-filled heart; the *grappolo*, a cluster of marzipan grapes, each one filled with preserves; and the *trionfo di gola*, literally the triumph of gluttony. This is a dome-shaped cake covered with green marzipan and decorated with marzipan curls and rosebuds, with a marzipan fruit on top—ours had an apricot. Cutting into the cake reveals the rococo construction of pistachio and squash preserves between layers of pastry and *pan di Spagna* (sponge cake) all held together with pastry cream or *Biancomangiare* (page 37). Here is how Mary described the *trionfo* in her book *Pomp and Sustenance: Twenty-Five Centuries of Sicilian Food*: "If its outward appearance was touchingly naïve, within the golden stripes of *pan di Spagna* framed bright green chips of pistachio and greeny-gold cubes of glistening *zuccata*, which floated in the pale *biancomangiare* like so many tesserae from the mosaic wall of an Arab-Norman chapel."

We also created a filled sun. I had had Iachetta, one of Sicily's most talented ceramicists, make a medallion for me; it has a smiling face

RIGHT: *Tangerine peels steeping for Mandarinetto (page 70).*

with chubby cheeks and eight rays. I took the medallion to Cillari, who makes the best marzipan molds, and he made a mold for me. Now I can make a marzipan sun whenever I like, to give as a gift. It will be my signature!

Marzipan is very easy to make, and it lasts forever in the refrigerator. You can use it to form fruits and vegetables by hand or in molds if you have them. Palermitani (those who live in Palermo) call these *Frutta di Martorana* after the Martorana convent where the nuns were particularly adept at making the fruits look very lifelike. Paint them with simple vegetable food colorings, the kind you find on every supermarket shelf, mixing the colors yourself rather than buying fancy premixed ones. It's more in the simple and frugal spirit of the nuns.

Among the other marzipan delicacies were *conchiglie*, marzipan seashells filled with preserves, and *cassata*, the elaborate cake, covered with tinted marzipan, that Sicilians serve often at family celebrations and always at Easter. The nuns also made *dolci di riposto*, pastries filled with preserves, and *dolcetti al liquore*, pastries filled with rum-soaked raisins, that could be kept in the cupboard to serve to guests when they came by. Maria Grammatico, who lived at the San Carlo convent for many years, still makes many of these tidbits; she gives recipes for them in her autobiography, *Bitter Almonds*, written with Mary Simeti.

Another common convent sweet was *bocconcini*, sometimes called *muccuneddi*. These little preserve-filled pastries are made with an almond dough and baked. I've managed to duplicate the ones from the Convento di San Michele in Mazzara, but other convents used to make them too, each following its own tradition. There were countless other baked pastries based on almond dough as well as fried pastries filled with pastry cream. Just thinking about them makes me want to beg the nuns again to give me the recipes, even though nuns are known to be stubborn.

One of the most unusual of the convent sweets is the green pistachio couscous garnished with chocolate and preserved squash that is the pride—if one can say that of a convent—of the Convento di Santo Spirito in Agrigento. The nuns still make it on special order for visitors. It was introduced to American readers by Nick Malgieri in his book *Great Italian Desserts*, which includes some other specialties of the Santo Spirito as well.

LAMB

Spring in Sicily is the time of the lamb. The ewes that are mated in September deliver in March, in time for Eastern lamb. Some of the male lambs are slaughtered while they are still nursing for their stomachs, which is used for *caglio*, or rennet, for cheese making. The others—all but a chosen few—are castrated and slaughtered about a year later.

The meat of baby lamb is tender with a very delicate flavor. We use it for *angello in fricassea*, which is like a *blanquette de veau* made with lamb, and for *Agnello al Vino* (page 75), in which pieces of meat are roasted with wine. The meat should be cooked on the bone for maximum flavor. If your guests are fussy, take the meat off the bone before serving rather than before cooking.

PASQUETTA

Easter is, of course, a very important holiday, the holiest of holy days, defining Christianity in Sicily as elsewhere. But the days of Holy Week, between Palm Sunday and Easter Sunday, are a solemn time. On Good Friday, twelve men of the parish stand in for the Apostles at the Last Supper. Each one gets a big sugar lamb, like the *pupi de cena* (sugar statues) that mark *I Morti* (All Souls' Day); a round loaf of *Pani di Cena* (Easter Sweet Rolls, page 73), glazed and decorated with colored sugar sprinkles; and the same trousseau of a head of romaine lettuce, a fennel bulb, a citron, and an orange that is presented to the *verginedde* on the feast of San Giuseppe (page 23). At the end of the ceremony, the pastor washes the feet of the "Apostles," just as the Pope does in Rome.

Pane di cena is normally formed into rolls, not loaves. The bakery sells them, but many women still make the rolls at home on Good Friday, using baking powder or baker's ammonia (ammonium carbonate) as a leavener rather than yeast. By one of those curious coincidences, Carol Field discovered these sweet rolls at the bakery in Vallelunga and has a recipe for them in her book *Celebrating Italy*. I asked her if I could include it in my book because it has the kind of precise directions for bread making that American readers like, and she very kindly said, "Of course."

ABOVE: *Sea salt, an essential flavor of Sicily, dries on rocks high above the sea.*

There is another kind of Easter bread, called *pupo con l'uovo*. For this bread, the dough is wrapped around one, two, or even three eggs in the shell, and the whole loaf is baked, eggs and all.

The joyous celebration of Easter comes on Easter Monday, called *Pasquetta* in Italian, when all of Sicily heads out-of-doors to feast on the traditional dishes of spring. There's lamb, lamb, lamb, and great coils of sausage with bay leaf and onion tucked in between.

Fires for grilling are going full steam. And when the fires die down, stuffed artichokes are roasted in the embers. We call these *carciofi alla brace*, and they are always served on this day. You cut off the tips of the leaves and spread them apart, either with your thumbs or by holding the artichoke by the stem and pressing it down on a flat surface. Then you push a mixture of minced garlic, dried oregano, salt, and pepper down between the leaves. Just before roasting, you drizzle the artichoke—actually drench it—with olive oil. Then you place the artichokes in the coals and cook, turning them from time to time, for about 45 minutes, until the outer leaves are charred. These are discarded to get at the tender inner leaves and the heart. Well worth the effort!

Many pasta dishes are prepared and carried to the picnic: *Pasta con le Prime Fave* (Spaghetti with Early Fava Beans, page 62), which can also be made with peas; *Pasta con i Mazzareddi e Ricotta* (Perciatelli with Wild Greens and Ricotta, page 64); but mostly *lasagne al forno*. One reason for having the lasagne is that it can be easily transported.

There are probably as many recipes for lasagne as there are Sicilians but basically it is lasagna noodles—they used to be homemade, always, but now the lazy ones buy them in town—layered with a *ragù* sauce with meat—like the one in *Sformato di Patate al Ragù* (Potato Timbale with Meat Sauce and Peas, page 200)—and béchamel sauce. Some people put peas in their lasagne; some people put lots of cheese. It's all a matter of personal preference.

Dessert on this occasion is *Cannoli* (page 34), both regular size and little ones, two bites. Molds for these tiny cannoli are sold in Italy but not elsewhere to my knowledge. Those are the official desserts, but anyone who has a different specialty is welcome to bring it to the picnic. When I asked Graziella Chimera, who came to work for me a few years ago, what she has on *Pasquetta*, she said dreamily, hungrily, "You eat all day long. You start in the morning and keep going until night." That's *Pasquetta* in Sicily.

THE RECIPES

FAVE A SPEZZATINO
Braised Fava Beans

This way of preparing vegetables is particularly well suited to *le prime fave*, the very first fava beans to be picked, and to other first-of-the-season vegetables, whether peas or artichokes or zucchini. These early favas don't have to be peeled; they are crunchy and juicy and the peel of the bean is good to eat. (The peel of later favas is tough and does have to be peeled.)

THIS MAKES ENOUGH FOR 2 PEOPLE AS A SIDE DISH.

1 small red onion, finely chopped
¼ cup (60 ml) olive oil
1½ cups (1½ lb/675 g) fresh or frozen fava beans (see Note)
Salt and freshly ground black pepper
½ cup (125 ml) water
3 tablespoons chopped flat-leaf parsley

Sauté the onion in the olive oil until golden. Add the favas, salt and pepper to taste, and the water. Cover and simmer over low heat until tender, 10 to 15 minutes, keeping in mind that Sicilians like their vegetables cooked through. Sprinkle with the parsley and remove from the heat.

NOTE. *Fresh fava beans are available in the spring in food specialty shops and in grocery stores catering to an Italian, Iranian, or Near Eastern clientele. One pound (450 g) of favas in the shell yields about 1 cup of shelled favas. Frozen beans are available all year round.*

VARIATION. *Pasta con le Prime Fave* (Spaghetti with Early Fava Beans). While the beans are cooking, cook ½ pound of spaghetti in lots of boiling salted water until al dente. Drain and toss with the fava bean mixture. Serve immediately. This makes enough for 4 people as a first course.

RIGHT: *Some people decorate salads with the mauve petals of the wild marsh mallow.*

PASTA CON I MAZZAREDDI E RICOTTA
Perciatelli with Wild Greens and Ricotta

In Sicily, we make this with wild greens and homemade sheep's-milk ricotta. Though broccoli raab is less bitter and cooks faster, it is a good substitute for the wild greens, and ricotta salata can stand in for the ricotta. If you can't find ricotta salata, use feta, cut into cubes or crumbled over the top.

THIS MAKES ENOUGH FOR 4 TO 6 PEOPLE.

2¼ pounds (1 kg) mixed greens, such as broccoli raab, chard,
    escarole, kale, collards, or mustard greens, or a combination
¼ cup (60 ml) olive oil
1 clove garlic, minced
Salt
Ground hot pepper
1 pound (450 g) perciatelli or bucatini
¼ pound (100 g) ricotta salata, sliced ¼ inch (less than
    1 cm) thick
½ cup (60 g) grated pecorino or parmesan

Wash and trim the greens. Cook them, uncovered, in plenty of boiling salted water until tender, about 10 minutes. Remove from the water with tongs to save the water for cooking the pasta. Drain well. Coarsely chop the greens.

Combine the oil, garlic, and greens in a large sauté pan and sauté, turning until everything is coated. Continue to sauté until cooked through, adding water as needed to keep the greens moist. Season to taste with salt and hot pepper and remove from the heat.

Cook the pasta in the water from the greens until tender. Drain, reserving 1 cup of the water. Toss with half of the greens and the reserved pasta water. Spread with the remaining greens and arrange the ricotta salata slices on top. Serve immediately, passing the grated cheese at table.

The village of Pollara, built high above the sea on Salina in the Eolian Islands. Crystalline waters lap its crescent-shaped lava beach.

**CLOCKWISE FROM
TOP LEFT:**
*Cockles and
clams are served
fresh from the
sea. One last
cherry tomato
hangs on tena-
ciously as the
vine withers. A
full ear of wheat
awaits the cutter,
no longer the
scythe. Home-
made Busiati
(page 159), a
kind of maca-
roni, are left to
dry in the sun.*

CLOCKWISE FROM LEFT: *An evergreen carob tree offers shade and color when the sun beats down on the dusty terrain. Homemade raw estratto (page 176) retains the bright color and fresh taste of just-picked tomatoes. The summer flavors of tomato and basil bring fusilli to life in this pasta salad (page 191). Potato salad with green beans and onions (page 239) is perfect served at room temperature for lunch.*

CLOCKWISE FROM LEFT: *Babaluci cling to the stalks of bushes, stripping them of all their leaves. These small snails are cooked in bianco, with garlic and parsley, or in rosso, with tomato sauce (pages 148 and 149).* OVERLEAF: *Malvasia grapes ripen on the vine in Salina.*

THESE PAGES: *Shaved ice flavored with fruit, mint, or almond is sold on street corners in Palermo. The vendor, Uncle Vincenzo by name, puts some ice in a cup, scraping more if need be, and pours the syrup over. His sign advertises the flavors available.*

THESE PAGES: *Making caciocavallo cheese begins with clabbering cow's milk with rennet and letting it rest until the stirring stick stands straight up. The milk is then broken into curds and whey. The curds are strained, stirred, and massaged, then left to ferment overnight.* **OVERLEAF:** *Next day, the cheese maker works the pasta filata (page 110) and forms it into balls.*

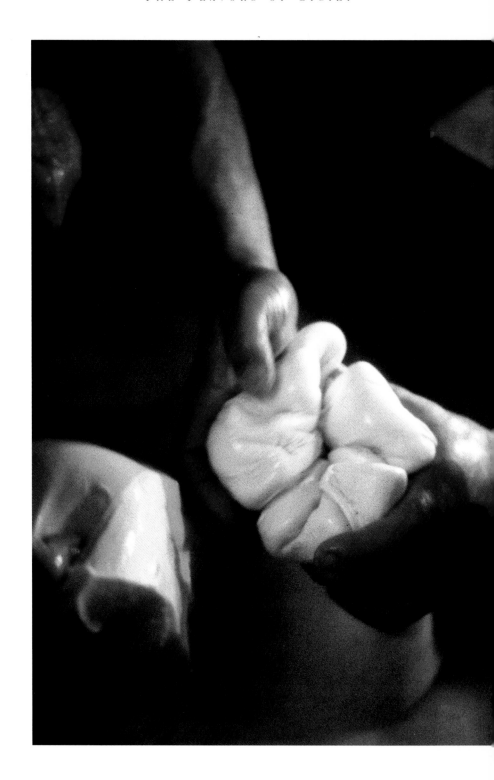

Sea urchins from the waters around Sicily cannot be surpassed. It's not easy to split open the urchins to get at the coral roe.

PASTA CON I CARCIOFI
Spaghettini with Baby Artichokes

This delicate artichoke dish makes an elegant first course. Cleaning the artichokes is tedious work, but you won't regret it.

THIS MAKES ENOUGH FOR 4 PEOPLE AS A FIRST COURSE.

2 lemons
8 to 10 baby artichokes (1½ lb/750 g)
½ cup (125 ml) olive oil
1 small red onion, very thinly sliced
2 cloves garlic, very thinly sliced
½ cup (125 ml) white wine
Salt
Ground hot pepper
¾ pound (350 g) spaghettini
3 tablespoons chopped flat-leaf parsley

Squeeze one of the lemons into a bowl of cold water. Cut the other in half to use to wipe your hands and the artichokes while handling them. Clean the artichokes (see Note). Slice them lengthwise as thin as possible; drop the slices into the lemon water.

Drain the artichokes. Combine ¼ cup of the olive oil with the artichokes, onion, and garlic in a large sauté pan over high heat. Sauté, tossing with 2 spoons, just until al dente, about 10 minutes.

Add the wine and cook briefly to evaporate some of the alcohol. Add salt and hot pepper to taste. Set aside until the pasta is done.

Boil the spaghettini in plenty of salted water until al dente. Drain and pour in a serving dish. Top with the artichoke mixture. Toss and drizzle with the remaining ¼ cup olive oil. Sprinkle with the parsley and serve immediately.

NOTE. *Always work with a stainless steel knife, a cut lemon, and a bowl of lemon water when cleaning artichokes. Break off the tough outer leaves of the artichoke and cut the inner leaves off about ¾ inch (2 cm) from the tip. Cut off the hard part of the bottom. Rub the artichoke with the cut lemon. Cut in two lengthwise and drop one half into the lemon water. Remove the choke, rub again with lemon, and drop into the water. Remove the choke of the other half. Continue until all are done.*

VERDURA SALTATA

Braised Greens

Use as much or as little oil as you like. The Sicilian preference is for a lot of oil. The population is divided, however, on lemon juice.

THIS MAKES ENOUGH FOR 4 TO 6 PEOPLE.

4½ pounds (2 kg) greens, such as chard, escarole, kale,
  collards, mustard greens, broccoli raab, or a combination
¼ to ½ cup (60 to 125 ml) olive oil
3 cloves garlic, minced
½ teaspoon crushed red pepper
Salt
1 lemon, cut into wedges (optional)

Wash and trim the greens. Boil them in lots of salted water until limp, about 10 minutes. Drain, reserving the water, and chop into large pieces.

Combine the oil, garlic, and red pepper in a large sauté pan. Add the chopped greens and toss until all of the pieces are coated with oil; sauté until cooked through. Add water as needed to keep the greens moist. Add salt to taste. Serve at room temperature with the lemon.

ABOVE: *Iris bloom in the fields and in the flower gardens.*

FINOCCHI AL FORNO
Baked Fennel

This is the dish to make when fennel is plentiful and cheap.

THIS MAKES ENOUGH FOR 6 PEOPLE.

4½ pounds (2 kg) fennel bulbs
Salt and freshly ground black pepper
¼ cup (30 g) grated caciocavallo or parmesan
½ cup (120 ml) olive oil or 3½ tablespoons (50 g) butter

Wash and trim the fennel bulbs, cutting away the stalks, base, and outer leaves. Quarter the bulbs and remove any tough core.

Blanch the fennel in boiling salted water until tender, 8 to 10 minutes. Drain well.

Preheat the oven to 400° F. (200° C.). Lightly oil or butter a baking dish large enough to hold the pieces in a single layer.

Place the pieces of fennel close together in the baking dish. Sprinkle with salt and grind lots of pepper on top. Spread the cheese evenly over the fennel and drizzle with the olive oil or dot with the butter.

Bake until the cheese is golden and the fennel juices are bubbling, about 10 minutes. Run under the broiler if the top is not golden enough. Let stand for 10 minutes before serving.

INSALATA DI POLLO CON OLIVE E LIMONE
Chicken Salad with Green Olives and Lemon

A great salad for a buffet or picnic, very refreshing. The slices of citrus add a colorful touch.

THIS MAKES ENOUGH FOR 8 PEOPLE.

1 large chicken (4½ lb/2 kg), whole or cut up
3 stalks celery
1 small carrot
3 sprigs of parsley
1 small onion
1 clove garlic
1 chicken bouillon cube
1 thin-skinned orange, such as a Valencia
1 thin-skinned lemon or lime
1 cup (120 g) slivered pitted green olives (see Note)
1 very small red onion, finely chopped, or 2 tablespoons
   chopped chives
1 tablespoon mayonnaise
¼ cup (60 ml) yogurt
1 tablespoon wine vinegar
Salt and freshly ground black pepper
¼ cup (15 g) fresh mint leaves, chopped

Put the chicken in a saucepan, cover with water, and bring to a boil. Make a bouquet garni with 1 celery stalk, the carrot, and the parsley, and add it to the pot. Add the onion, garlic, and bouillon cube. Simmer over low heat until the chicken is tender, 1 to 1½ hours.

Lift the chicken out of the water and let it stand. When cool enough to handle, remove the meat and cut it into bite-size pieces. Discard the skin and bones. Save the broth for another purpose. Place the chicken pieces in a serving bowl.

Scrub the orange and lemon and cut each in half. Remove the seeds and slice 1 half of each as thin as you can. Squeeze the other half for juice. Add the slices and the juice to the pieces of chicken. Cut the remaining 2 celery stalks into julienne strips. Add the celery, olives, and red onion to the chicken. Mix together the mayonnaise, yogurt, vinegar, and salt and pepper to taste. Pour over the salad and turn to coat all of the meat and vegetables; sprinkle with the mint. Let stand for 2 hours before serving. Serve at room temperature.

NOTE. *You will need about 1½ cups (200 g) large green olives with pits to get 1 cup (120 g) slivered pitted olives.*

POLLO ALL'ARANCIA
Orange Roasted Chicken

I call this my medieval chicken because of the combination of savory spices and orange juice. Hot peppers came later, of course, from the New World.

THIS MAKES ENOUGH FOR 4 TO 6 PEOPLE.

> *1 medium onion*
> *Sprigs of rosemary, sage, and/or thyme*
> *1 medium-size chicken (about 3½ lb/1,6 kg)*
> *1 cup (250 ml) fresh orange juice*
> *1 cup (250 ml) white wine*
> *1 teaspoon ground hot pepper*
> *Salt*

Preheat the oven to 400° F. (200° C.).

Put the onion and herbs in the cavity of the chicken. Place it, breast side up, in a roasting pan. Combine the orange juice and wine and pour half over the chicken. Rub the outside of the chicken with the hot pepper and salt to taste, massaging them well into the skin. Roast until the chicken is golden, or even a little burned, about 20 minutes.

Pour in the remaining 1 cup of the juice and wine. Scrape the bottom of the pan.

Reduce the oven temperature to 325° F. (160° C.). Roast, basting the chicken from time to time, for 40 minutes longer.

Remove the pan from the oven and leave the oven on. Cut the chicken into serving pieces. Dip each piece into the juices to coat all sides and put back in the pan. Roast for 20 minutes more.

Serve hot or at room temperature.

GELATINA DI SANGUINELLI
Blood Orange Gelatin

Blood-orange juice makes this gelatin a beautiful red color, like straw-berries. I've given large quantities because it is such a great party dessert—it always creates a sensation. The gelatin can be made with other kinds of citrus juice.

THIS IS ENOUGH FOR 8 TO 10 PEOPLE.

6½ cups (1,5 l) freshly squeezed blood-orange juice
3 envelopes (7 g each) unflavored gelatin
2½ cups (500 g) sugar

Strain the juice through a double layer of rinsed cheesecloth or a paper coffee filter. Soften the gelatin in 3 cups of the juice.

Bring the remaining 3½ cups of juice to a boil in a saucepan. Add the sugar and stir to dissolve. Remove from the heat as soon as it dissolves and stir in the juice with the gelatin. Pour into a pretty glass bowl and allow to cool. Cover with plastic wrap and refrigerate overnight.

NOTE. *Before serving, score deeply in a pattern of squares or diamonds. That way the gelatin stays pretty after you've served the first portions.*

MANDARINETTO
Tangerine Cordial

Homemade cordials, particularly those based on our bountiful citrus, are very Sicilian. When I make this one, I add a little *Vino Cotto* (page 223) after straining the peels; it turns the cordial amber instead of the greenish yellow color it normally has.

THIS MAKES ABOUT 3 PINTS (1,5 L) OF CORDIAL.

8 tangerines
2 cups (500 ml) 90-proof vodka
2 cups (400 g) sugar
2 cups (500 ml) water

Scrub the tangerines and zip off the peel. Remove and discard any white filaments and cut the colored zest into strips. Save the fruit for another purpose. Put the peel in a 2-quart (2-l) glass jar and pour on the vodka. Cover and let stand in the sun for 10 day, shaking from time to time.

Dissolve the sugar in the water in a saucepan and bring to a boil. Reduce the heat and simmer for 5 minutes. Let cool.

When cooled, add the syrup to the vodka mixture. Cover and let stand in a cool dark place for 10 days.

Filter through several layers of clean napkin or filter twice through coffee filters. Pour into a nice bottle and cork tightly. Let stand for at least 2 months before drinking.

VARIATIONS. Substitute the peel of 4 large lemons, 3 large oranges, or 2 large grapefruit for the tangerine peel.

PASTA REALE
Marzipan

This is the recipe I've perfected after three years of experimenting with marzipan. It has not been tested in the United States because the sale of bitter almonds is banned. For a recipe that has been tested, see the Variation at the end of the recipe.

THIS MAKES ABOUT 4½ POUNDS (2 KG) MARZIPAN.

2¼ pounds (1 kg) blanched almonds
20 ounces (50 g) bitter almonds
1⅓ pounds (600 g) confectioners' sugar, sifted (7½ cups
  when sifted)
¼ cup (60 ml) honey
Pinch of salt
¼ cup (60 ml) water
Green food coloring (optional)

Grind both types of almonds to a fine powder in a nut grinder or food processor. If using the processor, mix in a little of the sugar to prevent the almonds from turning to nut butter.

Combine the nuts, the rest of the sugar, the honey, salt, and water. Knead together, adding the food coloring, if using, bit by bit until you get the shade you want. Knead just until the mixture comes together.

Form into a log, wrap with plastic, and refrigerate for at least 3 hours before using. Store in the refrigerator for up to 6 months.

VARIATION. Substitute 2 cups (300 g) blanched almonds, 2 cups (400 g) sugar, and ⅓ cup (80 ml) water and omit the honey. Add a drop of vanilla extract and 1 teaspoon almond extract. Proceed as in the recipe. This makes about 1¾ pounds (800 g) marzipan.

PANI DI CENA
Easter Sweet Rolls

These buns are made on Good Friday. This recipe is adapted from Carol Field's recipe in *Celebrating Italy*.

THIS MAKES 10 TO 12 ROLLS.

SPONGE
1 teaspoon (2 g) active dry yeast
2 teaspoons sugar
½ cup (125 ml) milk, warmed to 105° F. (40° C.)
¼ cup (40 g) pastry or unbleached all-purpose flour

DOUGH
2 large egg yolks
½ cup (125 ml) milk (cold if using the food processor)
2 teaspoons vanilla extract (optional)
9 tablespoons (125 g) unsalted butter, lard, or margarine,
   at room temperature (cold if using the food processor)
3⅓ cups (500 g) pastry or 3 cups (450 g) unbleached
   all-purpose flour
½ cup (100 g) sugar
1 teaspoon salt

GLAZE
1 egg white, beaten

To make the sponge, stir the yeast and the sugar into the warm milk and let sit until foamy, about 10 minutes. Stir in the flour. Cover well with plastic wrap and leave until it is frothy and bubbly, 1 to 1½ hours.

To make the dough by hand, stir the egg yolks, milk, and vanilla, if using, into the sponge. Mix in the butter. Combine the flour, sugar, and salt and add in 3 additions, stirring for about 3 minutes. Knead on a lightly floured board, adding as little flour as possible, until silky and elastic, 5 to 6 minutes.

To make the dough in a mixer, put the sponge in the mixer bowl with the paddle attachment, add the egg yolks, milk, vanilla, if using, and butter, and mix about 1 minute. Add the flour, sugar, and salt and mix on low speed. Change to the dough hook and knead for about 3 minutes on medium speed. This dough won't come entirely away from the sides or bottom of the bowl. Knead briefly on a lightly floured work surface.

To make the dough in a food processor, put the flour, sugar, and salt into the processor fitted with either the dough blade or steel blade. Pulse 2 or 3 times to mix. Place the sponge and cold butter, cut into 8 or 9 pieces, on top of it. Mix the egg yolks, cold milk, and vanilla, if using, in a cup and, with the motor running, pour the mixture down the feed tube. Process until the mixture forms a dough. Process 30 seconds longer to knead.

For the first rise, put the dough in an oiled container, cover tightly with plastic wrap, and let rise until doubled, 2 to 2½ hours.

For the shaping and second rise, divide the dough into 10 to 12 pieces, form each into a round, and set on oiled or parchment-lined baking sheets. Cover well with towels and let rise again until the rolls have about doubled, about 45 minutes.

Preheat the oven to 400° F. (200° C.).

Just before baking, imagine a cross in the centers of the rolls and snip little V-shaped cuts in each quadrant so they will open up. Brush the tops of the rolls with beaten egg white and bake 20 to 25 minutes. Cool on a rack.

NOTE. *The rolls are often glazed with a simple sugar icing and decorated with colored sugar sprinkles.*

AGNELLO AL VINO
Roasted Lamb with Red Wine

The best lamb to use for this dish is from an animal no less than two months old, no more than four or five; the meat will cook in less than half an hour. Since that size is difficult to find if you don't have your own supplier, I would suggest using lamb neck and breast or shoulder, all tasty, succulent cuts, though they do take longer to cook. Have the butcher cut up the meat for you.

THIS MAKES ENOUGH FOR 6 TO 8 PEOPLE.

> *4½ pounds (2 kg) lamb with bones, such as lamb neck and*
> *   breast or shoulder, cut into 3½ inch (8-cm) pieces*
> *4½ pounds (2 kg) red or white new potatoes, peeled and*
> *   sliced ¼-inch (a little less than 1-cm) thick*
> *1 red onion, coarsely chopped*
> *2 or 3 sprigs of fresh rosemary*
> *Salt and freshly ground black pepper*
> *⅓ to ½ cup olive oil*
> *2 cups (500 ml) dry red wine*
> *1 cup (250 ml) water*

Preheat the oven to 350° F. (170° C.).

Layer the meat, potatoes, and onion in a large roasting pan and put the rosemary sprigs on top. Season with salt and pepper to taste and drizzle with olive oil. Roast for 15 minutes.

Remove the pan from the oven, and pour 1 cup of the wine over everything. Scrape the bottom of the pan with a spatula to get up all the brown bits and pieces of onion stuck to it. Return to the oven and cook, stirring a couple of times, until the meat is tender, 20 to 30 minutes longer, depending on the age of the lamb. Remove the meat and potatoes to a serving platter and keep warm.

Place the roasting pan directly on the burner. Pour in the remaining 1 cup wine and the water. Reduce over high heat, scraping the bottom of the pan and stirring, until the liquid reduces to a sauce. Taste for seasoning, pour over the lamb and potatoes, and serve.

RIGHT: *Artichokes are one of the first vegetables to appear in spring.*

MAGGIO

May is a magical moment for flowers in Sicily. Even in the city and along the highways, trees are in bloom—acacia trees, covered with the yellow flowers the bees love so much and elderberries, which look like scented white umbrellas. Here and there a jasmine bush blooms, its flowers like tiny white stars. Tall mallow plants with mauve blossoms line the streets.

High in the mountains, it is like a fairyland. Flowers carpet the earth. Rare tiny wild orchids, mauve, purple, yellow, and white, bloom side by side with the more common cyclamens, violets, and irises. Wild peonies come into flower late in the month; they are so extraordinary that it's worth a special trip for the show. In the countryside, patches of mustard that were green a month ago turn yellow as the plants set seed. Wild fennel and asafetida, which we call ferula, grow in profusion.

LEFT: *Pink-blossomed wild thyme flourishes in the arid soil of Sicily.*

WILDFLOWERS

∞

Thin-stemmed red poppies sway in the wheat fields, catching even the slightest breeze; the ones that are cultivated for their seeds stand tall with luminous white flowers. Sweet daisies and mayflowers beckon to the passerby. The spotted blue flowers of black cumin, also called love-in-the-mist, never fail to catch the eye. Wild roses, planted in old wine casks and *giare*, or earthenware jars, are blooming in their corners. Geraniums and scented geraniums add splashes of bright color.

Other plants that are called weeds when they grow in places where the farmer doesn't want them, namely the vegetable gardens or, especially, the vineyards, include the invasive chicory. Its bright blue flowers trick people into transplanting it, and you often see it growing at the doorway. A very peculiar plant is the *pelosedda*, a relative of comfrey. Carmelo Di Martino, caretaker of Case Vecchie and a font of folk wisdom, uses the leaves to wrap his feet when they get very hot; he says it cools them off.

HERBS

∞

One thing I know from personal experience is that a cup of chamomile tea will put me right to sleep. In May, my courtyard at Case Vecchie is covered with wild chamomile, which even the hens can't destroy with all their scratching and pecking. I'm not too keen on picking it after they've been there, so I find some that's been growing undisturbed elsewhere and dry the blossoms for tea. We spread it out on large sieves and dry it in the shade—not the sun as some advise—so that it doesn't turn gray or brown. When it's completely dry, we store it in jars. One big basket of flowers makes one small jar. This wild chamomile has a much better flavor than the cultivated one.

Other herbs, like sage, are in bloom at this time, but we don't do anything with the flowers, just leave them for the bees. Sometimes I put borage flowers or nasturtium or calendula in salad or on cheese just because they are so pretty. The men push the flowers aside with an expression that clearly says, "How ridiculous women are!" Women, generally more open to novelty, will take a bite and say, "Looks pretty but doesn't taste much." So much for edible flowers in Sicily.

Herbs are, however, used extensively in Sicilian cooking, both as flavoring and, in the case of borage, as a cooked dish. Leaves and wild borage are cooked and served with pasta exactly as in *Pasta con i Mazzareddi e Ricotta* (page 64). The leaves can also be simply boiled and drizzled with olive oil and lemon juice.

Sicilians have great belief in the tonic qualities of borage and bitter greens. If they don't live in the countryside, they will make an effort to visit, arriving with huge sacks to fill with greens. One day I saw a man parked at the gate to Regaleali, and when I approached him, he asked my permission to pick some wild greens *"per rinfrescarmi lo stomaco,"* that is, to make his stomach like new again.

The herbs used most for flavoring, in addition to wild fennel, are such garden herbs as mint, parsley, basil, sage, rosemary, thyme, and bay. Perhaps oregano should top that list since it is used so extensively—always dried, never fresh. Coriander, or cilantro, is grown for the seeds, which are put in pecorino cheese, not for the leaves. The flavor of cilantro is foreign to the Sicilian palate; in fact, I tasted it for the first time in a restaurant in San Francisco in 1994. When I got home and looked it up in my grandfather's agrarian encyclopedia, about 150 years old, I found the plant described as smelling like bedbugs (people then could tell bedbugs were in the neighborhood by the smell, imagine!) and very bad for your health. Fashions do change.

Usually we use the herbs in combination, as in *Spaghettini all'Insalata* (Pasta Salad with Olives and Capers, page 88), which is flavored with mint, basil, parsley, and dried oregano. For *Frittatine Verdi in Insalata* (Strips of Herb Pancake in Salad, page 89), thin pancakes made with mint, basil, parsley, and sage are torn up and tossed with a green salad or a tomato salad.

May is too early for tomatoes at Regaleali, and most of Sicily, but we can buy tomatoes grown in Pachino in southern Sicily. It's a new variety, bred to bear early. These particular tomatoes are watery—you wouldn't want to make a sauce with them—but they are quite good for salad. It's nice to have them around in May.

Once we have basil to pick, we go crazy with it. Sicilian basil is very perfumed and pungent; one would think a little goes a long way. On the contrary, Sicilians can't get enough of it. Even a dish in which you wouldn't expect to find a lot of basil, like *Insalata di Tacchino* (Turkey Salad, page 90), might take a whole cup of basil leaves.

FRUITS

May is the month for strawberries—luscious juicy ones from the cultivated beds, heavenly scented ones from the Madonie Mountains, the
famous *fraises des bois* or wild strawberries. I'm always looking for
new ways to preserve them, ways that will make the most of their
extraordinary flavor. At one point, I revolutionized my strawberry jam,
following the directions in a French recipe book. The berries are
cooked in a sugar syrup the first day and then cooked again the next
day. This *Marmellata di Fragole* (Strawberry Jam, page 96) is sweet
and full of whole pieces of fruit. I also make *sciroppo di fragola* (strawberry syrup), which we pour on vanilla ice cream or ricotta.

The perfume of wild strawberries is captured in *Liquore di
Fragoline* (Wild Strawberry Cordial, page 96), which requires no special equipment or skills, just an iron will to keep from tasting it before
it matures. It can also be made with cultivated strawberries.

While strawberries are plentiful, I make *Gelatina di Fragole* (page
163). It is certain to become one of your favorite gelatin desserts too.
You can serve it in a pretty bowl or in individual glasses. Another good
way to end a meal is with granita. Follow the recipe for *Granita di
Pesche* (page 166), substituting one pound of strawberries for the
peaches.

Other fruits in season in May in Sicily are loquats, cherries and sour
cherries, and tiny apricots the size of a big cherry that are so sweet and
juicy, eating them is like drinking drops of honey. These are not suit-
able for a fruit tart—it would be a waste—but strawberries, cherries,
and sour cherries are all good for *Crostata di Frutta Fresca* (Fresh
Fruit Tart, page 97). Use whatever fruit is in season when you make it:
peaches, nectarines, plums, mirabelles.

TUNA

It's easy to see the seasons of fruits and vegetables as they come and go
but hard sometimes to visualize the seasons of the creatures of the
deep. Yet, like salmon and shad, every spring the tuna come back to
their traditional spawning grounds. These powerful migratory fish
swim thousands of miles to return to the seas off the western coast of

Sicily to mate. There they are netted and killed, some of them in the *mattanza*, a ritual slaughter that dates back to Arab times. As a happy consequence, prices fall, and one feels free to indulge in tuna dishes.

Tuna has always been a favorite fish for Sicilians. It keeps longer than any other, and so it could be shipped inland in the days before refrigeration. In port towns, tuna was preserved under a sweet-and-sour *Cipollata* (Onion Topping, page 95); the dish is very similar to the famous *saor* of Venice. It is still a popular way to prepare tuna. For this, the fish is sliced rather thin and fried, then covered with topping and sprinkled with lots of mint leaves. The dish is left out at room temperature; the longer it stands, the better it tastes.

Two very special tuna treats are associated with tuna season: *lattume* and *ventresca*, called *surra*, an Arab word, in dialect. *Lattume*, the Sicilian word for tuna milt, comes from the expression *latte di pesce*, literally "fish milk." It looks like white liver.

Lattume is cooked like brains, simmered in salted water with bay leaf until opaque. It is then left to cool and is sliced. The slices are dipped in an egg batter and fried like cutlets or served with a dressing of olive oil, lemon juice, salt, and parsley. This dish is called *lattume con olio, limone, e prezzemolo*.

Ventresca is the fatty underbelly of the fish, a choice morsel, or *boccone prelibato* as we would say. When Mario Lo Menzo, my parents' *monzù* chef, cooks it at Case Grandi, it is usually reserved for my father, who has always been able to digest any amount of fat without a problem even after he reached his eighties. I recall one evening, though, when Mario wasn't there, my mother served a very clever second course. Three bowls were brought out and placed on the table. The first had sliced boiled potatoes seasoned with olive oil, chopped parsley, and salt and pepper; the second, pitted green olives with celery, garlic, and oregano; and the third, preserved *ventresca*. Each of us mixed some of the three ingredients in personal proportions on the plate. It was like a very sophisticated—yet very simple—*insalata di patate col tonno* (potato salad with tuna).

Sometimes the simpler version of *insalata di patate col tonno* has a little *bottarga*, or dried, salted tuna roe, grated on top. *Bottarga*, called *uovo di tonno* in Sicily, is sometimes available in specialty food stores

OVERLEAF: *Like onions, cherry tomatoes are hung to preserve them.*

and delicatessens in Italian-American neighborhoods.

Tuna meat is often grilled or baked. For *Tonno al Forno* (Baked Tuna, page 92), a large piece of fish is studded with garlic and herbs, much as one would prepare a leg of lamb for roasting. Leftovers can be used to make a pasta sauce or *Riso con Tonno Fresco* (page 93), a rice salad with tuna and lots of mint. Actually, these dishes are so good, it's worth baking or grilling extra tuna for the purpose.

Another very popular way to prepare tuna is to cook it in a sauce on top of the stove, either a wine sauce or a rich tomato sauce. If there is any left over, the fish and sauce can then be used to dress pasta. Nothing is wasted in the Sicilian kitchen.

Very fresh fish is wonderful raw. *Carpaccio di Tonno* (Tuna Carpaccio, page 91) makes a fantastic first course. Swordfish also can be marinated and eaten raw, but the two kinds of fish are not interchangeable. Swordfish, for example, can be marinated for only thirty minutes—tuna can be marinated much longer—and it would never be served with a mayonnaise sauce made with mustard and vinegar. On the other hand, raw tuna would not be put on pasta as is the swordfish in *Fettuccine al Pesce Spada* (page 197).

PRESERVED FISH

Over the centuries, preserved fish products have played an important role in the Sicilian diet. Drying and salting were and still are the two common methods, smoking not being in the Sicilian repertoire. Cod is both air-dried and salted. *Baccalà*, or salt cod, is more popular in eastern Sicily than in the western parts, though it is far from unknown there. It even has a place on the *verginedde* tables (page 23) in Valledolmo on San Giuseppe's Day.

Anchovies and sardines are salted. Salted anchovies are the mystery ingredient in many dishes in this book; if you can't find them, you can substitute canned anchovies, but the dish won't have the same depth of flavor. Salted sardines lend savor to anything they are added to. Just one in a pot of tomato sauce used to remind a whole peasant family of the taste of fish. In *Insalata di Lattuga Nostrana con Sarde Salate* (Romaine Lettuce Salad with Salted Sardines, page 94), on the other hand, they add a surprisingly subtle touch.

Canned tuna is an important pantry ingredient. It is used in salads with potatoes, as mentioned, or with rice, as in *Insalata di Riso con Pomodoro, Tonno, e Capperi* (page 113), and in quick pasta dishes with anchovies or with tomato sauce. Canned tuna is the basis of *Salame di Tonno* (page 157), a poached fish pâté in the shape of a salami, and *Pesce del Contadino* (page 203), in the shape of a fish. This simple dish is a great favorite at the annual Ferragosto buffet (page 172) at my parents' villa in Mondello.

THE WINE CELLAR AT CASA MAZZARINO

My husband Vences's paternal grandfather, Count Giuseppe Lanza di Mazzarino, was an exceptional gourmet, a good skipper, a fine shot, and a ladies' man. He had an extraordinary collection of wines, for which he transformed the carriage house at Casa Mazzarino in central Palermo into a wine cellar. The walls were so thick they kept the wines at the ideal temperature all summer and winter long. When World II was nearing Sicily, a quick-witted butler, in the absence of the family, decided to have the cellar sealed. Fortunately, it survived the fighting and bombing and escaped the attention of rowdy American troops, who had discovered they liked Sicilian wine.

Nonno Peppino, as Vences and the others called his grandfather, had started his collection around 1880, and it included many vintages from before the spread of phylloxera, the vine disease that devastated the vineyards of Europe. When I married into the family and went to live at the Casa Mazzarino in 1957, many bottles still lay on the shelves. Thanks to the butler's foresight, the family went on drinking the wines, toasting Nonno Peppino with a Gruaud-Larose or a Château Lafite from time to time.

The Count had collected French wines from Bordeaux, Burgundy, Chablis, Sauternes, and Champagne. He had wines from Spain and Portugal, from South Africa and Australia, the very first wines from there. He loved Liebfraumilch and always ordered several cases when he went on shooting parties in Germany.

Opening one of those dream bottles was a ritual that took place only when we had no guests to dinner. The precious vessel was carried to the dining room in trembling hands. The bottles were dark in the fashion of the day and covered with decades of dust and cobwebs. The labels were virtually unreadable. It didn't matter: All eyes were turned to the one chosen to open the bottle, usually Giuseppe, the oldest son, or Vences, or occasionally the butler. Some of the wines were undrinkable, and the sparkling wines were flat. But others were fantastic.

One corner of the cellar was reserved for Italian wines—Chianti, Barbera, Barolo. Sicilian wines were well represented too: table wines from many different wineries, including Camastra from the Tasca estate, Signora from my sister Costanza's in-laws, and of course, the potent cherry-colored Dorilli from the Mazzarino estate near Vittoria. This was the wine we always drank for lunch, which was a more intimate and less demanding meal than dinner. In addition to table wines, there were bottles of Malvasia and Marsala still bearing the English names of Woodhouse, Whitaker, and Ingham.

The assortment of sherry, port, and Malaga, Cognac and whisky, eaux-de-vie, and sweet liqueurs was unusually complete. Sweet liqueurs were very much appreciated by the ladies in the old days. There was also some rum that had been transported in barrels on a sailing ship from Jamaica to be bottled when it reached its final destination, the wine cellar of the Casa Mazzarino, in 1896. Sixty years later, Vences offered this very strong, almost black rum to guests in our own house. You could only have one sip it was so strong, but the flavor was exceptional.

In Nonno Peppino's day, dinner was an elaborate affair with many courses, each accompanied by a different wine. For each wine there was a different glass, clear for red wine, green or red for the white wines, which were not transparent as they are today. Glasses were shorter then as well, not long stemmed and likely to topple.

The wines too have changed. Experts say that the quality of the prephylloxera wines has never been—and never will be—matched. Other changes in wine making have also altered the character of the wine. The old strong wines of Sicily have given way to more refined wines, better appreciated by the modern palate. My grandfather and then my father led the way with the wines of Regaleali. While in the mainstream of European wines, they retain characteristics arising from the soil and climate that distinguish them from mainland wines. My brother Lucio and his two sons, Giuseppe and Alberto, are carrying the Tasca approach to wine making into the twenty-first century.

ABOVE: *The first growth climbs the trellises.*

THE RECIPES

SPAGHETTINI ALL'INSALATA
Pasta Salad with Olives and Capers

This recipe was inspired by a dish made famous by the Duca di Salaparuta, founder of Corvo, the huge Sicilian winery. He was a vegetarian and wrote a vegetarian cookbook. The dish sounded so refreshing, I decided to try it with a few changes to bring it more up to date although it is very good his way, with just lemon juice, olive oil, parsley, and salt and pepper.

THIS MAKES ENOUGH FOR 4 PEOPLE.

½ cup (30 g) mint and basil leaves
2 tablespoons flat-leaf parsley leaves
2 cloves garlic
2 tablespoons fresh lemon juice
½ cup (125 ml) olive oil
1 teaspoon dried oregano
1 pound (450 g) spaghettini
12 Sicilian green olives, pitted and cut in half
1 tablespoon capers, rinsed

Set aside some of the basil and mint leaves for garnish. Chop the rest together with the parsley, garlic, and lemon juice in a food processor or blender. With the motor running, slowly pour in the olive oil. Stir in the oregano. Transfer to a serving bowl.

Cook the spaghettini in boiling salted water. When the pasta is al dente, drain it. Set the colander in a bowl of salted cold water with ice cubes for 2 seconds. Drain again. Pour into the serving bowl and mix thoroughly. Top with the olives, capers, and reserved whole basil and mint leaves. Serve at room temperature.

FRITTATINE VERDI IN INSALATA
Strips of Herb Pancake in Salad
Add pieces or strips of these delicate herb pancakes to a salad.
THIS MAKES ENOUGH FOR 8 PEOPLE.

PANCAKES
   4 large eggs
   2 tablespoons all-purpose flour
   ½ cup (125 ml) milk
   1 clove garlic, pushed through a press
   1 cup (60 g) mixed leaves of mint, sage, basil, and
      parsley, chopped
   Salt
   Butter
VINAIGRETTE
   2 tablespoons wine vinegar
   2 tablespoons fresh lemon juice
   2 tablespoons white wine
   ½ cup (125 ml) olive oil
   Salt

   3 pounds (1,35 kg) ripe tomatoes or 3 heads lettuce

Lightly beat the eggs and work in the flour, using a wooden spoon or
whisk. Whisk in the milk. Add the garlic, herbs, and a pinch of salt.
Lightly butter a crêpe pan or skillet and make large, very thin pancakes. Set aside to cool.

   To make the vinaigrette, combine the vinegar, lemon juice, wine, oil,
and salt to taste and mix well.

   Just before serving, tear the pancakes into bite-size pieces or cut into
strips and place in a serving bowl with the tomatoes or lettuce. Dress
with just enough of the vinaigrette to coat everything lightly and toss
the salad. Tomato salad can stand, but a green salad should be made
at the last minute.

INSALATA DI TACCHINO
Turkey Salad

This meat salad is ideal hot-weather food and is very economical to prepare with turkey legs. Save the broth to use as stock in soups or sauces.

THIS MAKES ENOUGH FOR 4 PEOPLE.

2¼ pounds (1 kg) turkey leg (2 drumsticks or 1 large thigh)
1 large onion
2 carrots
2 stalks celery
1 chicken bouillon cube
1 cup vegetables pickled in vinegar, such as pickled beets, drained
Juice of ½ orange
Juice of 1 lemon
2 tablespoons red wine vinegar
2 teaspoons Worcestershire sauce
Pinch of ground hot pepper
1 cup (60 g) basil leaves, torn
½ cup (125 ml) olive oil
Salt
¼ pound (100 g) mixed salad greens or romaine or arugula,
  cut into ¾-inch (2-cm) ribbons (about 4 cups)

Put the turkey leg in a medium saucepan and add the onion, carrots, celery, and bouillon cube. Pour in enough water to cover, and bring to a boil. Reduce the heat and simmer until the meat is done, 45 to 50 minutes. Using a slotted spoon, remove the turkey and vegetables. Set aside to cool.

Bone the meat and cut into strips about ⅜ inch (1 cm) wide; you should have about 2½ cups. Cut the cooked vegetables and pickled vegetables, if necessary, into similar-size strips. Put everything in a serving bowl.

Whisk together the orange juice and lemon juice, vinegar, Worcestershire, hot pepper, basil, olive oil, and salt to taste. Pour over the turkey and vegetables and mix well. Let stand at room temperature for at least 2 hours.

Just before serving, stir in the salad greens.

CARPACCIO DI TONNO
Tuna Carpaccio

Serve this with mayonnaise seasoned with mustard and vinegar.

THIS MAKES ENOUGH FOR 8 PEOPLE AS AN APPETIZER.

½ pound (250 g) fresh tuna
Juice of 1 lemon
Juice of ½ orange
Salt
Ground hot pepper
1 clove garlic, very finely minced or pushed through a press
2 tablespoons chopped flat-leaf parsley or 1 teaspoon
    dried oregano
Olive oil

Thinly slice the fish, cutting with the grain. Arrange the slices in a large shallow dish. Mix the lemon and orange juices and pour over the fish. Marinate at room temperature for 1 hour.

Remove the fish from the juice, letting the excess drip off. Do not rinse. Arrange on a serving plate and season with salt, hot pepper, and the garlic. Sprinkle with the parsley, drizzle with olive oil, and serve.

ABOVE: *Wild poppies and marguerites bloom in a meadow.*

TONNO AL FORNO
Baked Tuna

Serve this baked tuna with mashed potatoes. If there is any left, use it for *Riso con Tonno Fresco* (opposite) or as a topping for pasta, as described at the end of the recipe.

THIS MAKES ENOUGH FOR 6 TO 8 PEOPLE.

3 cloves garlic
½ cup (30 g) mint leaves
2 salted anchovies, filleted and rinsed, or 4 canned anchovy fillets
3 pounds (1,5 kg) fresh tuna, in 1 or 2 pieces, 2 inches
   (5 cm) thick
Salt and freshly ground black pepper
¼ cup olive oil
1½ cups (375 ml) white wine
Juice of 1 lemon
1 sprig of rosemary

Preheat the oven to 375° F. (190° C.).

Chop the garlic, mint, and anchovies and mix them together. With the tip of a knife, make holes in the tuna, about 1¼ inches (3 cm) deep and about 2½ inches (6 cm) apart. Fill the holes with the garlic mixture. Rub the fish with salt and pepper and the rest of the mixture, if any remains.

Put the fish in a roasting pan or baking dish and drizzle with the olive oil. Bake for 10 minutes.

Remove from the oven, pour 1 cup of the wine and the lemon juice into the pan, and scrape the bottom with a wooden spatula. Put the rosemary in the pan. Put the fish back into the oven. Reduce the heat to 350° F. (180° C.), and cook until done, turning once, 20 to 30 minutes, depending on how thick the fish is. Test by inserting the tip of a knife; it should go in easily. Remove from the oven. Set the fish aside on a serving dish and keep it warm while you make the sauce.

Place the roasting pan on the stovetop over low heat. Add the remaining ½ cup wine and simmer for 5 minutes. Taste for seasoning. Strain the sauce over the fish.

To serve, push a spoon into the fish and break off pieces. Do not cut or slice the fish.

VARIATION. *Pasta con Tonno Fresco* (Pasta with Fresh Tuna). Combine 1 small red onion, chopped, and ¼ cup olive oil in a sauté pan over medium heat and cook until the onion is soft, about 5 minutes. Stir in 1 cup flaked cooked tuna and any leftover sauce and heat just to warm through. Cook ¾ pound (350 g) spaghetti in boiling salted water until al dente. Drain and transfer to a serving dish. Pour the tuna sauce on top and toss. Add 2 to 3 tablespoons more olive oil if the dish seems dry. Sprinkle generously with chopped parsley and serve. Serve toasted breadcrumbs at the table. This makes enough for 4 people as a first course.

RISO CON TONNO FRESCO
Rice Salad with Fresh Tuna

This is one good way to use leftover tuna—so good, in fact, that it's worth making extra.

THIS MAKES ENOUGH FOR 4 PEOPLE AS A FIRST COURSE.

1 cup (200 g) long-grain rice
¼ cup (125 ml) olive oil
½ small red onion, finely chopped
1 clove garlic, minced or pushed through a press (optional)
¼ cup (30 g) chopped mint leaves
1 cup (packed) flaked cooked tuna (6 to 7 oz/180 to 200 g)
¼ cup white wine
Salt and freshly ground black pepper

Cook the rice as described on page 113. Drain.

Place the rice in a serving bowl and add only as much oil as needed to keep the rice from sticking. Let cool for 10 minutes.

Stir in the onion, garlic, and mint. Stir in the flaked fish. Add the wine and oil to taste—a Sicilian would add a lot. Season to taste with salt and pepper. Let stand at room temperature for 1 hour. Taste for seasoning again before serving.

INSALATA DI LATTUGA NOSTRANA CON SARDE SALATE
Romaine Lettuce Salad with Salted Sardines

You could make this salad with other greens, but they would have to be strong, as romaine is, to stand up to the salted sardines. The orange juice—it could as well be grapefruit or tangerine—softens the vinaigrette. I always put some citrus in my green salads.

THIS MAKES ENOUGH FOR 6 PEOPLE.

3 salted sardines or 6 salted anchovies, filleted
1 large head romaine lettuce
¼ cup (60 ml) fresh orange juice
1 tablespoon wine vinegar
⅓ cup (75 ml) olive oil
Pinch of ground hot pepper
Salt
2 tablespoons chopped flat-leaf parsley

Wash the sardine fillets under running cold water, blot dry, and cut into long strips. If using anchovies, halve lengthwise. Set aside.

Wash and dry the lettuce, stack the leaves, and cut crosswise into strips ⅜ inch (1 cm) wide. Put in a serving bowl.

Mix together the orange juice, vinegar, olive oil, hot pepper, and salt to taste. Just before serving, whisk the dressing, pour it over the lettuce, and toss to mix. Garnish with the strips of sardines, sprinkle with the parsley, and serve.

CIPOLLATA
Onion Topping

This topping goes on fish and various fried foods, like winter squash or meat cutlets. It is put on while still hot so its flavor penetrates the other food. In Sicily, we use our mild red onions. You can use red onions or other sweet onions—Vidalias, or Mauis, or Walla Wallas—for this.

THIS MAKES ABOUT 2 CUPS OF TOPPING.

3 pounds (1,35 kg) red onions, sliced
1½ cups (375 ml) olive oil
2 cups (500 ml) water
1 cup (250 ml) wine vinegar
2 tablespoons sugar
1 tablespoon salt
1 cup (60 g) mint leaves

Combine the onions and the olive oil in a large sauté pan and cook over low heat until soft and translucent, about 5 minutes. Cover and cook for 10 minutes, shaking the pan from time to time.

Add the water, cover, and cook until the onions are very soft, 8 to 10 minutes. Stir in the vinegar, sugar, salt, and mint leaves. Use hot.

ABOVE: *Wild chamomile is the best for tea.*

MARMELLATA DI FRAGOLE
Strawberry Jam
THIS MAKES 4 HALF-PINT (250-ML) JARS OF JAM.

2 quarts (1 kg) strawberries
2½ cups (500 g) sugar
2 cups (500 ml) water
Grated zest and juice of ½ lemon
Grated zest and juice of ½ orange

Wash and hull the strawberries. Cut any very large ones in half.

Combine the sugar with the water in a large saucepan and stir to dissolve. Bring to a boil and boil, uncovered, until the syrup reaches the thread stage (230° F./110° C. on a candy thermometer). Add the strawberries and lemon and orange zests and juices and cook for 40 minutes. Remove from the heat and let stand for 24 hours.

The next day, bring the mixture back to a boil and cook for 20 minutes. Check the consistency: Drop a spoonful onto a plate; if the mixture spreads only slightly, it is ready to be put into jars. Ladle into hot sterilized jars, leaving ¼ inch (less than 1 cm) of headspace. Cover and process in a hot-water bath (page 211). Store in a cool dark place for at least 2 months before using.

LIQUORE DI FRAGOLINE
Wild Strawberry Cordial
For the lucky few who know where the wild strawberries grow.
THIS MAKES ABOUT 3 PINTS (1,5 L) OF CORDIAL.

10 ounces (300 g) wild strawberries
2 cups (500 ml) 90-proof vodka
1¾ cups (350 g) sugar
2 cups (500 ml) water

Clean the wild strawberries and put them in a jar. Pour in the vodka, tightly close the jar, and put in a cool, dark place for 15 days.

Combine the sugar and water in a large saucepan and heat until the sugar dissolves. Remove from the heat and let cool. Filter the alcohol through several layers of clean napkin or filter twice through coffee filters. Combine with the syrup. Mix well, pour into bottles, and seal. Let stand for at least 2 months.

CROSTATA DI FRUTTA FRESCA
Fresh Fruit Tart

I often make a quick tart with fruit that is left in the fruit basket. The shell is partially baked first so that the fruit doesn't cook for too long.
THIS MAKES ENOUGH FOR 10 PEOPLE.

2²/₃ cups (400 g) all-purpose flour
¼ cup (50 g) sugar
Pinch of salt
2 large eggs
½ pound (2 sticks/250 g) butter, softened
About 2½ pounds (1 kg) peaches or plums, peeled
2 tablespoons packed brown sugar

Put the flour, sugar, and salt in a bowl and mix together. Make a well, add the eggs, and mix in. Add the butter and mix with your fingers. Knead just until the dough comes together; it will be soft. Let it rest for at least 20 minutes.

Preheat the oven to 350° F. (175° C.).

Butter and flour an 11-inch (27-cm) tart or springform pan. Pat the dough into the bottom of the pan and against the sides, even with the top of the tart pan, or about 1 inch up the sides of a springform. Place a sheet of foil on top and fill with dried beans. Bake for 30 minutes. Remove the beans and save them for the next time. Remove foil.

While the shell is baking, prepare the fruit, cutting it into slices, halves, or quarters depending on the size. Arrange it in the tart shell and sprinkle with the brown sugar. Bake for 20 minutes. Remove from the oven and as soon as the pan is cool enough to handle, remove the sides. Let the tart cool on a rack.

VARIATION. *Biscotti* (Cookies). Take a little piece of leftover dough, roll it into a ball, and flatten it. Place the disks, very close together, on a foil-lined baking sheet. Brush with marmalade. Bake at 350° F. (175° C.) for about 30 minutes.

GIUGNO

Lost in the sea somewhere between Sicily and North Africa is the tiny island of Pantelleria. The climate is harsh—the wind always blows, hot in summer, cold in winter. Barren volcanic slopes reach down into rough seas. Tenacious plants, like the caper, grow in patches of dusty soil nestled between the black lava rocks.

The only water is rainwater, and the Pantescans, as the people of Pantelleria are known, have learned to cherish every drop. The roofs of their houses are domed; the rain rolls off and is channeled into a cistern.

The houses, called dammusi (an Arab name), are cube shaped with volcanic-rock walls sometimes three feet thick. The walls and dome keep the house cool in summer and warm in winter. The domes are whitewashed; they seem to glow in the brilliant sunshine.

LEFT: *A small black dammuso, with its white domed roof.*

PANTELLERIA

Two volcanoes dominate Pantelleria, Montagna Grande and Monte Gibele. The slopes of Montagna Grande are thickly covered with vegetation, the famous *macchia mediterranea*—bushy oak and maritime pines, rock roses (*Cistus*), honeysuckle, myrtle, and holly. The air is cool, real mountain air.

Along the coast, windbreaks of black and rust-colored rocks protect the caper beds, row upon row of caper plants. The vineyards, vegetable gardens, and dwarf olive and fruit trees also grow on terraced slopes. In the olive groves, the trees are barely knee high; the enormous trunks sticking through the leaves are the only sign that they are trees, not some bizarre kind of bushes.

Some houses have a round walled garden, *uno giardiano pantesco*, about fifteen feet in diameter, which is entered through a low archway. The stone walls, built without mortar or cement, are made as high as the lemon trees they were originally designed to shield from the relentless wind.

Every June, my sister Costanza, her husband, Paolo Camporeale, and I go to Pantelleria for a little holiday. It is not so hot and windy in June nor as crowded as in August, when the rich and famous come carrying their bottled water. Paolo pioneered Pantelleria many years ago, long before it was discovered by the jet set. Now he owns several houses on the island so there is plenty of room for the family, and we always invite a few special guests.

One year I invited the four friends I call my American Pillars after the name of a rose that grows in my garden: Mary Simeti, a native New Yorker married to a Sicilian, who has lived in Sicily all of her adult life; Faith Willinger, an American with a consuming interest in Italian food and wine, who has lived in Florence for many years; Ann Yonkers, who came to appreciate the flavors of Sicily when she tested the recipes for my first book, *The Heart of Sicily*; and Susan Derecskey, a convert to Sicilian food and customs, who helped me write *Heart* and continued to work with me on this book. She was with us only in spirit. Over the years, the Pillars and I have shared many a culinary adventure. In Pantelleria, we had a great time—cooking, eating, and tooling around in a rickety rented car to look at what was being grown, made, and marketed on the island.

CAPERS

One day we went to visit the Cooperativa Agricola Produttori Capperi, the caper producers' cooperative. The co-op was founded in 1971 with the goal of increasing production as well as promoting the sale and distribution of Pantelleria's capers worldwide. The co-op, which also assists the growers in coping with the complicated regulations and mountains of paperwork generated by the government in Rome, is a noble attempt at survival—something everyone engaged in agriculture, including me and my family, faces every day.

The capers of Pantelleria are famous throughout the world. Capers love sun and heat, and the wild plant has always flourished in the volcanic soil of the island. It has been domesticated for centuries, but only since 1960 have techniques become specialized and the best varieties systematically selected for cultivation.

Large, juicy, and bursting with strong aromas and flavor, the caper, actually the bud of the caper plant (*Capparis spinosa*), is harvested from May until the end of August. Each grower's family goes out at first light to pick capers, stripping the buds from the stems, which will bear new buds in about a fortnight. The pickers work until noon when the sun gets too hot. They spread out the capers to dry in the sun for a day. Then they take them to the co-op.

At the co-op sheds, the capers are weighed and dumped into large plastic barrels to be cured in sea salt. These used to be wood. It was believed that the salt had to come into contact with wood to melt and draw off the juice of the capers, but the curing seems to work just as well in plastic.

After a week or ten days, the capers are drained and transferred to fresh containers with more dry sea salt. After another week or so, they are calibrated by machine; the sizes range from 7 mm to 14 mm (about ¼ to ½ inch), far larger than the tiny nonpareil capers from Spain found bottled in vinegar in American supermarkets. The capers are then transferred to new containers and salted again. The containers are closed and set aside for two months. Finally, the capers are ready to eat. They keep in excellent condition like this for two years.

Some of the caper buds are left on the vine to go to seed. Their bloom is short-lived: four or five delicate rose-tinged white petals that drop after only one day, leaving the long purple stamen that is particular to the caper. The fruit, called caperberries in English, *zucchinette* in Pantelleria, and *zuccotti* in the Eolian Islands, looks like a tiny green zucchini—as the names suggest—about the size of the nail of your little finger. They are picked unripe and pickled in vinegar. Though they are not as good as capers, caperberries can be substituted for them in many dishes, such as *Insalata di Riso con Pomodoro, Tonno, e Capperi* (Rice Salad with Tomatoes, Tuna, and Capers, page 113), nibbled like olives, or dropped into a dry martini.

Capers are also preserved in vinegar, though normally not by the Pantescans, who feel salted capers are superior because you taste the caper not the vinegar. (I agree.) Growers Salvatore and Dominica Ferrandes, however, discovered an old family recipe, which leaves the capers looking like fresh ones, big and unwrinkled. In this process, the capers are cured in sea salt, rinsed in good vinegar, drained and dried, then packaged in plastic. These capers are very good, like a mild pickle. Unfortunately, they are not appreciated in Italy, but Dominica, being Swiss, found a way to export them to Switzerland, where they are.

Capers have been known since antiquity for their power in flavoring meats and fish and sauces, notably the *garum* of the Roman era and, in modern times, French sauces like *sauce ravigote* and *sauce tartare*. I would rinse them for such delicate sauces or for complex dishes like *vitello tonné* (called *vitello tonnato* in northern Italy). For salads or other simple preparations, I just use them as is and add less salt to the dish.

The Pantescans themselves use capers mostly in sauces for fish and as an added flavor for composed salads, such as *Insalata Pantesca* (Tomato Salad with Potatoes and Black Olives, page 114), which is very good served with canned mackerel; and for *Coniglio all'Agrodolce* (Rabbit in Sweet-and-Sour Sauce, page 114), a stew that uses a full half cup of capers.

Individual growers and the co-op also make two kinds of caper paste. One is simply pureed capers with vinegar and *peperoncino* (ground hot pepper), the other pureed capers and sun-dried tomatoes; both are preserved under oil. They are very flavorful. I find they are excellent on *bruschetta*, on pasta, or thinned with olive oil and mixed into a pasta, rice, or potato salad.

MUSTAZZUOLI PANTESCHI

The first time I went to the co-op to taste the caper paste, there was none available, and I was told to come back the next day. This was to be my last stop for food before leaving the island. I had also been try-ing for days to locate a woman who makes *Mustazzuoli Panteschi* (page 128), the most elaborate pastries I had ever seen. Mary had given me one for Easter, which I had kept as a clue to tracking down its cre-ator; Mary had her name but no address.

So that last day, I picked up Alessandro Leone, the photographer who took the pictures for this book, at the airport. Our immediate objective was to photograph the *dammusi* against the rays of the set-ting sun. It was a little early, so we drove to the co-op first. Timing is not the strongest attribute of the Pantescans, and the jars of paste, not surprisingly, were not there. But we did find someone who knew the woman I'd been looking for. He led us to her house; we never would have found it without a guide.

We called out, but there was no answer. So, we went up to the first floor, and as we turned the corner, there, as if by magic, was a wood-burning oven built into the gray rock. The door was open, and there was a tray of these extraordinary pastries looking right at me. I started getting all excited. Suddenly, the man of the house appeared. The fol-lowing conversation ensued:

Alessandro: "Are you Signor D'Aglietta?"

The man: "So they say."

I was desperate to know where and who the person who made these wonderful pastries was, but Alessandro went on with the formalities:

Alessandro: "What strange weather!"

Signor D'Aglietta: "To speak of the weather is a waste of time."

Our host pulled out three chairs and opened a bottle of wine, made from his own grapes. I tried to say we were in a hurry, the photos, the sunset . . .

"Signora," he said, "life lies ahead of you."

Not a bad compliment, but not what I wanted to hear at that moment.

Finally, Maria, freshly showered and all dressed up, appeared. We asked her if the sheet of pastries we saw was the only one. No! Sheets and sheets of the *mustazzuoli* had been specially ordered (the pastries are normally made only for Easter), and she had made many different shapes for the occasion.

Alessandro went up on the roof with the *mustazzuoli*, while Maria and I sat down, and she gave me her recipe. It was an impossible recipe, with imprecise quantities and incomplete directions. The pastry was a simple pastry dough, which the Pantescans make with leaf lard (vegetable shortening can also be used). The filling was a paste of dried fruit and almond flour, flavored with orange peel, cinnamon, and mint, and held together with honey. The paste is rolled into ropes, placed on strips of pastry, and rolled together. These ropes are shaped into rings or leaves. Then the dough is snipped to create baroque pastries that look almost too good to eat. The art is passed from mother to daughter, and some women are known to have the feel for it in their fingertips.

ZIBIBBO GRAPES

The Zibibbo table grapes of Pantelleria are almost as well known as the capers, at least in Italy. Large and golden, almost pink, with an incredible perfume, the grapes fill your mouth with juice the moment you bite into one.

The grapes are also dried. Everyone who has grapes dries some, but Salvatore Ferrandes's *uva passa di zibibbo* is outstanding. You can scarcely taste the peel, so carefully have the grapes been dried. He picks them when they are ripe but not overripe and lays them out on screens, turning them over every morning and every evening until they are dry but still soft inside. You cannot imagine how wonderful they are.

Marmellata di Zibibbo (Zibibbo Grape Jam, page 127) is another way to prolong the pleasure of the grape. The grapes are so sweet, you can use less than half as much sugar as you usually would need for jam. The only drawback is peeling and seeding the grapes.

Some of the local grapes are made into the famous *passito di Pantelleria*, a dessert wine, very strong, sweet, and flavorful. It goes down ever so smoothly, and if you're not careful, you might finish your meal sleeping under the table.

THE VEGETABLES OF PANTELLERIA

One day, Anna Belvisi, the caretaker's wife, brought us a flask of her own *passito* to taste; she was very proud of it—and rightly so! She also brought a basket of vegetables, including some *zucchine pantesche*, from her garden. These zucchini—pale green, striped with darker green and perfectly oval—are, as far as I know, grown only on Pantelleria. Like the Zibibbo, they are incredibly sweet.

With the Pillars, Costanza, and I all cutting and chopping, we cooked the zucchini for lunch, stuffing them with potatoes, almonds, cheese, and the flesh of the zucchini itself. You can substitute pattypan squash or a scaloppine, a cross between zucchini and pattypan squash, for the Pantescan squash in the recipe for *Zucchine Pantesche Ripiene* (Stuffed Pantescan Zucchini, page 116). It won't taste quite the same as the local variety, but it will be in keeping with the local philosophy.

Pesto pantesco, one of the island's specialties, is a perfect example of that philosophy, which is an instinctual attitude toward food and life in its purest form. I must have asked a dozen women how they make pesto. No two replies were the same—although each one swore hers was *the* authentic recipe. The only ingredients found in every recipe were garlic and olive oil; the only direction, to let the pesto stand for a day to let the flavors develop. Other than that, one woman uses tomatoes and basil and another, tomatoes and parsley; a third uses basil in summer and parsley in winter. One seasons it with dried oregano, another with ground hot pepper, a third with both. One has almonds, another black olives, and so on.

In line with the Pantescan philosophy, I concocted my own pesto for pasta, used in *Spaghetti al Pesto di Case Vecchie* (Anna's Pasta with Pesto, page 120). It has tomatoes and mixed herbs—whatever and how much there is in the garden the day I make it—as well as ground hot pepper and almonds.

Pasticcio di Verdure Pantesco (Layered Vegetables, Pantelleria Style, page 121), best reflects the cooking style of the island: cook with what you find in your garden that very day and make the dish the way *you* want it to be. It's made with zucchini, eggplant, green peppers, potatoes, and tomatoes. My recipe tells you how much to use and how thick to cut each vegetable, but this is contrary to the fatalistic Pantescan approach, namely, to use what you have and cut "as the knife goes in." The first time we made this, we used only six eggs for sixteen people because that was all we had in the house, but it's better with about one egg for every two people.

THE FRUITS OF PANTELLERIA

After lunch, Anna Belvisi invited us to her place to pick plums. We were teasing Ann Yonkers that she would have to pick from the highest branches of the tree because she was the tallest, but when we got there, no tall tree was to be seen. The orchard was hugging the ground, all dwarf trees, and soon we were all bending—Ann folded herself in three—to pick the plums, which grew under the branches. As we were leaving, we asked Anna where their bay was. Not right there, she said, but she promised to send it with her husband the next day.

We expected a handful of leaves, but when he came by, he was carrying so many branches, he looked like a bush of bay walking in. He also brought us more of those sweet little plums from his trees and some figs and white peaches.

The perfume of the fruit was so powerful it completely overwhelmed the aromas of Paolo's *Zuppa di Pesce* (Fish Soup, page 124), which we were eating when he arrived. (When Paolo catches the fish, he considers it his privilege to make the soup himself, his way.)

A PICNIC ON THE CLIFFS

The weather in Pantelleria changes every minute. You wake up in the morning, look out your window at the sea, and see a big menacing cloud on the horizon. You think it bodes no good—it might bring the scirocco, the wind from Africa—and you cancel the plan to go swimming that day. A little while later, the dark cloud vanishes completely, leaving clear blue skies behind; luck is with you, and you decide to go after all.

When we go swimming, we spend the day. It's not a casual outing. The land is high above the sea, and the car goes only to a certain point. You have to climb down the rocks carrying all your provisions on your back: snorkel masks, fishing knives, rubber mattresses to lie on atop the rocks (there is no sand), and, most important of all, the picnic. We pack all kinds of good things to eat—fruit, tomatoes, *Frittata al Forno* (Baked Frittata, page 126), and any other good picnic foods we can think of.

What we always take is a bottle of olive oil already seasoned with oregano, and lots of bread—these are a must. We find holes the wind and rough seas have carved in the rocks, leaving some dried sea salt behind. These are our bowls, and we pour the olive oil into them. They are perfect for dipping the bread that we're going to eat with the sea urchins that we catch.

Everyone joins the hunt. Some pick just a few; others are very good at it and bring back a lot. But first we have to find some limpets to use as spoons to eat the sea urchin roe. Costanza usually makes a rice salad, and we put some roe on top of that too. What a splendid meal it is, eaten under the sun at the edge of the sea.

NOCINO

Every June we pick green walnuts for *nocino*, a walnut liqueur. Traditionally, they are picked in Sicily on June 24, the feast of San Giovanni. It is the ideal moment to cut the walnuts in four with a knife. The quartered nuts are combined with alcohol, sugar, cinnamon, cloves, and lemon zest. The jars are sealed and left in the sun for forty days. Then the liqueur is strained, bottled, and put away until *I Morti*, All Souls' Day, November 2.

You probably can't buy *nocino*, so if you have a walnut tree, you really should make your own. It's simple to do and far superior to any commercially available *digestivo*. *Nocino* has a very mysterious flavor, almost medicinal, like some of those liqueurs and eaux-de-vie made since medieval times by closemouthed monks in northern Europe.

There is nothing secret about my formula—for every ten walnuts, use one cup (200 g) of sugar, a small piece of cinnamon stick, two whole cloves, a tablespoon of chopped lemon zest, and one quart or liter of vodka. In Sicily, we use pure alcohol diluted with water, but vodka works fine. Nor is the method sacrosanct: We sometimes pick the walnuts before the feast of San Giovanni because the weather was hotter than usual or the scirocco blew more than usual and the walnuts had started to turn hard. We might use whole lemons instead of just the zest because the lemons were particularly beautiful that year, and it seemed a shame to waste them. And then there have been the attempts to make the *nocino* lighter in taste. We always go back to the same recipe—which is lighter than the one we found in the old books.

CACIOCAVALLO CHEESE

The warm sunny days of June signal the resumption of caciocavallo cheese making. Homemade or artisanal caciocavallo depends on the heat of the day for fermentation. Also, at this time of year, the cows are fed hay and silage, which make their milk rich. In this respect, cacio-cavallo is unlike pecorino, which is made from fall to spring, when the days are cool and the sheep are eating grass.

When I am in my sitting room at Case Vecchie in Regaleali, I can watch the cows across the way at Tavernola as they graze in the cool months or munch on hay in the four very hot months that make up summer in Sicily. Once the estate was mine, but I sold it in 1957 to the Messina brothers, butchers from nearby Valledolmo.

My great-uncle Alessandro had left Tavernola to me, but at the time making a living from the land looked hopeless. My uncle had a herd of sixty Modicana cows, a tall, skinny, all-purpose breed, good for work, meat, and milk. It was the practice then for landowners to exchange herds, walking them from one place to another to graze. No wonder they looked like ghost cows! Those sixty cows didn't give as much milk as the eighteen Swiss cows my grandfather kept at Regaleali.

Over time, the Messina brothers, Tufanio and Calogero, have developed a healthy dairy herd of stout cows with big udders that show what they are good for. The Messinas also fixed up the old barns and built new ones. They sell the steers for meat—they no longer do the slaughtering or butchering themselves—and they also sell milk. They save some of the milk to make butter and cheese for the Tasca family, but not for sale.

RIGHT: *A cheese-making corner at Tavernola. A cauldron for making ricotta sits in the wood-burning stove; to the left stands an old-fashioned balance scale.*

CHEESE MAKING

The cheeses the Messinas make are caciocavallo and ricotta. The process takes place over two days. It starts when *una noce* (about one tablespoon) of lamb rennet is stirred into a huge wooden bucket of milk (forty liters or about ten gallons) to clabber it. When the stirring stick stands up straight in the mix—after about half an hour—a bucket of hot water is poured in to break the clabbered milk apart into curds and whey.

The curds are stirred, and then the whey is drained off and poured into a giant cauldron to be boiled for ricotta. The curds meanwhile are put in a tilted wooden box and massaged gently to squeeze out more whey, which is added to the rest. Half a bottle of whey saved from the day before is added to the cauldron—without a dose of this super-acidic whey, the ricotta won't come to the surface—along with a handful of sea salt and a cup of magnesium sulfate. (The Messinas say the magnesium sulfate is not necessary, but they always do it that way.) The fire is lit under the cauldron, and the whey comes to a boil. What rises to the top is skimmed off as ricotta (literally, twice-cooked) cheese.

The curds meanwhile are put back in the big bucket and some of the hot whey is poured over them—to cook them, as the Messinas say. Once the liquid cools off completely, the curds are wrapped in a damp towel that was dipped in whey the day before and left to ferment overnight. Between this wrapper and the summer's heat, optimum fermentation is reached in twenty-four hours.

PASTA FILATA
∞

The next day, the curds are unwrapped and each package is cut into three pieces. On the inside, little holes, a sign of fermentation, are visible. At this point, making the *pasta filata* begins.

Pasta filata refers to any cheese—mozzarella is a familiar one—for which the curds are heated, and then stretched and kneaded, and finally molded into the typical shape. Such cheese has great elasticity.

That is why caciocavallo is the ideal cheese to use in dishes in which the cheese is baked, as in the *Zucchine Pantesche Ripiene* (page 116) or the *Sformato di Patate al Ragù* (page 200); grilled or fried, as in *Formaggio al Pomodoro* (page 230), or in *Frittata al Formaggio* (page

47). Caciocavallo is the most famous cheese of Sicily, more famous than pecorino, and since it is not so strong, we eat it often, both on a cheese platter and in such dishes as *Insalata di Linguine con Prosciutto e Formaggio* (page 123).

When Calogero makes the *pasta filata*, he takes his pocket knife and cuts the fermented curds in three, then cuts each piece lengthwise into thin slices, dropping them into a bucket on the floor between his feet. He then covers the strips of cheese with very hot water and works the cheese with a stick, pushing it against the sides of the bucket—the way laundry used to be done with a stick in a tub—until it melts into a paste or dough. The idea is to get out all the holes and air bubbles and excess acidity and have the cheese in one place.

As soon as the water cools enough to handle the cheese, Calogero works it with his hands. With the bucket in place between his feet, he pulls up the cheese with both hands, squeezes it, folds it over, and squeezes it some more; now it looks as if he's wringing out the laundry. Then, he dips it back in the hot water and starts all over again. The temperature of the water in the bucket is very important—it shouldn't get too cold or the cheese "dough" won't be stringy enough to work; nor should it be too warm. (I thought it was pretty hot when I touched it, but maybe my hands are not used to it.) The result is a shiny dough that when it is pulled up by one end, the rest comes up with it.

Next, Calogero starts molding the cheese into a ball, grasping it by the neck and constantly pulling the outside around and tucking it in. Finally, he drops each ball into a brine solution, where it is left to float for several hours—twenty-four hours for a two-pound (one-kilo) ball, twelve hours for a one-pound (half-kilo) ball.

When the cheese is removed from the brine, the balls are tied together with a length of straw, two by two in the characteristic *a cavallo*, or saddlebag, arrangement. The pairs of cheese are hung over a rod to dry. (Some Sicilians, proud of their Arab heritage, point out that the word "caciocavallo" comes from the Arabic word for cheese, *cashcavaj*. Similar ewe's milk cheeses, called *kashkaval*, are made throughout the Balkans, so it's hard to know what the origin of the word is.)

Caciocavallo cheese can be eaten fresh or after it's been aged. At two months, it is still mild and soft; at four months, it is spicier but still buttery; after six months, it becomes *piccante*—sharp and dry.

Caciocavallo is also made in *scalone*, or blocks, though the Messinas make only the balls. The cheese is exactly the same, but it is molded into a brick shape, which is easier to handle for distribution and sale.

The day Calogero showed me how he makes the cheese, he also made a sort of mozzarella. He took a piece of cheese, pulled it into a long rope, tied a knot at the end, and cut it off. He kept doing that, dropping each knot into a bowl of cold water as he cut it. Of course, I had to taste one. It was delicious—warm and chewy and full of flavor. I took some home to make *Insalata Cafona* (Asparagus and Mozzarella Salad, page 117).

ABOVE: *Caper plants sometimes grow out of a crevice in a rock. The buds will be picked or left on the vine to flower and ripen into caper-berries, which look like olives and can be used instead in a dry martini.*

THE RECIPES

INSALATA DI RISO CON POMODORO, TONNO, E CAPPERI
Rice Salad with Tomatoes, Tuna, and Capers
If you like, you can substitute caperberries for the capers. Caperberries are the fruit of the caper bush; you can buy them in jars in specialty food shops or by mail order (page 252).
THIS MAKES ENOUGH FOR 6 PEOPLE AS A FIRST COURSE.

2¼ pounds (1 kg) ripe tomatoes, peeled and cut into small pieces
1 teaspoon sugar
Salt
2 cans (6⅛ oz/173 g each) solid white tuna
1 small red onion, coarsely chopped
1 clove garlic, minced
2 tablespoons capers or 2 to 3 tablespoons caperberries, rinsed
½ cup (125 ml) olive oil
2 tablespoons fresh lemon juice, or more to taste
Pinch of ground hot pepper
2 cups (400 g) long-grain rice, cooked (see Note)
½ cup (60 g) chopped fresh herbs, such as basil, parsley, mint,
*   or dill, or a combination*

Place the tomatoes in a colander and sprinkle with the sugar and salt. Set aside to drain for at least 20 minutes.

Empty the tuna into a strainer and rinse under running water. Drain well, flake with a fork, and place in a salad bowl. Add the onion, garlic, and capers and mix well. Add the olive oil, lemon juice, hot pepper, and the tomatoes. Add the rice and mix well. Sprinkle with the chopped herbs. Let cool, stirring from time to time. Serve at room temperature.

NOTE. *To cook the rice, bring a large saucepan of salted water to a boil. Add the rice and bring back to a boil. Stir and reduce the heat to a simmer. Cook until tender, 15 to 20 minutes. Drain.*

INSALATA PANTESCA

Tomato Salad with Potatoes and Black Olives

This light, refreshing summer salad can be made more substantial with the addition of canned mackerel or, if you prefer, sardines.

THIS MAKES ENOUGH FOR 4 TO 6 PEOPLE.

6 medium-size red or white new potatoes (1½ lb/675 g), scrubbed
4 ripe or green tomatoes (1 lb/450 g), sliced ⅜ inch (1 cm) thick
1 small red onion, thinly sliced
12 oil-cured black olives, pitted
1 tablespoon capers, rinsed
1 can (4⅜ oz/125 g) mackerel packed in olive oil (optional)
½ cup (125 ml) olive oil
2 teaspoons dried oregano
Salt

Boil the potatoes in salted water until tender, 20 to 35 minutes, depending on size. Drain. When cool enough to handle, peel and cut into bite-size pieces.

Combine the potatoes, tomatoes, onion, olives, and capers in a serving bowl. Drain the mackerel, if using, break each fillet in half, and add. Pour the olive oil over and sprinkle with the oregano and salt to taste. Turn carefully to coat. Serve at room temperature.

CONIGLIO ALL'AGRODOLCE

Rabbit in Sweet-and-Sour Sauce

The people of Pantelleria raise rabbits for meat. They don't have as much taste as wild rabbits, but this sauce is so flavorful, it doesn't matter. If you don't eat rabbit, try the sauce with the meat from a poached turkey drumstick or a couple of chicken thighs.

THIS MAKES ENOUGH FOR 4 PEOPLE.

1 small rabbit (2¼ to 3 lb/1 to 1,5 kg), cut into pieces
1 lemon, cut in half
2 bay leaves
¼ cup (60 ml) white wine
Vegetable oil, for frying the rabbit

SWEET-AND-SOUR SAUCE

1 large onion, roughly sliced
¼ cup (60 ml) olive oil
1 pound (450 g) ripe tomatoes, coarsely chopped
3 tablespoons sugar
1 cup (250 ml) wine vinegar
Pinch of ground cinnamon
1 cup (200 g) pitted green olives, cut in half
½ cup (80 g) capers, rinsed

¼ cup (40 g) toasted almond flour (see Note)
Salt

Put the rabbit pieces in a saucepan, add ½ lemon and the bay leaves, and cover with water. Bring to a boil. Remove from the heat and drain. Sprinkle the rabbit pieces with the wine and brown them in vegetable oil. Set aside.

To make the sauce, combine the onion and the olive oil in a medium saucepan over medium heat and sauté until the onion is soft, about 5 minutes. Add the tomatoes and cook until very thick, about 20 minutes. Dissolve the sugar in the vinegar and stir in. Stir in the cinnamon. Add the olives and capers.

Place the rabbit in a skillet and cover with the tomato mixture. Sprinkle with the almond flour. Cook, covered, until the rabbit is tender (a fork should go easily into the flesh), about 30 minutes.

Taste the sauce and adjust the seasoning with sugar, vinegar, or salt. Serve at room temperature.

NOTE. *Almond flour is available in some gourmet food shops or by mail order (page 252). Toast it in a small dry skillet or in the microwave. Or toast ¼ cup (35 g) raw or blanched almonds in the oven or microwave, combine them with 1 tablespoon of the sugar from the recipe, and grind them to a fine powder in a coffee mill or spice grinder.*

ZUCCHINE PANTESCHE RIPIENE
Stuffed Pantescan Zucchini

On Pantelleria, they grow a kind of summer squash that I have never seen elsewhere. It is round and striped light and dark green; the flesh is amazingly tender and sweet. The nearest substitute is pattypan squash or, if you can find it, a new variety called scaloppine, which looks like a big pattypan but is dark green in color. Garden-variety zucchini can also be used.

THIS MAKES ENOUGH FOR 8 PEOPLE AS A FIRST COURSE.

4 large scaloppine squash or 8 medium zucchini (4½ lb/2 kg)
1 pound (450 g) waxy potatoes, peeled and cut into ⅜-inch
  (1-cm) dice (about 2 cups)
½ cup (125 ml) olive oil
Salt and freshly ground black pepper
¼ cup (50 g) almonds, coarsely chopped (see Note)
2 salted anchovies, washed and filleted, or 4 canned
  anchovy fillets
1 pound (450 g) ripe tomatoes, coarsely chopped
1 large clove garlic, chopped
½ cup (125 ml) milk
½ cup (60 g) grated caciocavallo, parmesan, or other
  grating cheese
¼ cup (30 g) fine dry breadcrumbs (optional)
Ground hot pepper

Scrub the scaloppine and cut crosswise in half. (Cut zucchini lengthwise in half.) Remove the flesh, leaving a shell about ¼ inch (1 cm) thick. Steam the squash shells briefly to soften them, about 3 minutes.

Cut the flesh into ⅜-inch (1-cm) dice. Mix with the potatoes and sauté in ¼ cup of the olive oil, until softened, about 8 minutes. Season to taste with salt and black pepper. Stir in the almonds; set aside.

Preheat the oven to 350° F. (175° C.). Liberally oil a baking sheet with 2 tablespoons of the remaining olive oil.

Sauté the anchovies, tomatoes, and garlic in the remaining 2 tablespoons olive oil, stirring constantly, until the anchovies melt and the mixture comes together. Add to the stuffing mixture.

Pour the milk into the sauté pan and stir in the cheese. Add the breadcrumbs if the mixture seems too wet. Season to taste with hot pepper. Add the cheese mixture to the stuffing mixture and mix everything together. Stuff each squash shell, mounding the stuffing and letting it cover a bit of the shell.

Place the stuffed zucchini on the baking sheet and cover with foil. If using scaloppine, bake for 45 minutes; if using zucchini, bake for 30 minutes. Uncover and bake for 10 minutes more. Serve at room temperature.

NOTE. *If the almonds are flavorful, use them raw. Otherwise, toast them.*

INSALATA CAFONA
Asparagus and Mozzarella Salad

This being a summer dish, we always keep some asparagus in the freezer for unexpected guests. Everyone loves it. The name in Italian suggests that it is not a dainty dish, but I think it is rather elegant.

THIS MAKES ENOUGH FOR 4 TO 6 PEOPLE AS AN APPETIZER.

1 pound (450 g) fresh asparagus, trimmed, or frozen asparagus
1 pound (450 g) plum tomatoes
½ pound (225 g) fresh mozzarella, cut into bite-size pieces
Salt and freshly ground black pepper
3 to 4 tablespoons olive oil
1 teaspoon dried oregano

Cook the asparagus in boiling salted water until tender. Drain and cool.

Cut any very long asparagus into 2 or 3 pieces. Cut the tomatoes into pieces about the same size as the mozzarella. Combine the asparagus, tomatoes, and mozzarella in a bowl. Stir salt and pepper to taste into 3 tablespoons of the olive oil in a cup and pour on top. Turn to coat. Add more olive oil if needed, keeping in mind that this salad should not be too oily.

Transfer to a platter and pat the salad together into a mound. Sprinkle with the oregano. Serve at room temperature.

OVERLEAF: *A Sicilian variety of eggplant, called Tunisian, is striped lavender and cream color. The flesh is very tender and sweet. Zucca lunga zucchini are in season at the same time.*

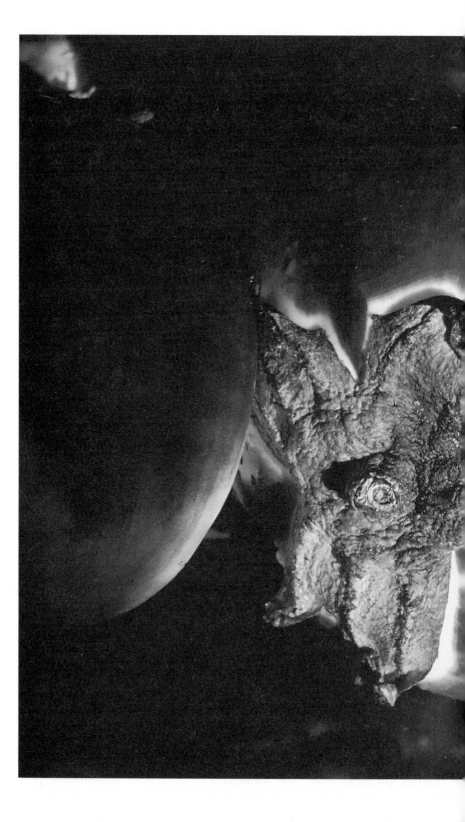

SPAGHETTI AL PESTO DI CASE VECCHIE
Anna's Pesto with Pasta

This is my rendition of the famous Pantescan pesto, for which no two recipes are alike. I just go out into the garden and pick as many herb leaves as I think I'll need and proceed from there. The pesto tastes better if it sits for a day.

THIS MAKES ENOUGH FOR 4 PEOPLE.

2 cups (120 g) mixed herbs, such as mint, parsley, basil, and sage
2 cloves garlic
4 small ripe tomatoes (½ lb/250 g), cut up
1 teaspoon sugar
Salt
Ground hot pepper
⅓ cup (80 ml) olive oil
1 pound (450 g) spaghetti
¼ cup (40 g) slivered almonds (see Note)

Combine the herbs, garlic, and tomatoes in a food processor and process until roughly chopped. Add the sugar and the salt and hot pepper to taste. With the machine running, pour in ¼ cup of the oil. Process just until blended. Scrape into a bowl or jar. Pour the remaining oil on top. Refrigerate overnight to let the flavors develop.

Just before serving, cook the spaghetti in plenty of boiling salted water until al dente. Drain. Stir the pesto and toss with the pasta. Sprinkle the almonds on top and serve.

NOTE. *If the almonds are very flavorful, use them as is; otherwise, toast them lightly to heighten the flavor.*

PASTICCIO DI VERDURE PANTESCO

Layered Vegetables, Pantelleria Style

You may think this layered vegetable dish is just one more rendition of ratatouille, but the tomato and egg topping is unique and gives the dish an entirely different aspect from that classic Mediterranean vegetable stew. Served with bread for sopping up the juices, it is a good lunch or light supper dish.

THIS MAKES ENOUGH FOR 8 TO 10 PEOPLE.

1 large or 2 medium eggplants (1½ lb/700 g)
Salt
¼ cup (60 ml) olive oil
5½ pounds (2,5 kg) ripe tomatoes, coarsely chopped
3 cloves garlic, chopped
½ cup (30 g) basil leaves, torn if very large
Freshly ground black pepper
Vegetable oil, for frying
3 medium zucchini (about 1½ lb/700 g), partially peeled and
*   cut into ⅜-inch (1-cm) slices*
5 medium potatoes (about 1¼ lb/600 g), peeled and cut into
*   ¼-inch (0,5-cm) slices*
3 small or 2½ large red or green bell peppers, cut into ¾-inch
*   (2-cm) strips*
6 large eggs, lightly beaten

Peel the eggplant, entirely if the skin is tough or in stripes if not; cut into ⅜-inch (1-cm) slices. Sprinkle with salt and let stand for 20 minutes.

Combine the olive oil, tomatoes, garlic, and basil in a large sauté pan over low heat. Cook, without stirring, until the tomatoes start bubbling, about 10 minutes. Season to taste with salt and pepper and stir, scraping the bottom. Cook, stirring from time to time, until the tomatoes start to melt and the sauce begins to thicken, 15 to 20 minutes, depending on how juicy the tomatoes are.

Heat about ⅜ inch (1 cm) vegetable oil in another large sauté pan over medium-high heat and fry the zucchini slices until browned on both sides. Remove and drain on paper towels. Spread in a single layer over the bottom of a large serving dish; a 15 × 10 × 2-inch (37,5 × 25 × 5-cm) dish is a good size. Lightly salt the zucchini.

Add more oil to the pan if needed and heat it. Fry the potatoes until cooked through and lightly browned on both sides. Taste a slice to be sure the potatoes are done since they will not be cooked further. Drain and spread over the zucchini slices. Lightly sprinkle with salt.

Blot the eggplant slices dry. Add more oil to the pan if needed and heat it. Fry the eggplant until browned on both sides. Drain and spread over the potatoes. Do not salt this layer.

Reduce the heat to medium-low, add more oil to the pan if needed, and heat it. Add the bell pepper strips, cover, and fry until soft. Put the peppers on top of the eggplant. If you have more vegetables than fit in a single layer in the dish, start layering again in the same order.

Raise the heat under the tomatoes to medium-low. Pour the eggs over the tomatoes. Let stand until the eggs begin to set, about 1 minute. Then, stir with a fork until the sauce is well mixed and thickened, about 3 minutes. Spoon evenly over the vegetables, covering them completely. Let the *pasticcio* cool. Serve at room temperature. Do not refrigerate.

ABOVE: *Zucchini blossoms are wonderful braised or stuffed and batter-fried. We have them all summer, as long as the plants are putting forth flowers.*

INSALATA DI LINGUINE CON PROSCIUTTO E FORMAGGIO

Linguine Salad with Ham and Cheese

This method of preparing pasta for salad is very effective. A quick dip in ice water stops the cooking and brings the pasta rapidly to room temperature. Be sure to let the salad stand for a good two hours to give the flavors time to develop.

THIS MAKES ENOUGH FOR 6 PEOPLE.

*½ pound (225 g) ripe tomatoes, peeled, seeded, and cut
  into pieces
Sugar
Salt
1 pound (450 g) linguine
1 cup (250 ml) olive oil
1 cup (180 g) julienned cooked ham
1 cup (120 g) julienned caciocavallo or emmentaler
½ cup (60 g) grated parmesan
½ cup (30 g) basil leaves, shredded
Juice of 1 lemon
1 tablespoon wine vinegar
1 tablespoon dried oregano
1 teaspoon ground hot pepper
¼ cup (30 g) chopped flat-leaf parsley*

Put the tomatoes in a colander and lightly sprinkle with sugar and salt. Let drain while cooking the pasta.

Bring a large pot of salted water to a boil. Add the linguine and cook until al dente. Drain and soak the colander in a bowl of salted ice water for 1 minute. Drain again. Pour the pasta into a serving bowl.

Pour on some of the oil and toss to coat to prevent sticking. Add the tomatoes, ham, caciocavallo, parmesan, and basil. Mix the lemon juice, vinegar, oregano, and hot pepper with the remaining oil; pour over the pasta. Toss and add salt to taste. Let stand at room temperature for at least 2 hours, stirring from time to time.

Just before serving, taste and adjust the seasonings. Sprinkle with the parsley and serve.

ZUPPA DI PESCE
Fish Soup

In Pantelleria, we made this fish soup with two *cernie* (groupers),
weighing two pounds each, and one scorpion fish, the one that is called
rascasse in French. The soup is best when made with an assortment of
flavorful lean fish, such as grouper, snapper, monkfish, or tilefish. Buy
what looks best in the market the day you go. If you have fish stock on
hand, use that in place of the water and fish bouillon cubes.

THIS MAKES ENOUGH FOR 6 PEOPLE.

2 large onions, chopped
5 cloves garlic, chopped
¼ cup (60 ml) olive oil
2 cups (500 ml) white wine
4 cups (1 l) water
1 fish bouillon cube
10 threads saffron
Salt
Ground hot pepper
¼ cup (40 g) all-purpose flour
¾ cup (90 g) chopped flat-leaf parsley
About 6 pounds (2,7 kg) mixed whole fish, such as rockfish,
    grouper, snapper, or tilefish, cleaned and cut crosswise into
    3 pieces

Choose a shallow sauté pan or skillet that is large enough to hold all
the fish. Sauté the onions and garlic in the oil until golden. Add the
wine and boil for a few minutes to reduce slightly. Add the water, bouillon cube, saffron, and salt and hot pepper to taste. Simmer until the
bouillon cube dissolves. Mix the flour into 1 cup of the broth and pour
back into the pan. Add ½ cup of the parsley.

Gently slip the fish into the pan, the thickest pieces first, thinnest
pieces last. The broth should come three quarters of the way up the
fish. Simmer until the eyes of the fish turn opaque, about 20 minutes.
Very carefully transfer the fish to a serving bowl. Pour the broth on top.
Sprinkle with the remaining ¼ cup parsley. Serve at room temperature.

RIGHT: *Swimming in the sea this morning, in the soup pot tonight.*

FRITTATA AL FORNO
Baked Frittata

Almost any kind of frittata is good picnic fare—you might want to have *Frittata al Formaggio* (page 47), or *Frittata di Verdura Amara* (page 48), or *Frittata di Pomodoro, Cipolla, e Basilico* (page 23) in season—but this one is particularly light and airy. Season it with *Fuoco*, my homemade hot pepper sauce, or ground hot pepper.

THIS MAKES ENOUGH FOR 6 PEOPLE AS A SIDE DISH.

1 pound (450 g) ripe tomatoes
Sugar
Salt
1 small red onion
Olive oil or butter, for the baking dish
2 tablespoons fine dry breadcrumbs, for the baking dish
6 large eggs, separated
½ cup (60 g) grated caciocavallo or parmesan
½ cup (30 g) basil leaves, torn
½ teaspoon Fuoco (page 234) or ground hot pepper to taste

Peel the tomatoes if the skins are tough, seed them, and cut into ⅜-inch (1-cm) cubes. Put in a colander and lightly sprinkle with sugar and salt. Let drain for at least 20 minutes.

Meanwhile, peel and thinly slice the onion. Let stand in cold salted water for 20 minutes. Drain and pat dry. (You can also blanch the onion in boiling water for 1 minute. Drain and pat dry.)

Preheat the oven to 350° F. (175° C.). Lightly oil or butter an 8-inch (20-cm) round or square baking dish and coat the bottom and sides with the breadcrumbs.

Squeeze the water out of the tomatoes and onion. Lightly beat the egg yolks and add the tomatoes, onion, cheese, basil, and *Fuoco*. Season with salt to taste.

Beat the egg whites to soft peaks. Fold into the egg yolk mixture. Scrape into the baking dish.

Bake until golden brown and dry on the inside (you can check with a toothpick), 25 to 30 minutes. The frittata will puff like a soufflé, and then fall as it cools. Serve warm or at room temperature.

MARMELLATA DI ZIBIBBO
Zibibbo Grape Jam

Zibibbo grapes have a fantastic perfume; not surprisingly, they make a very sweet and aromatic jam. You can substitute any flavorful table grape, one that is large enough to make peeling and seeding easy. Muscat, a fall grape that is sometimes also available in spring from South America, is a good stand-in for the Zibibbo.

THIS MAKES 4 HALF-PINT (250-ML) JARS.

3½ pounds (1,6 kg) Zibibbo grapes
1¼ cups (250 g) sugar
1 cup water

Peel and seed the grapes. Stop when you have 2¼ pounds (1 kg). You will have some left over.

Combine the sugar and water in a large saucepan and stir together off the heat. Bring to a boil over low heat. When the syrup reaches the thread stage (230° F./110° C. on a candy thermometer), add the grapes. Simmer for 30 minutes. Remove from the heat and set aside for 24 hours.

The next day, bring the mixture back to a boil and boil again for 15 minutes.

Ladle the jam into hot sterilized jars, leaving ¼ inch (less than 1 cm) of headroom. Cover and process in a hot-water bath (page 211). Store in a cool dark place for at least 2 months before using.

MUSTAZZUOLI PANTESCHI
Pastries from Pantelleria

Maria D'Aglietta makes her *mustazzuoli* filling with dried figs and raisins, but I have had more luck with this recipe, which I got from Signora Pasqua Liceti, who got it from her great-grandmother Pasqualina. The pastries used to be made especially for Easter, but now they are made in the summer to be sold to tourists who buy them for their beauty, not their symbolic value.

MAKES 4 DOZEN.

DOUGH

4 cups (600 g) bleached all-purpose flour
1/3 cup (65 g) sugar
Pinch of salt
5 tablespoons (70 g) vegetable shortening
About 1 1/2 cups (375 ml) cold water

FILLING

3/4 cup (250 g) honey
1/4 cup (60 ml) water
1 cup (200 g) sugar
2/3 cup (100 g) almonds, toasted and ground
1/2 cup (25 g) sesame seeds, toasted
2 1/2 tablespoons (35 g) vegetable shortening
2 teaspoons grated lemon zest
1 cup (250 g) couscous
1/4 teaspoon mint extract
1/2 teaspoon vanilla extract
1/2 teaspoon ground cinnamon

To make the dough, combine the flour, sugar, and salt in a large bowl or on the counter and make a well. Add the shortening and work it in with your hands or a pastry cutter until it is the consistency of oatmeal. Gradually add as much water as you need to make the dough stick together. Do not overwork it. Set aside in a cool place for 2 hours.

Make the filling about 30 minutes before you plan to form the pastries. Grease a baking sheet and set it aside.

Combine the honey, water, sugar, almonds, sesame seeds, vegetable shortening, and 1 teaspoon of the lemon zest in a saucepan, preferably nonstick. Bring to a boil and gradually add the couscous, stirring as you sprinkle it on. Cook, stirring constantly, until the mixture comes away from the sides of the pan, about 7 minutes.

Remove from the heat and stir in the mint and vanilla extracts, cinnamon, and remaining 1 teaspoon lemon zest. Pour out the mixture onto the baking sheet. As soon as it is cool enough to handle, take pieces of filling and roll them into sausages about ½ inch (1,5 cm) in diameter.

Pinch off a piece of dough and roll it out into a rectangle about ⅛ inch (3 mm) thick and 2¼ inches (6 cm) wide. Place a sausage of filling on the dough, bring up the sides, and roll it under your hands into a rope about ⅜ inch (1 cm) thick. Continue with all the dough and all the filling. If the filling gets too stiff to work, warm it in a low oven.

Cut a length of the rope about 5 inches (13 cm) long and form a ring. Or cut longer lengths to form leaves, spirals, and other shapes, as in the photographs following page 160 and on page 248. Using a sharp paring knife and embroidery scissors, cut out windows and other shapes as in the photograph. If your kitchen is very warm or humid and the dough resists cutting, place the pastries briefly in the freezer or refrigerator.

Preheat the oven to 350° F. (175° C.). Sprinkle 2 baking sheets with semolina flour or cornmeal or line them with parchment paper. Place the pastries close together on the baking sheet and bake in the middle of the oven for 15 minutes, or until the filling is bubbling. The dough will not brown. Remove from the oven and cool on racks. Repeat with the second sheet.

LUGLIO

The street markets of the old city of Palermo—la Vucciria near the port, Ballarò behind the Casa Professa, and il Capo—resemble the bazaar more than they do the tidy markets of, say, Venice, where fish and shellfish are displayed with awesome precision. In Palermo, the fishmongers just spread out their wares in the square.

Sacks of beans and jars of olives crowd the shopkeeper out of his minuscule shop and onto the sidewalk. Merchandise spills out from hole-in-the-wall shops. Fry shops and food stands do a brisk business.

Whatever is plentiful and in season—be it long-stemmed artichokes, green cauliflower, or lemons—is piled high on pushcarts or sold from the back of pickup trucks parked, probably illegally, on adjacent streets.

Palermo is blessed with an abundance of fresh fruits and vegetables seldom seen elsewhere.

LEFT: *Sand lilies are found on a few pristine beaches in Sicily.*

SICILIAN VEGETABLES

Vegetable stores, whether in the downtown markets or in residential neighborhoods, set up their displays following ancient eye-catching formulas. The arrangement of fruit on one side of the entrance to the shop and vegetables on the other looks exactly the same today as it does in drawings from the Middle Ages.

At sunset, the fresh vegetables are joined by huge copper cauldrons full of steaming cooked vegetables—artichokes in spring, green beans in summer, and potatoes all year round—and baking pans laden with roasted bell peppers, crunchy baked onions, and violet eggplants, the famous sweet Tunisian eggplant. It's a big help in summer to have all of those wonderful vegetables already cooked for you.

Usually I buy some for a salad, but one hot summer day when I was thinking of how refreshing a bowl of vichyssoise would taste, I had an inspiration. Instead of potatoes and leeks, why not combine some of those Sicilian vegetables in a cold soup, a Sicilian vichyssoise. My brother-in-law Giuseppe, who is quite a culinary adventurer, was coming for dinner. He always enjoys my improvisations, so I went ahead and bought a baked eggplant, an onion, a roasted pepper, and a couple of boiled potatoes. I pureed them together with ripe tomatoes, fresh herbs, broth, and wine. A heavy hand with seasoning at the end—cold soup often needs it—and *Ecco!* Sicilian vichyssoise.

Now I make the soup in large quantities, as I do *Gaspacho* (page 147). Gazpacho is Spanish, not Sicilian, but I follow an old recipe my father-in-law found in Seville and brought home to please his young wife. She, Conchita Ramirez de Villa Urrutia, was the daughter of a Spanish diplomat, born in Istanbul and educated in English boarding schools, but Spanish to the core. I never addressed her as anything but "Contessa."

The Contessa had no clue as to where or what a kitchen was, though she did like to eat and was fussy about her food right up to the end. (She died at ninety-two, complaining about and picking at whatever was served her, eating little more than thickly buttered bread.) My in-laws had a *monzù* chef, Don Mimi he was called—Don being a universal term of respect—at the Casa Mazzarino, their palazzo in the center of Palermo where I went to live as a bride. I missed my country food, but Don Mimi made all kinds of extraordinary dishes, and my father-in-law, like my own father, was a connoisseur, a *fin bec* as the French would say. My father-in-law told him how to make the soup, but Don Mimi surely gave it a touch of fantasy, for it is as much Sicilian as Spanish. I have the recipe written in Don Mimi's hand.

STREET VENDORS

In Palermo, vendors still cry their wares. The vegetable man, the fishmonger, the cheese seller, all sing out like raucous birds, calling you to their stands. The music and the words of these songs, like the art of display, date back to a time before time.

Other vendors with just one item to sell join the chorus. The candymaker, operating with a dented pan over a gas burner for cooking caramel and a marble slab to pour it out on, still makes *caramelle* (hard candies) before your eyes. The carob-flavored ones are good to soothe a cough. The *stigghiole* seller sets up his charcoal grill on a corner and before you know it, the neighborhood is full of smoke and the smell of grilled lamb innards. His cries are superfluous—the aroma attracts the faithful—but traditional.

There are vendors for boiled octopus, huge purple creatures sold by the piece, and for iced watermelon and roasted chestnuts in their season. Before refrigerators became commonplace, the iceman sold blocks of ice, kept covered with a canvas blanket.

Someone else sells flavored shaved ice. He is identified by his tool, the *grattarola*, or scraper. On his cart, drawn by a bicycle or, more likely nowadays, a motor scooter, he has a hand scraper, a covered block of ice, a row of syrup bottles—lemon, mint, anise, *orzata* (almond syrup), all of the Mediterranean flavors imaginable—and a row of glasses. Using the *grattarola*, the vendor scrapes some ice into a glass, pours on a shot of syrup, and there you have it: instant granita, instant gratification. This quickie granita is surely the forefather of the satiny granitas whose fame has spread far beyond the shores of Sicily.

It's easy to make granita at home. The traditional ones are *Granita di Caffè* (page 164) and *Granita di Limone* (page 165), and then there are the fruit granitas, like *Granita di Pesche* (page 166). You can substitute just about any kind of fruit for the peaches, whatever you fancy. My favorite is apricot.

One of the most curious vendors is the fire seller. You see him at night or on Sunday, usually in Il Capo. He has a large square of hot coals with a grid over them, and people rent a corner to cook on it. (Similarly, after they've finished baking bread, village bakers rent out the oven to people who don't have one at home.)

In the old days, many vendors went from door to door. They were very often country people selling prickly pears or mulberries, wild fruits so commonplace they weren't sold in the market. I particularly remember a man who came to the door in Mondello with a cow to be milked on demand. You don't see that anymore, but the grandsons, or perhaps great-grandsons, of those peddlers now parade up and down the beach, hawking corn on the cob, *pizzette* and *sfincionelle* (small thin- and thick-crusted pizzas), and *ciambelle* (doughnuts).

ACQUA E ZAMMÙ

One of the last of the itinerant vendors to disappear was the *acquavitaro*, sometimes called *acquaiolo*, or water seller, who sold water by the glass. The water could be had with or without *la nuvola*, or cloud, so called because the water gets cloudy when *zammù*, an extract of anise (*Pimpinella anisum*), is added. The liquor probably took away the stale taste of the water—and surely made the glass of water more profitable for the *acquavitaro*. In any event, *acqua e zammù* (called *acqua e anice* in Italian) became a very popular Sicilian drink.

This *zammù* is an ancient concoction, probably dating back to Arab times. What is used these days is Anice Unico Tutone, made and bottled in Palermo. The distillery, located behind the Palazzo Aiutamicristo in the old town, has been in the Tutone family for five generations. Alfredo Tutone, of the youngest generation, graciously showed me around the plant one day, pausing to let me examine the old labels and posters with such slogans as "Water and Anice Unico, To Refresh Your Memory of Sicily," but not revealing the family's secret formula. By law, the liquor has to be labeled *"anice per acqua"* to indicate that it is for mixing with water, not for drinking straight like Sambuca, a sweet liqueur that became fashionable not so long ago.

The *acquavitaro* would set up his stand, actually a special folding table, at a busy spot in the market or on a crowded sidewalk. In the shade under the table stood the earthenware bottles of cold water, and on top, held steady by metal rings, stood the water glass and the *zammuttiera*, or *zammù* bottle. This special bottle, a glass balloon with a silver or metal spout that measures out the exact amount of the liquor, has become something of a collector's item in recent years.

Acquavitaro or no, one of the most rooted habits of Palermitani when they are thirsty—and in summer, one is always thirsty in Palermo—is to drink a glass of iced water, with or without *zammù*. Before we had refrigerators, we had iceboxes, and the two things we kept in them were meat, to keep it from spoiling, and water, to keep it cold.

As long as I can remember, every day after lunch, my father has a glass of *acqua e zammù*. My mother brings it to him—only she knows exactly how much *zammù* to splash in the glass. When I see them looking into each other's eyes as they perform this little ceremony, I marvel at how close they are, how after more than sixty years of marriage they can still flirt over a simple glass of water.

ANISE, DILL, AND LICORICE

Another way to enjoy anise's refreshing and digestive powers (it is a carminative, often recommended to nursing mothers to calm their baby's colic) is in *Biscotti all'Anice* (Anise Biscuits, page 167). These light little biscuits are perfect with a dish of *Granita di Limone* (page 165). Anise is also used for *caramelle*, good sucking candies.

Some people think anise is the same as dill, which is a completely different plant though with a light aniselike taste. It is, actually, closely related to our wild fennel and can be substituted for it in a pinch in certain dishes. Dill grows like a weed in Sicily; in July, the fields and roadsides are covered with it. Although it supposedly originated in southern Europe—and what could be more southern Europe than Sicily?—dill is not part of the Sicilian repertoire. It is more commonly found in central and northern European cuisines, especially in combination with fish, cucumbers, and sour cream. I have started to use it myself, though, on salads and in the herb mixtures I make to garnish soup and fish dishes.

It's also easy to confuse anise with licorice, which has a similar flavor but with a somewhat bitter aftertaste. Although the plant is culti-

vated by the French—they are great fanciers of licorice and even lov-
ingly describe very dark eyes as "licorice drops"—licorice grows wild
in Sicily. It has a very long tap root, which I have seen children sucking on. In the war against weeds at Regaleali, Vincenzo Curcio, who is
in charge of the land, doesn't always win against licorice because it is
so difficult to pull out of the ground.

IL FESTINO

In mid-July, all of Palermo turns out for Il Festino, which honors Santa
Rosalia, the patron saint of Palermo, whom the citizens affectionately
call La Santuzza. It's a lively, joyous celebration that goes on for six
days, culminating in fireworks in the old harbor. Il Festino commemo-
rates the intercession of Santa Rosalia, which saved the city from a
devastating plague in 1624.

Rosalia had renounced the world in 1159 and died as a hermit on
Monte Pellegrino, the huge rock formation that broods over Palermo.
Almost five hundred years later, when the plague was at its peak, she
appeared in the dream of a hunter and commanded that her bones be
exhumed from the cave where she had died and paraded through the
city. And, the story goes, the plague receded before them.

Now, centuries later, the silver reliquary holding her bones is
removed from the cathedral and carried through the streets, which are
lined with booths and stalls set up for the occasion and festooned with
crepe-paper ribbons, flags, and banners. Palermitani are great ones for
eating on the street, and vendors sell all kinds of food for snacking—
watermelon, ice cream, and cotton candy; and *scaccio*, an old mixture
consisting of toasted nuts, sunflower and squash seeds, favas, and
chick peas that used to be made by the nuns. A favorite treat is
Babaluci del Festino (pages 148 to 149), snails cooked with a liberal
dose of garlic, with or without tomato sauce. People walk along with
the snails, picking at them and sucking them from their shells.

GIO'S BUFFET

On the night of the sixth day, a display of fireworks, the most elaborate
in Sicily, is launched in the harbor of Palermo. The sea and all of the
beautiful old palazzi facing it are lit up by them.

My brother-in-law Gioacchino Lanza Tomasi, the adopted son and heir of Giuseppe di Lampedusa, author of the novel *The Leopard*, always offers a lavish cold buffet that evening at the Palazzo Lampedusa. The house has a terrace high above the old promenade— now a four-lane highway—skirting the marina. Gio, a renowned musicologist and opera director, now director of the Italian Cultural Center in New York City, and his wife, Nicoletta, invite a mix of family, friends, intellectuals, society people, and, in recent years, the new "in" group, the Greens—left-leaning environmentalist ideologues.

As befits Gio's heritage, the table is laid with great splendor. A huge mahogany table covered with Belgian linen sits in the middle of the room. An extraordinary eighteenth-century faïence centerpiece— white with red tulips—is surrounded with soup tureens and oval bowls filled with fruits and flowers, all from the same Tuscan factory called Doccia or sometimes Ginori. Two twelve-branched silver candelabra with candles burning are at either end of the table.

The meal matches the opulence of the setting: boiled lobster decorated with giant prawns; *pesce coricato*, Sicilian dialect for lying fish, in fact, a giant poached sea bass lying on a silver platter; another enormous silver platter with all different kinds of raw fish, the latest culinary fad; and, more traditional, heaps of fried small fish that are eaten with the fingers. Another classic Sicilian fish dish, *sarde a beccafico*— that is, stuffed sardines that look like little birds—completes the fish offerings.

There is always *vitello tonné*, cold veal with tuna sauce, and a *piatto di carne fredda mista* (sliced cold meats decorated with aspic). Some of the meats are home-cooked—chicken, roast beef, braised beef, and *Falsomagro* (Meat Roll, page 149)—and some are purchased from the *salumeria*, such as prosciutto, cooked ham, and *lingua salmistrata* (corned tongue).

Lately, though, people are not all that keen on meat, and so there are even more vegetable dishes on the table than ever: rice and pasta salads; *Timballo alla San Giovannella* (Eggplant Timbale, page 151); *Melanzane Arrosto con Aglio e Menta* (page 235) and *Peperoni Arrosto con Olio e Aceto* (page 232), or roasted eggplant and peppers and stuffed bell peppers.

But Gio is not only a Tomasi, he is a Lanza di Mazzarino, and so there are three tureens of *Gaspacho* (page 147). It is served with gar-

nishes of croutons and diced vegetables. Another family dish is
Insalata di Casa Mazzarino (Mazzarino Salad, page 153), a kind of
slaw of thinly shredded cabbage and carrots with apples, dressed with
a light lemony mayonnaise.

Desserts are no less sumptuous. In addition to fresh fruit, there are
gelatins, pastries, and cookies. Matching footed crystal bowls hold *Gelo
di Melone* (Watermelon Pudding, page 162), decorated for the occasion with jasmine flowers, chocolate flakes, candied squash, and
chopped pistachios, and, in the best tradition of the Sicilian aristoc-
racy, *Biancomangiare* (page 37) with pistachios and cinnamon. This is
Gio's downfall: He can't resist. It is also what Don Fabrizio, Prince of
Salina, ate at the Ponteleone's ball in *The Leopard:* "He savored the
subtle mixture of blancmange, pistachio, and cinnamon in the dessert
he had chosen. . . ."

Before long, all of the good food and wine and the noise and the light
make everyone feel quite giddy.

MENFI, GRISI, AND PERNICE

Spectacular though the fireworks, and impressive the food at Gio's,
may be, it's good to get back to simpler pleasures. For a few years,
Fabrizia and Luca, my daughter and her husband, have rented a house
on the sea near Menfi, and I try to spend July 26, Sant'Anna's day, my
onomastico (name day), with them. They chose Menfi because they
were looking for a clean, safe beach to take a vacation with their children, Ruggero and Virginia. The beach there on the southern coast of
Sicily is wide and stretches about sixty miles from Porto Palo to
Siculiana, and the water is clear, so cold and bracing I sometimes think
each dip makes your body a year younger.

Here and there are patches of wild lilies (*Pancratum maritimus*), *i
gigli degli antichi* as they are called. The Greeks ate the seeds of this
plant and used its down to line their footwear because it is so very soft.
From mid-July to mid-August the plants pop out of the sand without
any warning, first the bud, then the flower, then the whole plant with
leaves. People of my parents' generation remember when the beaches
everywhere in Sicily were covered with *i gigli*, but now Menfi is one of
the few places where they are found. They've been declared an endan-

gered species, and it is forbidden to pick them, but people do, of course, since there is no one around to enforce the law.

The first time I went to visit my children at Menfi, we decided to go to the pizzeria at Porto Palo, a small picturesque harbor just for fishing boats, as a special treat. We stopped to talk to the fishermen, who were mending their nets in the late afternoon sun. The Sirenetta, as it is called (we picked it because Virginia is crazy for mermaids), is just a hut on the beach serving pizzas that taste remarkably good in the setting. The classic one there is called *"Rianata"* for the oregano that is sprinkled on top; it is drizzled with olive oil first, of course. *"Biancaneve,"* or Snow White, has white cheeses on top.

When I asked the pizza boy, a chubby fellow with a pigtail and one earring—all the rage at the time—what is Porto Palo's most famous recipe, he replied without hesitation *Pasta con Gamberetti* (Spaghettini with Shrimp in Wine Sauce, page 153). This simple preparation is superb when the shrimp are very fresh. Red shrimp are quite plentiful in the seas off Porto Palo; they are brought in almost daily. We had shrimp every way we could think of, including *Gamberetti Marinati* (Marinated Shrimp, page 154) and *Gamberoni Freddi al Limone* (Jumbo Shrimp with Lemon, page 155). The jumbo shrimp also are used to garnish cold lobster and *pesce coricato*.

SNAILS

One evening we walked down to the sea at sunset. It was very beautiful to behold, yet I couldn't help noticing the clusters of snails clinging to the bushes along the path. These *babaluci*, as we call them, are of the family *Helix aspersa*, small snails with a brownish spiral around the shell. In July, they are called *babaluci del Festino*, and in June, *babaluci di San Giovanni*, names that I suppose are meant to remind us that they are with us all summer long, at least in western Sicily. I remember seeing them once in September at Segesta, the site of a famous Greek temple and theater.

Until then, I had never prepared snails from scratch, always being in too much of a hurry. This time, though, I decided those little devils were not going to escape my curiosity. The next day the children and I took our sand pails and started picking. The snails were sleeping, and it was hard to pull them off; even so, we picked plenty.

When I got home, I started asking what to do with them. First, I was

told, you have to soak them in warm water until you see their horns
sticking out; this is to make sure they are all alive. Then, after rinsing
them a couple of times, you put them in a pan with clean cold water on
a very low fire until they poke out their horns again—this time looking for the life they are leaving behind. You cook them for about five
minutes, skimming the foam, and then pour them into a colander to
rinse them and let all of the water drain out of the shells. Now they are
ready to be prepared, either *in rosso*—red, with tomato—or *in
bianco*—white, with garlic (pages 148 to 149). These are the snails
that are sold on the streets of Palermo during Il Festino.

WHEAT BERRIES

Whenever I visit the children, I take as much food with me as I can
carry, often including a *Salame di Tonno* (Tuna Salami, page 157),
which Ruggero really likes. Children often fuss about their food, but
he, I'm proud to say, is already a connoisseur. I also pack a container
of *Insalata di Grano con Pomodoro, Tonno, e Capperi* (Wheat Berry
Salad with Tomatoes, Tuna, and Capers, page 156), which Fabrizia
loves but which Luca calls bird food.

Wheat berries are traditionally used in Sicily for *cuccìa*, a sweet
pudding that is eaten on Santa Lucìa's day in December. It occurred to
me that there might be a savory version. When I asked my father about
it, he recalled that Donna Lorita, who cooked for the Tasca family in
the country when he was a boy, used to make a *cuccìa* seasoned with
olive oil, salt, and what she called "spices," by which she meant black
pepper. (Ground hot pepper came to our table later when some Swiss
doctors told us it was more healthful.)

I asked around some more and found that in all of the villages
around Regaleali in central Sicily and in the nearby Madonie
Mountains, the classic *cuccìa* is not sweet but savory! My friend
Francesca di Carpinello remembers that as a child growing up in
Polizzi, she ate a kind of soup, *Zuppa du Grano Duro* (Wheat Berry
Soup, page 158), in the kitchen with the maids; only the sweet version,
on the other hand, was served in the dining room. She still likes the
soup and makes it at least once a year when she makes the sweet version for the rest of the family. She seasons hers with olive oil, bay

leaves, and black pepper and mixes in some grated caciocavallo or pecorino cheese. Mine is a bit heartier, with vegetables, white beans, and herbs in addition to the wheat berries.

When Nonno, my paternal grandfather, was alive, wheat—hard durum wheat—was the main crop at Regaleali as in the rest of Sicily. In those days, the wheat was sown by hand and the ground worked with the *zappa*, a short hoe that is still used in the vineyards. Our first threshing machine arrived at the Vallelunga train station one day in 1925. Nonno drove the tractor, as he always did on important occasions, which pulled the thresher up to Case Grandi. Next in the convoy was my father, driving the car all alone for the first time; he was thirteen years old.

Nonno's wheat usually won first prize in all of the competitions. I used to ride with him in an old Jeep as he inspected the fields, golden spikes waving in the breeze of the *tramontana*, the north wind that comes down across the mountains. From time to time, he would abruptly stop the Jeep, jump out, and stride across the field to pluck out an errant stalk of oat or undesirable variety of wheat.

We still grow some wheat at Regaleali, but it is sown by machine. No more hoes, either. Since we don't use any herbicides, there are quite a few wild oats among the wheat, but we sift them out after threshing.

In the old days, the bran had to be laboriously removed from the wheat berries at home before cooking, but nowadays the berries sold in the stores, usually health-food stores, have had the bran removed. (Hard durum wheat berries such as we have in Sicily are not available in the United States; kamut and spelt, two ancient strains of hard wheat, are good substitutes. Be careful not to buy the tiny berries of soft wheat; you will be very disappointed if you do.)

Graziella Chimera, who works for me at Case Vecchio, explained to me how the bran was removed in her family. Their method was *stricato 'ntu canale*, which means "scrubbed in the tile" in Sicilian dialect. The tile in question is a long, curved roof tile that used to be formed on a woman's thigh. The tile would be turned over and filled with warm water and wheat berries. Then they were scrubbed by hand—a gloved hand to avoid tearing the skin—with the same motion as for washing clothes in a sink, pushing the berries back and forth until all of the bran had come off. Next they were cooked, just covered with water, no salt, for forty-five minutes, removed from the heat, and literally put

under a blanket (*ammantato* in dialect) to cool slowly. This method results in a thick puree, which is seasoned very simply with olive oil, salt, and pepper.

Another way, told to me by Liboria Di Martino, Carmelo's wife, was to combine the amount of wheat berries you wanted with hot water and, after a few minutes, put it all in a *sacco di iuta* (hemp sack). The sack was then beaten with a stick until all of the bran had separated from the kernels. This method also results eventually in a thick puree. To leave the berries intact, soaking them in several changes of water is sufficient.

BUSIATI

Though wheat has become less important as a cash crop in Sicily in recent years, particularly since the postwar land reforms and changes in the world wheat market, its central role in the diet and economy of Sicily dates back at least two thousand years, when Sicily was known as "the granary of Rome." Bread is a sacred food, a gift of God not to be wasted. And pasta is served once a day, every day.

The first written record of pasta in Sicily is in a twelfth-century

LEFT AND ABOVE: *Carmela and Rosa form busiati, rolling out the dough until it is long and thin, then hanging the macaroni to dry.*

manuscript; it probably had been around earlier, one of the many food-stuffs the Arabs introduced to Sicily. These days, most of the pasta eaten is machine-made dried pasta, which is of excellent quality, but long before there was such a thing as a macaroni factory, pasta was made at home, with the dough rolled out and cut into ribbons or twisted into shapes.

Another form that used to be made at home is *Busiati*, a long nar-row tube (page 159). For this pasta the dough is rolled around a *buso*. The word means knitting needle, but the *buso* is actually the stalk of a tough grass with long plumes called *disa*. This grass is soaked in water to make it more pliable and then used to tie up the vines and bind sheaves of wheat. For purposes of pasta making, the grass is soaked and then dried in the sun until it is straight and stiff.

I had heard that the women of Grisi still make *busiati* by hand. About a forty-minute drive from Palermo, Grisi is in the valle del Belice earthquake zone, not far from Gibellina, now the site of a Summer Arts and Music Festival. Once a charming little village, Grisi was badly damaged in a quake a few years ago and was very slow to rebuild. I got an introduction to two sisters, Carmela and Rosa, locally acclaimed *busiati* experts. Alessandro and I met the sisters at Rosa's place—one of those new houses that look unlived in—even though Carmela was the chief pasta maker.

She got right to work—we didn't even pause for coffee—pouring out flour onto the counter. She made the well, cracked in eggs, and stirred them in with her hand, adding a little water to make the dough come together. In the old days, eggs were not used in homemade pasta; I don't know if she used them simply because she had them—now with electric lights in the henhouses we have eggs all year round, not just in summer—or because the palate has become more sophisticated. (It is true, though, that fettuccine noodles made without eggs, while light and white and exquisite, don't hold the ribbon shape; they break up when cooked.)

She kneaded the dough thoroughly, put half aside for tagliatelle, and cut the rest into small pieces. She and Rosa rolled the pieces into little ropes, placed a *buso* on each one, and rolled it under their fingers until the dough thinned out and covered the entire length of the *buso*. Then they pulled out the *buso* and hung the *busiati* over the edge of a plastic basket to dry.

When the *busiati* were all done, Carmela rolled out the other half of the dough with a rolling pin—no pasta machine for her!—until it was so thin you could read a newspaper through it. Then she cut it into tagliatelle. The sisters gave us a tray of *busiati* and one of tagliatelle to take with us. In Sicily, this kind of homemade pasta is always eaten with tomato sauce in summer, meat *ragù* in winter; we had it that evening, and it was delicious.

AN ENCHANTED PLACE

The next stop on the food tour that day was Pernice, the home of my nephew Filiberto Camporeale, Costanza's son, and his wife, Domitilla. They are wonderful hosts, and I knew I could count on them when I asked if we could stop by for lunch and a dip in their pool. I asked Domitilla to make her specialty, *Sformato di Riso Freddo al Pomodoro* (Rice Ring Filled with Tomatoes, page 160). As a second course we had *Pesce del Contadino* (Fish Mousse, Peasant Style, page 203), a simple dish made with canned tuna and potatoes. She asked me to make the salad, and I made *Insalata di Cetrioli* (Cucumber Salad, page 161). For dessert, we had *Gelatina di Fragole* (Strawberry Gelatin, page 163), which Domitilla has made part of her repertoire, served with *Taralli* (Lemon Cookies, page 168), which I had bought in Grisi because they looked different from mine.

Pernice has been in the Camporeale family forever. The farmhouse is surrounded by vineyards, and Filiberto makes wine, which is sold from the barrel in his own *bettole* (wine shops) in Palermo. He also grows melons—both watermelon and muskmelon—and orchard fruits, peaches and apricots.

When Filiberto and Domitilla married, they adapted Pernice to their liking. They repainted the faded exterior walls of the house bright pink and planted flowers everywhere—red and pink geraniums and begonias in old *giare* and purple bougainvillea and orange trumpet vines that creep up the walls of the courtyard and across the roofs. The children, Costanza and Paolo, keep busy doing the things children do in the country—catching toads, watching spiders spin their webs, daydreaming. Cats and dogs wander at will through the courtyard, and when the spirit moves them, caged birds sing. It is truly a magical place.

ABOVE: *An inkfish like squid, cuttlefish is still plentiful in the Mediterranean. It is sepia colored, recalling its Italian name, seppia.*

THE RECIPES

GASPACHO
Gazpacho

This recipe is much simpler than the one I have from Don Mimi. I sometimes think the *monzù* chefs complicated everything just so no one else could copy their recipes!

THIS MAKES ENOUGH TO SERVE 4 TO 6 PEOPLE.

4½ pounds (2 kg) ripe tomatoes
1 medium-size red onion, coarsely chopped
2 cups (120 g) basil leaves
½ cup (60 g) breadcrumbs
1 tablespoon salt
1 tablespoon sugar
3 to 4 tablespoons (45 to 60 ml) olive oil
2 tablespoons red wine vinegar (optional)
Basil leaves, for garnish
Cubed raw vegetables, such as cucumbers, red and yellow bell
   peppers, carrots, onion, and zucchini
Croutons

Cut up the tomatoes and puree them in a food processor. Working in batches if necessary, add the onion, basil, and breadcrumbs and puree until smooth.

Transfer the tomato mixture to a fine-mesh plastic strainer. Using a wooden spoon, push the puree through the sieve. At the end, make a fist and scrub as much through as you can.

Season with the salt and sugar. Slowly stir in the oil, adding as much as you like. A Sicilian would like a lot. Check the seasoning and adjust if necessary. Refrigerate for at least 1 day or up to 1 week.

Just before serving, taste and adjust the seasoning. Add vinegar to taste. Put some ice cubes in the soup if you like. Decorate with whole basil leaves and serve. Pass the vegetables and croutons.

NOTE. *If you don't have a food processor, pass the tomatoes through a food mill, using the finest blade. Mince the onion and basil and stir them into the puree. Stir in the breadcrumbs and continue with the recipe.*

BABALUCI DEL FESTINO IN BIANCO
Snails with Garlic and Parsley

Although many kinds of live snails are sold in Sicily as well as Italy and other mainland European countries, in America only canned large snails (escargots) are available. The can contains a dozen snails, enough for one or at most two people as an appetizer or first course. With small Sicilian snails, a portion would be ten times that. The idea is to eat them with your fingers, either on the street or at home, sucking them out. There is even a proverb in dialect, *"Fimmine vasate, vavaluci sucati,"* literally, kissed women, sucked snails, which means that the noise is the same.

THIS MAKES ENOUGH FOR 1 OR 2 PEOPLE AS A FIRST COURSE.

1 medium-size red onion
4 cloves garlic, minced
¾ cup (180 ml) olive oil
1 can (7 oz/198 g) snails
1 cup (120 g) chopped flat-leaf parsley
½ cup (125 ml) white wine
½ teaspoon ground hot pepper
Salt

Sauté the onion and garlic in the olive oil in a medium sauté pan over medium heat until soft, 7 to 8 minutes. Add the snails and stir to coat. Add the parsley, wine, hot pepper, and salt to taste. Cook, uncovered, until tender, about 10 minutes. Remove from the heat. Serve at room temperature.

BABALUCI DEL FESTINO IN ROSSO
Snails with Tomato Sauce
Serve these snails with bread for sopping up the sauce.
THIS MAKES ENOUGH TO SERVE 2 PEOPLE AS A FIRST COURSE.

1 large red onion
4 cloves garlic, minced
¾ cup (180 ml) olive oil
1 pound (450 g) ripe tomatoes, peeled and chopped, or 1 can
    (14 oz/420 g) Italian plum tomatoes, drained and coarsely
    chopped
1 can (7 oz/198 g) snails
1 tablespoon salt
1 cup (120 g) chopped flat-leaf parsley
½ cup (125 ml) white wine
½ teaspoon ground hot pepper

Sauté the onion and garlic in the olive oil in a medium saucepan over medium heat until soft, 7 to 8 minutes. Add the tomatoes and cook, uncovered, until the sauce thickens somewhat, about 10 minutes.

Stir in the snails, salt, parsley, wine, and hot pepper. Cover and simmer until the snails are tender, about 10 minutes. Serve at room temperature.

FALSOMAGRO
Meat Roll
Meat (or fish) rolled around a stuffing is a typically Sicilian dish—simple, economical, and flavorful. Depending on the occasion, the roll is braised in *ragù* or, as here, broth and wine. Large meat rolls filled with combinations of spinach, cheese, hard-boiled eggs, and/or a Sicilian stuffing of breadcrumbs, pine nuts, and currants are very popular. In this version, the filling consists of a cheese pancake—halfway between a crêpe and a frittata—and prosciutto or mortadella. When the meat is sliced, the fillings make an attractive pinwheel design.

Be sure to let the roll cool thoroughly before slicing it; otherwise it will fall apart. To serve *Falsomagro* hot, put the slices back together with a skewer or two and reheat the roll in the sauce. *Falsomagro* is

also delicious served at room temperature. In that case, use the sauce
as a topping for pasta or rice or on stuffed cabbage.

1¼ to 1½ pounds (600 to 700 g) flank steak (see Note)
3 large eggs
½ cup (125 ml) milk
2 tablespoons chopped flat-leaf parsley
½ cup (60 g) grated caciocavallo or parmesan
Salt
¼ pound (100 g) prosciutto or mortadella, thinly sliced
½ cup (125 ml) olive oil
2 cups (500 ml) red wine
1 large onion, coarsely chopped
2 beef bouillon cubes
3 tablespoons all-purpose flour
Freshly ground black pepper

Butterfly and pound the meat, if the butcher hasn't already done it for
you, until it is ⅜ inch (1 cm) thick. Set aside.

Mix the eggs with the milk, parsley, caciocavallo, and a pinch of salt.
Using a large nonstick skillet or a greased, well-seasoned one, make 1
or 2 pancakes large enough to cover the steak.

Place the pancake on the steak and cover with the prosciutto, leaving a ¾-inch (2-cm) margin on all sides. Roll up the steak, going with
the grain, and tie tightly.

Choose a heavy pan that holds the roll rather snugly. Sear the roll in
the oil. When you think it is going to burn, add ½ cup of the wine and
cook until it evaporates. Continue searing the meat, adding the onion
when it is almost completely brown on all sides. Add more wine and
scrape the bottom of the pan. Add enough water to cover; add the rest
of the wine and the bouillon cubes. Bring to a boil. Lower the heat and
simmer until the meat is tender when pierced with a fork, 45 to 60
minutes. Remove the meat roll and let it cool. Don't cut it while it is hot
or it will fall apart.

Skim the sauce and pass it through a food mill or puree it in a food
processor. You should have 5 to 6 cups. Transfer the sauce to a small
saucepan. Allowing 1 tablespoon flour for every 2 cups of sauce, make

a slurry with the flour and ½ cup of the sauce. Whisk the slurry into the rest of the sauce and simmer until thickened, about 10 minutes.

Season to taste with salt and pepper. Slice and serve the meat warm with the sauce or serve it at room temperature.

N O T E. *The cut of beef closest to ciambella, which is what we use in Sicily, is flank steak. It is very tender and cooks quickly. Have the butcher butterfly and pound it for you.*

TIMBALLO ALLA SAN GIOVANNELLA
Eggplant Timbale

Sicilians are very fond of timbales, whether the shell is pasta, pastry, potatoes—as in *Sformato di Patate al Ragù* (page 200)—or, as in this dish, eggplant. The San Giovannella is a kind of "macaroni pie," a cousin of the one served to "the major citizens" of Donnafugata in *The Leopard.*

THIS MAKES ENOUGH FOR 8 PEOPLE.

2 eggplants (2¼ lb/1 kg)
Salt
3 tablespoons (50 g) unsalted butter
½ cup (60 g) dry breadcrumbs
Vegetable oil, for frying
1 pound (450 g) perciatelli
3 cups (750 ml) thick tomato sauce, preferably homemade,
    with meat (page 200) or without (page 229)
1 tablespoon dried oregano
3 tablespoons chopped fresh basil or 1 teaspoon dried basil
1 cup (120 g) mixed grated parmesan, caciocavallo, and pecorino
Freshly ground black pepper

At least 1½ hours before serving, peel the eggplants and slice them lengthwise ⅜ inch (1 cm) thick. Salt and let stand in a colander for 30 minutes.

Meanwhile, use 1 tablespoon of the butter to lightly coat a 10-inch (25-cm) mold with 3-inch-wide (8-cm) sides or a 10-inch (25-cm) springform pan. Coat evenly with 2 tablespoons of the breadcrumbs.

Blot the eggplant slices dry. Fry the slices in the oil in a large skillet over medium-high heat until lightly golden on both sides. Drain on paper towels. Set some slices aside for the top of the timbale. Line the bottom of the mold or pan with some of the others, making an attractive arrangement since, when the timbale is unmolded, the bottom will be the top. Line the sides with the rest of the slices, slightly overlapping them and letting them hang over the edge of the pan. If you have any slices left over, set them aside to make a layer in the middle. Set aside.

Preheat the oven to 350° F. (180° C.).

Cook the perciatelli in boiling salted water for 3 minutes, or until less than al dente since it will cook further in the oven. Drain and return to the pot.

Warm the tomato sauce if cold. Stir 2 cups of the sauce, the oregano, basil, and cheese into the pasta. Add salt and pepper to taste. Spoon half into the lined mold. Cover with a layer of eggplant if you have slices left over and add the rest of the perciatelli. Lightly press down with your hands to spread the pasta mixture to the sides. Fold the overhanging slices of eggplant over the pasta and cover completely with the reserved slices.

Sprinkle the top with the remaining breadcrumbs and dot with the remaining 2 tablespoons butter. Bake for 25 minutes, or until golden brown on top.

Remove from the oven, put a platter on top, and invert the pan. Let stand for at least 10 minutes before unmolding. Remove the sides and bottom of the pan. Serve with the remaining sauce on the side.

NOTE. *If you prefer, brush the eggplant slices with oil and broil them until lightly browned. Grease the pan generously with butter. The dish will be less oily.*

INSALATA DI CASA MAZZARINO
Mazzarino Salad

Since my in-laws had lived all over the world, many non-Sicilian dishes appeared on their table. Over time, though, a Sicilian twist always crept in—the oranges in this cabbage salad, for example.

THIS MAKES ENOUGH FOR 6 PEOPLE.

½ small green or white cabbage (12 oz/350 g), cored and
  very thinly sliced
2 large carrots, cut into julienne
1 red apple, such as Winesap or Empire, scrubbed, quartered,
  cored, and sliced
1 orange, peeled, quartered, and sliced
2 tablespoons water
½ cup Mayonnaise (page 160)
Juice of ½ lemon or orange or vinegar, to taste
Salt and freshly ground black pepper

Combine the cabbage, carrots, apple, and orange in a large salad bowl.
  Stir the water into the mayonnaise to lighten it. Add the lemon juice and salt and pepper to taste. Pour the sauce over the salad ingredients and toss to coat. Let stand for at least 1 hour before serving.

PASTA CON GAMBERETTI
Spaghettini with Shrimp in Wine Sauce

The shrimp have to be perfectly fresh for this simple dish because they have nowhere to hide.

THIS MAKES ENOUGH FOR 6 PEOPLE.

1 pound (450 g) small shrimp (30 count)
2 cloves garlic, chopped
⅓ cup (80 ml) olive oil
½ cup (125 ml) white wine
1 pound (450 g) spaghettini
3 tablespoons chopped flat-leaf parsley

Peel and devein the shrimp.

Sauté the garlic in ¼ cup of the olive oil in a large skillet, just until the aroma rises. Add the shrimp and sauté until they turn opaque, about 2 minutes. Add the wine and boil for 2 minutes to evaporate the alcohol. Remove from the heat.

Cook the spaghettini in boiling salted water until al dente. Drain; transfer to a serving dish. Drizzle the remaining olive oil over the pasta, top with the shrimp and their sauce, and sprinkle with the parsley. Serve at once.

GAMBERETTI MARINATI
Marinated Shrimp

The shrimp I buy in Sicily, especially in Menfi where they are sold still wriggling, are so fresh that I was worried that this recipe wouldn't work with American days-old shrimp. But when Jennifer Wilkinson tested it, she found her tasters were intrigued by the flavor, and everyone wanted more.

THIS IS ENOUGH FOR 6 PEOPLE AS AN APPETIZER.

1 pound (450 g) small shrimp (30 count)
½ cup (125 ml) fresh lemon juice
½ cup (125 ml) fresh orange juice
1 small clove garlic, minced
¼ cup (60 ml) olive oil
Salt
Pinch of ground hot pepper
¼ cup (30 g) chopped flat-leaf parsley

Peel and devein the shrimp. Place in a glass dish.

Combine the lemon and orange juices and pour over the shrimp. Let stand for at least 30 minutes, turning once or twice.

Drain the shrimp and discard the marinade. Toss the shrimp with the garlic, olive oil, salt to taste, and the hot pepper. Sprinkle with the parsley. Eat right away, though they will still be good the next day. Refrigerate any leftovers.

NOTE. *For this dish, it is particularly important that the shrimp you buy be fresh, not previously frozen.*

GAMBERONI FREDDI AL LIMONE
Jumbo Shrimp with Lemon

You can prepare peeled and deveined shrimp the same way but you'll miss the pleasure of sucking out all the good things that are in the head.

THIS MAKES ENOUGH FOR 6 PEOPLE.

*2 pounds (1 kg) jumbo shrimp (8 to 10 count) in the shell,
  with heads if possible*
Salt
2 lemons, quartered
Sprigs of flat-leaf parsley, for garnish

Wash the shrimp under cold running water. Immerse in boiling salted water and cook just until the flesh turns opaque, about 3 minutes. Drain, transfer to a serving platter, and refrigerate for 10 minutes to firm the flesh.

Surround the shrimp with the lemon quarters and garnish the platter with the parsley.

ABOVE: *Sardines are one of the traditional flavors of Sicily, appearing fresh in the national dish of pasta con le sarde and salted in salads with pasta and tomato sauce.*

INSALATA DI GRANO CON POMODORO, TONNO, E CAPPERI

Wheat Berry Salad with Tomatoes, Tuna, and Capers

Kamut, a strain of wheat said to date back to ancient Egypt and now widely available in health-food stores, is a good substitute for Sicilian durum wheat. It is very similar in taste and texture when cooked. Spelt, though a bit chewier, is also acceptable. It too is available in health-food stores.

THIS MAKES ENOUGH FOR 3 TO 4 PEOPLE.

1 cup (200 g) durum wheat berries
1 bay leaf
Zest of ½ orange, in 1 piece or strips
Salt
1 pound (450 g) ripe tomatoes
Sugar
1 can (6⅛ oz/173 g) albacore or solid white tuna fish,
    rinsed and drained
1 tablespoon capers, rinsed and drained
½ small red onion, finely chopped
1 clove garlic, minced
Pinch of ground hot pepper
¼ cup (60 ml) fresh lemon juice
¼ cup (60 ml) olive oil
½ cup (30 g) fresh herbs, such as basil, parsley, mint, or
    whatever you have, chopped

Rinse the wheat berries, discarding any chaff. Soak in hot water to cover by ¾ inch (2 cm) for 24 hours, changing the water twice.

Drain and rinse the berries. Put them in a heavy saucepan with enough fresh water to cover by at least 2 inches. Add the bay leaf, orange zest, and 1 teaspoon salt and bring to a boil. Reduce the heat, cover, and simmer until the grains are separate and tender, like rice, neither mushy nor al dente, 30 to 45 minutes. Check frequently after 30 minutes. Drain, discarding the bay leaf and zest. Let the wheat berries cool thoroughly.

Peel, seed, and roughly chop the tomatoes. Place in a colander, sprinkle with salt and sugar, and let stand for at least 20 minutes.

Put the tuna in a serving bowl and flake it. Add the capers, onion, garlic, hot pepper, salt to taste, and the lemon juice. Add the tomatoes and toss thoroughly. Stir in the olive oil; add the wheat berries and half of the herbs. Let stand for several hours, if possible.

Just before serving, sprinkle the remaining ¼ cup herbs on top. The salad will keep well for a few days.

SALAME DI TONNO
Tuna Salami

This poached tuna pâté is ideal for a picnic or a casual lunch. Unlike the *Pesce del Contadino* (page 203), an uncooked tuna mousse, it can be cut into slices. Serve the slices with tomato salad or green salad.

THIS MAKES ENOUGH FOR 10 PEOPLE.

5 cans (6⅛ oz/173 g each) albacore or solid white tuna fish,
*   rinsed and drained*
4 large eggs
1 cup (120 g) grated parmesan
1 cup (120 g) fine dry breadcrumbs
¼ teaspoon freshly ground black pepper

Put the tuna in a food processor and process to very fine crumbs. Transfer to a bowl and knead in the eggs one at a time. Add the parmesan, breadcrumbs, and pepper and mix with your hand until well blended. The mixture should be like a paste; add more breadcrumbs if it is too loose.

Divide the mixture in two. Form each half into a salami shape about 8 inches (20 cm) long. Wrap each one in aluminum foil, twist the ends, and tie securely with string.

Place in a large saucepan, cover with water, and bring to a simmer. Cook for 20 minutes. Remove the pan from the heat, and let the salami stand in the water until cool.

Remove from the water, unwrap, and rewrap in plastic wrap. Store in the refrigerator. To serve, cut into thick slices.

ZUPPA DI GRANO DURO

Wheat Berry Soup

Be sure to use kamut or spelt, not the tiny red soft wheat berries.
THIS MAKES ENOUGH FOR 6 PEOPLE.

1½ cups (300 g) durum wheat berries, kamut, or spelt
1 large red onion, finely chopped
2 stalks celery, finely chopped
3 cloves garlic, peeled
2¼ pounds (1 kg) ripe tomatoes, peeled, seeded, and chopped,
*   or 1 can (14½ oz/411 g) Italian plum tomatoes, drained,*
*   seeded, and chopped*
6 cups (1,5 l) water
1 cup (250 ml) white wine
2 beef bouillon cubes
2 cans (14 oz/397 g each) small white beans, rinsed and drained
Salt
Ground hot pepper
BATTUTO CRUDO
¼ cup (30 g) chopped flat-leaf parsley
¼ cup (30 g) chopped basil
1 to 2 cloves garlic, minced
⅓ cup (40 g) grated pecorino

Olive oil

Rinse the wheat berries, discarding any chaff. Soak in cold water to cover by ¾ inch (2 cm) for 24 hours, changing the water twice.

Drain and rinse the berries. Put them in a heavy saucepan with the onion, celery, garlic, tomatoes, water, wine, and bouillon cubes. Bring to a boil. Reduce the heat and simmer, covered, for 30 minutes.

Stir in the beans and simmer until the wheat berries are tender and the beans are warmed through, 10 to 15 minutes longer. Season to taste with salt and hot pepper.

Combine all of the ingredients for the *battuto*. Ladle the soup into individual serving bowls. Drizzle with olive oil and sprinkle with the *battuto*. Serve hot.

BUSIATI O TAGLIATELLE
Homemade Macaroni or Tagliatelle

To make the *busiati* in the United States, use bamboo skewers, which are readily available in the supermarket, in place of *disa* grass. They are somewhat shorter, but are smooth and flexible.

THIS MAKES ENOUGH FRESH PASTA FOR 10 PEOPLE.

About 6 cups (1 kg) semolina flour
1 tablespoon salt
4 large eggs
About 1 cup (250 ml) warm water

Grind the flour, one half at a time, in a food processor until silky to the touch, about 5 minutes.

Transfer the flour to a countertop or large bowl, stir in the salt, and make a well. Break the eggs into the well and mix with your hand. Add the water, a little at a time, continuing to mix with your hand, until the dough just sticks together. If using a bowl, turn the dough out onto a work surface. Knead until smooth, about 20 minutes. Divide the dough in two and shape each half into a ball. Wrap in plastic and set aside to rest for 30 minutes

To make *busiati*, flatten the dough into a disk and roll it out into a rectangle about ⅜ inch (1 cm) thick. Cut into strips about ¾ inch (2 cm) wide. Place all but one strip in a plastic bag. Roll the strip you are working with under your hands into a long rope about ¼ inch (0,5 cm) thick. Cut it into finger-length pieces, 3½ to 4 inches (8 to 10 cm) long.

Place a skewer in the center of a piece of dough, bring up the sides, and roll under your fingers until the dough is almost the length of the skewer. Let stand to dry somewhat, 20 minutes to 1 hour, depending on the humidity in the air. Pull out the skewer and hang the pasta to dry. Continue until all of the dough is used.

To make tagliatelle with a rolling pin, flatten the dough into a disk and roll it out into a very thin (1/16 inch/15 mm), very large sheet, or pass it through a pasta machine until it is very thin. Cut the dough into strips the width you want them.

Fresh pasta will keep for 1 day at room temperature and for 1 week in the refrigerator. Cook in plenty of boiling salted water until al dente, 2 to 3 minutes.

SFORMATO DI RISO FREDDO AL POMODORO
Rice Ring Filled with Tomatoes

Our eggs come straight from the hen, and salmonella is not a problem. If you are concerned about the raw egg yolk in the mayonnaise, use your own recipe for it. Bottled mayonnaise will not have the right flavor.

THIS MAKES ENOUGH FOR 6 TO 8 PEOPLE.

3 cups (600 g) long-grain rice
1 cup (60 g) basil leaves, coarsely chopped
¼ cup (60 ml) olive oil
Salt and freshly ground black pepper

MAYONNAISE

1 egg yolk, at room temperature
Salt
2 cups (500 ml) vegetable oil
¼ cup (60 ml) fresh lemon juice

½ cup (125 ml) plain yogurt
Whole basil leaves, for garnish
1 pound (450 g) tomatoes, peeled and cut into bite-size pieces,
*   for serving*

Cook the rice as directed on page 113 until tender. Meanwhile, lightly oil a 9-inch (23-cm) tube pan (10-cup/2,5-l capacity) or angel food cake pan or line it with parchment paper.

Drain the rice and mix with the chopped basil, olive oil, and salt and pepper to taste. While the rice mixture is still warm, fill the mold, gently pressing down on the rice. Refrigerate until ready to serve.

For the mayonnaise, whisk the egg yolk until smooth. Stir in a pinch of salt. Whisk in some of the oil, a little at a time, until the sauce thickens. Whisk in some of the lemon juice. Continue whisking in the oil until the sauce is very thick. Whisk in the rest of the lemon juice.

For the sauce, whisk the yogurt into the mayonnaise and season to taste with salt. The sauce should be rather acidic. (You will have more than enough sauce; refrigerate the portion.)

When ready to serve, invert the mold onto a serving plate. Decorate with the basil leaves and fill the center with the tomatoes. Pass the sauce separately.

PREVIOUS PAGE: *Peperoncini Rossi Ripieni (page 233) sit on the windowsill of my kitchen at Case Vecchie.* **ABOVE:** *The Ferragosto buffet (page 172) at my parents' home.*

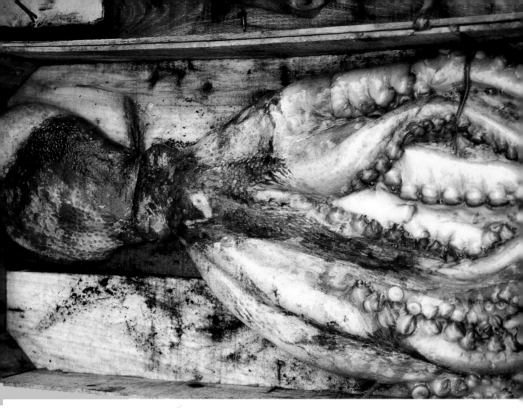

ABOVE: *Octopus is much appreciated in Sicily; it is sold by the piece by vendors.* BELOW: *The bay of Mondello, with the fishing village of Mondello Paese in the distance.*

ABOVE: *Bread in the shape of San Giuseppe's beard, sprinkled with white poppy seeds.* BELOW: *Ring- and leaf-shaped Mustazzuoli Panteschi (page 128), filled with sesame seeds and couscous. A tray of nut brittle.* RIGHT: *A San Giuseppe altar in Salemi, with angels, flowers, and animals sculpted from bread.*

CLOCKWISE FROM TOP LEFT: *A basket vendor sets up shop on a shady sidewalk. Straw is dried before storing. Boiled zucca lunga is sold on the street; a morsel sprinkled with salt and lemon juice is amazingly refreshing. Part of a vendor's stall for Il Festino, the feast of Santa Rosalia. The last of Palermo's donkey-drawn door-to-door vendors.* OVERLEAF: *Vineyards follow the rolling contours of central Sicily.*

LEFT: *Clusters of cherry tomatoes are hung from the rafters. Many fruits and vegetables keep well this way, much better than in the refrigerator.* ABOVE: *Rocks of volcanic tuff litter the countryside. They are piled up for fences.* BELOW: *Cows dot the hillsides.*

CLOCKWISE FROM TOP LEFT: *Licorice root is refreshing to suck in summer. Green walnuts and lemons steep in alcohol in the first step of making nocino (page 107). Green salad benefits from the crunch of radish. Loquats (page 54) and cherries are good to put in your fruit basket in late spring.*

CLOCKWISE FROM TOP LEFT: *My marzipan sun, who can smile on us night or day. Nacatole (page 188) from the Eolian Islands are filled with dried fruit and nuts. The Verginedde tables of San Giuseppe's day (page 23) are crowded with good things to eat. Amaretti (page 36) are a universal favorite.* **OVERLEAF:** *Chocolate, lemon, and other fruit granitas melt in the sun before they can melt in your mouth at this gelateria in the Eolian Islands.*

INSALATA DI CETRIOLI

Cucumber Salad

The Sicilian cucumber is long and twisted with a fuzzy dark green skin. Like hothouse or burpless cucumbers, it does not have many seeds. If you use a seedy type of cucumber, cut each cucumber lengthwise and remove the seeds. Though it isn't an authentic Sicilian flavoring, I sometimes add a bit of chopped dill to cucumber salad.

THIS MAKES ENOUGH FOR 8 PEOPLE.

2 long hothouse cucumbers, 6 Kirby cucumbers, or
* 4 regular cucumbers*
Salt
3 tablespoons olive oil
1 tablespoon red wine vinegar
Freshly ground black pepper
3 tablespoons chopped dill (optional)

Peel the cucumbers entirely or in stripes and slice as thin as possible. Put in a serving bowl. Combine the oil, vinegar, and pepper to taste, pour over the cucumbers, and turn to coat. Sprinkle with dill, if you like, and serve.

NOTE. *If your cucumbers are watery—Sicilian cucumbers are not—salt the slices and let stand in a colander for 1 hour. Squeeze the juice out of the cucumbers and blot dry.*

GELO DI MELONE
Watermelon Pudding

Because it is so sweet and juicy, watermelon eaten by the slice is a favorite summer food in Sicily. Its refreshing flavor is also appreciated in granita or in this classic pudding. For grand occasions, the pudding is garnished with jasmine flowers, cinnamon, chocolate, candied squash, and pistachios, otherwise just simply with jasmine flowers and a light sprinkling of cinnamon.

THIS MAKES ENOUGH FOR 8 PEOPLE.

1 small watermelon (5½ lb/2,5 kg)
1 cup (60 g) fresh jasmine flowers (optional)
½ cup plus 2 tablespoons (80 g) cornstarch
1 cup (200 g) sugar
Jasmine flowers, ground cinnamon, chocolate flakes, candied
squash or citron, and chopped pistachios, for garnish

Cut up the watermelon and scoop out the flesh. Coarsely chop the pulp, removing as many seeds as you can. Put through a food mill or mash with an electric mixer, using the paddle attachment. Drain through a colander and measure out 4 cups of juice. Add the jasmine flowers, if using, and let steep overnight.

Strain the watermelon juice and discard the flowers, if any. Whisk the cornstarch into ½ cup of the juice. Whisk the mixture into the rest of the juice in a medium saucepan. Place over low heat and add the sugar. Stir constantly until the mixture comes to a boil. Count to 60 and remove from the heat.

Pour into a glass bowl and let cool briefly. Refrigerate until set, 2 to 3 hours.

Just before serving, garnish with at least the fresh jasmine flowers and cinnamon. Add whatever other garnishes you like.

NOTE. *Add 1 to 2 tablespoons rose water, if desired, just before pouring the pudding into a bowl.*

GELATINA DI FRAGOLE
Strawberry Gelatin

This dessert is always an event. If you were raised on packaged gelatin desserts, you're in for a big surprise. I like to serve it in double martini glasses with a berry and a mint leaf on top.

THIS MAKES ENOUGH FOR 6 PEOPLE.

2 quarts (900 g) strawberries
Zest of 1 lemon, in large pieces
Juice of ½ lemon
Zest of 1 orange, in large pieces
Juice of ½ orange
4⅓ cups (1 l) water
3½ cups (700 g) sugar
2 envelopes (7 g each) unflavored gelatin
Strawberries, edible flowers, or mint leaves, for garnish

Combine the strawberries, lemon zest, lemon juice, orange zest, and orange juice in a medium saucepan. Add the water and sugar and bring to a boil over medium heat. Cook for 15 to 20 minutes, or until the berries are very soft and mushy.

Remove from the heat; remove and discard the citrus zests. Puree the mixture. Pour the puree through a fine-mesh strainer. (If you want a clear gelatin, line it with cheesecloth.) Measure the juice; you should have at least 4⅓ cups (1 l). If you have much more, make more gelatin, allowing 1 envelope of gelatin to every 2 cups of juice.

Sprinkle the gelatin over 2 cups of the juice in a medium saucepan and let soften. Add the rest of the juice and bring to a boil over high heat, whisking to dissolve the gelatin. Pour through a clean fine-mesh strainer, pushing down with a spoon in case any of the gelatin is not dissolved. Pour into a pretty serving dish or martini glasses, and refrigerate overnight.

Just before serving, decorate with berries, flowers, or mint leaves.

GRANITA DI CAFFÈ
Coffee Granita

Coffee granita is traditionally served with whipped cream in Sicily. You can omit it if you prefer. You can also reduce the amount of sugar if you find this too sweet, but whatever you do, be sure to use strong coffee.
THIS MAKES ENOUGH FOR 6 PEOPLE.

¾ cup (150 g) sugar
2 cups (500 ml) water
1¼ cups (300 ml) brewed espresso or very strong coffee
1 cup (250 ml) heavy cream, whipped (optional)

Combine the sugar and water in a saucepan and cook over medium heat until the sugar dissolves. Boil for 5 minutes to make a light syrup. Stir in the coffee and let cool.

Pour the mixture into metal ice trays or a shallow metal pan and freeze for at least 2 hours. Stir every 30 minutes to break up the ice crystals.

Just before serving, stir one more time and scoop into individual serving glasses. Garnish with the whipped cream, if desired.

GRANITA DI LIMONE

Lemon Granita

Few flavors in the world are as refreshing as lemon. I often think it's a pity lemons are not plentiful in Sicily in summer—their season ends in spring—but we do always manage to find some to make granita.

THIS MAKES ENOUGH FOR 6 TO 8 PEOPLE.

1½ cups (300 g) sugar (see Note)
4 cups (1 l) water
1 cup (250 ml) fresh lemon juice
1 teaspoon grated lemon zest

Combine the sugar and water in a saucepan and cook over medium heat until the sugar dissolves. Boil for 5 minutes to make a light syrup. Pour the mixture into a wide bowl and let cool in the kitchen or in the refrigerator.

Stir the lemon juice and zest into the syrup. Transfer to metal ice trays or a shallow metal pan and freeze for at least 2 hours. Stir every 30 minutes to break up the ice crystals.

Just before serving, stir again and scoop into individual serving glasses.

NOTE. *Use an additional ½ cup (100 g) sugar if you like the granita sweet or if your lemons are very sour; use ½ cup (100 g) less if you like the granita tart or if you have particularly sweet lemons.*

GRANITA DI PESCHE
Peach Granita

You can make this granita with about one pound of any fruit. The more perfumed the fruit, the better the granita will be. Use more sugar if the fruit is not very sweet.

THIS MAKES ENOUGH FOR 6 PEOPLE.

2 cups (400 g) sugar
4 cups (1 l) water
4 peaches (1 lb/450 g)
Juice of 2 lemons

Combine the sugar and water in a saucepan and cook over medium heat until the sugar dissolves. Boil for 5 minutes to make a light syrup. Pour the mixture into a wide bowl and let cool in the kitchen or in the refrigerator to save time.

Peel, pit, and cut up the peaches, dropping the pieces into the lemon juice to prevent them from discoloring. Pour the peaches and juice into a food processor and puree until smooth.

Stir the puree into the syrup. Transfer to metal ice trays or a shallow metal pan and freeze for at least 2 hours. Stir every 30 minutes to break up the crystals.

Remove from the freezer about 30 minutes before serving. Stir until the granita is of the desired consistency. Scoop into serving glasses and serve immediately.

VARIATIONS. *Granita di Pere* (Pear Granita). Substitute 1 pound (450 g) of pears, any variety or a mixture, for the peaches. Peel, core, and cut up the fruit, dropping the pieces into a bowl with the juice of 1 lemon. Puree the fruit with the juice. Continue as with the peaches.

Granita di Mele e Pere (Apple and Pear Granita). Substitute 2 apples and 2 pears for the peaches. Peel, core, and cut up the fruit, dropping the pieces into a bowl with the juice of 1 orange and 1 lemon. Puree the fruit with the juices. Continue as with the peaches.

BISCOTTI ALL'ANICE
Anise Biscuits

This recipe is from *Bitter Almonds*, the story of Maria Grammatico as told by Mary Taylor Simeti. Maria, who has a pastry shop in Erice, learned the skills of pastry making and confectionery from the nuns at the Istituto San Carlo, where she spent her childhood.

THIS MAKES 3½ TO 4½ DOZEN BISCUITS.

3 large eggs
¾ cup plus 2 tablespoons (170 g) sugar
½ teaspoon vanilla extract
½ teaspoon baker's ammonia or ½ teaspoon baking
  powder mixed with ½ teaspoon baking soda (see Note)
1¾ cups (260 g) all-purpose flour
1 tablespoon plus 1 teaspoon (10 g) anise seeds

Preheat the oven to 375° F. (190° C.). Line several baking sheets with parchment paper or foil. If using foil, grease it.

Lightly beat the eggs in a large mixing bowl. Add the sugar and vanilla and whisk until light and fluffy and a ribbon begins to form when the whisk is lifted from the bowl, about 8 minutes.

Mix the baker's ammonia (or the mixture) with the flour. Stir one quarter of the flour mixture into the beaten eggs. Fold in the rest of the dry ingredients in 3 additions. Fold in the anise seeds.

Scoop the batter into a pastry bag fitted with a large plain tip or use a large spoon. Pipe or spoon the batter onto the baking sheets, forming loaves, each 2 inches (5 cm) wide and 2½ to 3 inches (6 to 8 cm) long.

Bake for 20 to 25 minutes, or until golden. Remove from the oven and reduce the temperature to 300° F. (150° C.).

Cool the loaves for 10 minutes on the pans. Transfer to a cutting board and cut on the diagonal into slices ½ to ¾ inch (1,5 to 2 cm) thick. Lay the slices on an ungreased baking sheet and bake, turning once, until very lightly toasted, about 5 minutes on each side. Cool thoroughly on racks. Store in an airtight container.

NOTE. *Baker's ammonia (ammonium carbonate) is an old-fashioned leavener, which has the side effect of drying the pastry. It is available in many shops that sell cake and pastry supplies or by mail order (page 252).*

TARALLI
Lemon Cookies

In some places, these cookies are called *"cuddureddi"* from the verb *"incuddurare,"* to intertwine, because of the way the two ropes of dough are twisted around one another.

THIS MAKES ABOUT 3 DOZEN COOKIES.

COOKIE DOUGH
>   3½ cups (500 g) all-purpose flour
>   ½ teaspoon salt
>   2½ teaspoons baking powder
>   2½ teaspoons baking soda
>   6 tablespoons (75 g) granulated sugar
>   Grated zest of 1 lemon
>   6 tablespoons (90 g) unsalted butter, softened
>   1 cup (250 ml) milk
>   2 large eggs
>   1 teaspoon vanilla extract
>   Juice of ½ lemon

GLAZE
>   2 cups (160 g) sifted confectioners' sugar
>   Grated zest of ½ lemon
>   Juice of ½ lemon
>   2 to 3 tablespoons milk

Preheat the oven to 350° F. (180° C.). Lightly flour 2 or 3 baking sheets.

For the cookies, combine the flour, salt, baking powder, baking soda, sugar, and lemon zest in a mixing bowl or on the counter. Make a well and add the butter, milk, eggs, vanilla, and lemon juice and mix the dough with your hands until the mixture stretches out into a ribbon when you lift it out of the bowl with your hand. The dough will be very sticky.

Pick up 1 tablespoon of dough and roll it out without squeezing into a rope. Cut it in half and roll each piece into a rope about 10 inches (25 cm) long. Fold each rope in half and intertwine the 2 loose ends. Bring together to form a ring and pinch the ends to seal. Place the rings 1 inch apart on the baking sheets. Continue with the remaining dough.

Bake for 15 to 20 minutes, or until very lightly browned and puffed. Cool thoroughly on the pan.

To prepare the glaze, combine the confectioners' sugar, lemon zest, and lemon juice. Add just enough of the milk to make a medium-thick icing.

With a pastry brush, dust the excess flour from the bottom of the cookies. Dip the top of each cookie in the glaze and with your finger, spread the glaze evenly over the top of the cookie. Place on racks or clean pans until the glaze is dry.

Store the cookies in a tightly sealed container. They will soften as they stand.

N O T E . *I use 2½ teaspoons baker's ammonia (ammonium carbonate) when I make these cookies, but they were tested with baking powder and baking soda since baker's ammonia is not so readily available in the United States. You can get it by mail order (page 252), though. Besides leavening the dough, it has a drying effect. Cookies made with baking powder and baking soda are more cake-like than those made with baker's ammonia.*

A B O V E : *In her kitchen at Regaleali, Anna demonstrates how to form Taralli into a ring.*

AGOSTO

My parents and I both have homes in Mondello Valdesi, the seaside suburb of Palermo. I live there when I am not at Regaleali, and I usually stay there for most of August: Regaleali is too hot and has no water to spare for a refreshing dip, while in Mondello, you have the sea and its cooling breezes at your doorstep.

Not far from the fashionable neighborhood around the beach is the old fishing village of Mondello Paese. It used to be a charming, peaceful place where you could go in the early evening and watch the old men sitting in their beached boats mending the nets. The boats, painted in dazzling colors like the caretto siciliano (Sicilian cart) so they could be seen from afar at sea, would go out before dawn and bring the catch back to market by midmorning. Each fisherman had a stall around the piazza. You could be sure that the wriggling silver fish had just come out of the sea.

LEFT: *Golden melons slowly ripen under the summer sun.*

THE TWO MONDELLOS

Sometimes the fishermen from Mondello Paese would pedal their bikes over to Mondello Valdesi at midday, a big basket of sea urchins tied to the rack. The family would sit around a table in the garden and watch mesmerized as the man picked up one after another of the spiny creatures with his left hand and cut it open with just one stroke of his knife. Somehow he managed not to destroy the shell, an important skill since one wouldn't want to lose any of the golden roe, the edible part. The left hand, which performed this task all day long, was monstrous, swollen like a balloon from the urchin's spines.

Eventually the market was abolished—too dirty, the authorities said—and the wooden fishing boats were replaced with noisy motorboats that pollute the sea. A fountain with an improbable double-tailed mermaid rising out of it was erected in the middle of the piazza. Surrounding the fountain are restaurants and bars and a gelateria, all with garish neon signs on top. Many of the fishermen who used to bicycle around Mondello with their catch now own these restaurants—the Sariddus and the Pinellos, for example—where they serve fish and shellfish, including sea urchins. You can scoop out the roe and have it with a piece of bread and a few drops of lemon juice or with pasta in *Spaghetti con i Ricci* (Spaghetti with Sea Urchins, page 190).

FERRAGOSTO

On August 15, all of Sicily, like the rest of Catholic Europe, observes the Feast of the Assumption of the Blessed Virgin. Called *Ferragosto* in Italian, it is an occasion marked by fireworks. My parents have trimmed the shrubbery in front of their villa to create an unobstructed view of the bay and Mondello Paese from the terrace. The sunset is breathtaking every day; the fireworks on *Ferragosto* are spectacular.

My parents always have open house on the holiday. Mario Lo Menzo, their *monzù* chef, is on vacation for the month of August, but that doesn't stop them from inviting friends and family to join them for the evening. For many years, my mother's sister Maria Flugy and her husband, Nicolo, have spent the week at the house. The crowd usually numbers about forty, a few children included.

We all pitch in to prepare a cold buffet in advance of the festivities, with my mother, as always, determined to make all of the dishes her guests like best. Zia Maria is a great help in the kitchen. Her specialty is *Cotolette alla Tedesca* (Breaded Beef Cutlets, page 202), which are perfect for a buffet since they are much better cold than warm. My sister Rosemarie and I prepare *Pesce del Contadina* (Fish Mousse, Peasant Style, page 203), made with canned tuna.

I usually make a couple of pasta salads and maybe a rice salad, too. I always say I'll try something new but usually end up falling back on the old favorites, *Fusilli Mediterranei* (Fusilli with Tomatoes, Basil, and Black Olives, page 191), and *Insalata di Pasta Arrabiata* (Penne Salad with Herbs and Hot Pepper, page 192). *Riso con Melanzane, Menta, e Capperi* (Cold Rice with Eggplant, Mint, and Capers, page 198) is particularly refreshing.

Salvatore Campisi, who is in charge of the kitchen when Mario is away, makes a batch of *Caponata* (page 207) and a huge poached fish surrounded by jumbo shrimp and boiled potatoes. It's served with *Salsa Verde per il Pesce* (Green Sauce for Fish, page 208).

Usually I do the desserts—*Gelo di Melone* (Watermelon Pudding, page 162) and gelatins that slide down easily in the heat. I always make *Biancomangiare* (Blancmange, page 37) with almonds; the season for fresh almonds is very short and mid-August is the end of it. This is a good occasion to show how wonderful they are, and everyone in the family loves this very sweet, very Sicilian dessert.

Everything is ready and the table set long before the procession gets to the breakwater in front of my parents' house. It is timed to leave Chiesa Maria Santissima Assunta, the parish church of Mondello, so as to arrive at the breakwater just as the sun begins to set. The taller-than-life-size statue of the Virgin on a pedestal is lowered onto long poles. The bearers—a dozen of them—lift the poles onto their shoulders and carry the Virgin out of the church and through the streets of Mondello, followed by the faithful. As soon as we hear the band playing in the distance, we rush out to the sidewalk.

When the procession reaches the sea, the statue of the Virgin is carefully placed standing in a rowboat. It is pushed off to sea and rowed across the bay into the sunset. Other rowboats, lanterns swaying, follow. Soon the flotilla arrives in Mondello Paese, and the Virgin is reverently lifted out of her boat. The procession continues, with the people of Mondello Paese following in the train of the Virgin as she wends her way back on land to the church. Then the fireworks begin.

They are set off from the same breakwater from which the Virgin's boat was launched a few hours earlier. Brilliant flashes of colored light alternate with pops and bangs; it can be frightening. The first year Virginia, my granddaughter, stayed at Mondello for *Ferragosto*, she was terrified and very angry at us because the stars were falling down.

SNUFFBOX PEACHES AND OTHER CURIOSITIES

A few days after the fireworks one year, I was sunbathing at the Circolo del Vela, a private club on the beach, with a friend when out of the blue, she asked me if I knew anything about a peach called *pesca tabacchiera*, literally, "snuffbox peach," which she had heard grows only in Sicily. I had to admit I knew nothing about it. Soon the sun got uncomfortably hot, and we decided to find some shade. I walked over to my mother's to visit with her before lunch.

I asked her if she was familiar with this strange peach. To my amazement she said, "Of course. You remember, my brother planted them, but the fruit was so ugly no one wanted to buy it. They uprooted the trees and planted something else. I saw those peaches only this morning at Pizzichella's, but I didn't buy any because they were so dear." I rushed over to Pizzichella's, the best and most expensive fruit and vegetable store in Mondello, to buy some.

This peach is indeed very peculiar looking—flat and almost square with an indentation in the middle. In fact, it is being marketed as the "donut peach" in the United States. The fuzzy skin, pink on one side, yellowish on the rest, peels easily. The aroma is powerful even when the fruit is hard. When ripe, the flesh, which falls easily off the stone, is sweet and perfumed and fills your mouth with intense satisfaction. An incredible fruit.

A few days later, back at Regaleali, I was having lunch with my brother, Lucio, and I told him about my discovery with great enthusiasm. He didn't say anything, though I noted he was looking even more devilish than usual. When the fruit was served, what should appear in the basket but *pesche tabacchiere*, larger and healthier looking than the ones at Pizzichella's. His eyes shining, Lucio told me he was going to plant them—one hundred fifty trees—for a grappa that will be so special people will fight to have a bottle.

It seems that Salvatore Triffiletti, who is in charge of the bottling room at the winery, brought the peaches when he returned from vacation. He comes from Moio, a village near Taormina, and every year he brings us enormous juicy peaches from home; this year for the first time he brought the *tabacchiere*.

They grow around Mount Etna in eastern Sicily. Etna, alive and menacing, still erupting, dominates the entire island. All kinds of vegetation thrives in the volcanic soil—trees and vines, beautiful vegetables and fruits. Extensive vineyards and orchards of citrus, peaches, pears, and apples are planted on its slopes.

Some unusual varieties of fruit, like the *limoncella* apple, which also flourishes in the volcanic soil of Alicudi in the Eolian Islands, are still cultivated there. Locally called *pomocora*, it is a small oval yellow apple, fragrant but tart; it ripens in time for Christmas. Other old varieties are disappearing; only a few abandoned trees survive high on the mountain. One of those is the *pomogola*. It looks like a Granny Smith from the outside but is soft around the core. Commercial growers try to avoid this phenomenon, which they call "water core," because although the apples taste good, they won't hold for very long in storage. The water core results when an early frost causes some of the apple juice around the core to turn amber; it is incredibly sweet.

We're not sure how well the peaches will do uprooted from their familiar volcanic soil and transplanted to Regaleali. A few years ago when I was starting a fruit garden at Case Vecchie, I asked Triffiletti to bring me some peach branches. We grafted them onto bitter almond trees, the best host for peaches, but all we got was green Ping-Pong balls. This time, we planted two of the one hundred and fifty saplings in my garden, as near to the house as possible. Maybe Carmelo will take pity when he sees them and give them at least a little drink of water from time to time.

ESTRATTO

Another morning during one of my August interludes in Mondello, I was sitting on the terrace of my parents' home talking to Zia Maria. Like the rest of us, my aunt is very interested in food and food customs. Suddenly, in the middle of a perfectly innocuous conversation, she turned to me and said, "Around my country place, the *estratto* is not cooked. Why don't you try that yourself?" I answered, passionately, that it was impossible, *estratto di pomodoro* (sun-dried tomato paste) was always cooked. End of discussion. But even though I had been able to shut her up, however rudely, I couldn't shut up my own mind.

A little research revealed that, yes, in some parts of Sicily *estratto di pomodoro* is made without cooking the tomatoes. Thus the worst step of the process—standing in front of a roaring fire all the while stirring the tomatoes—could be eliminated.

When I returned to Case Vecchie, the tomatoes had been picked, and my assistants, Graziella and Maria, were getting them ready for Carmelo to boil them down, as I described in *The Heart of Sicily*. I announced, "Girls, not today but in a couple of days we're going to try to make *estratto* without boiling the tomatoes." They both stared at

ABOVE: *Two tons of tomatoes make two hundred pounds of estratto.*

me, disbelief and disappointment showing clearly in their eyes.

They were considerably more cheerful the next morning. It seems Graziella's mother said that she had heard of raw *estratto*, that so-and-so used to make it that way. With her stamp of approval on it, my idea no longer looked so crazy.

So we embarked on our experiment. We set up a dozen wooden tables in the courtyard of Case Vecchie, wherever they would catch the most rays of sunshine. As for cooked *estratto*, we squeezed as much juice out of the tomatoes as we could with our hands. The girls use their thumbs to make a hole the old-fashioned way, but I prefer to use a knife. We put the crushed tomatoes in slotted plastic crates and pressed out as much juice as we could with our hands.

The next step was to pass the tomatoes through the electric food mill. The sauce was thinner than with cooked tomatoes but still thick enough to pour on the wooden tables without running off, though we had to be very careful. For the raw *estratto* we didn't tilt the tables as we do for cooked-tomato *estratto*; we would have lost too much of the juice if we had. Only after the juice had been drying in the sun for an hour did we salt it.

As with the other, we kept spreading the paste as it dried and consolidating it as it shrunk, until we finally had only one table left out of the original twelve. It took a week, compared to three days for the cooked-tomato *estratto*.

But this *estratto* is well worth waiting for—it is red rather than rust colored and tastes acidic and fresh, like just-picked ripe tomatoes. It's so good, in fact, that Lucio and his sons, who live at Case Grandi near the winery, sneak into the kitchen at Case Vecchie to steal it to put on *bruschetta!* I myself like to use it for many dishes, including the *ragù* in *Sformato di Patate al Ragù* (Potato Timbale with Meat Sauce and Peas, page 200), which can be eaten warm or, even better, cold.

THE SUMMER KITCHEN

It's very quiet in the country in August. The family is in Mondello, and most of the winery and farm workers are on vacation. The courtyard of Case Vecchie, usually abuzz with activity, is still, empty except for the dogs sleeping in whatever spot of shade they can find. The gardens and vineyards are silently making their final effort before the harvest.

Times like this are very relaxing, and doing mindless chores is a good way to restore the soul. With no one running after you, you can do a hundred things in one day. We don't even stop to cook lunch. Graziella buys a sandwich for each of us at the bakery in Vallelunga.

The grandfather of the American hero sandwich, this one is made on a *sfilatino*, a long bread like a French *ficelle*. The owner's wife cuts the bread in half the long way and fills it with fillets of *sarde salate* (salted sardines), which she drizzles with olive oil and dusts with a mixture of oregano, salt, ground hot pepper, and grated pecorino. Eaten with a glass of wine, a sandwich like this is all you need to keep going until nightfall.

Mostly we do things like dry herbs and make lavender sachets. Two years in a row we experimented with so-called bastard saffron, actually safflower (*Carthamus tinctorius*), a flower that in the old days was used to dye silk.

Saffron is one of the ancient flavors of Sicilian cuisine. The saffron crocus (*Crocus sativus*), whose stigmas are dried to make the spice, still grows wild in the Madonie Mountains, but no one wants to go forage for it anymore. I planted some bulbs in my garden and had just about given up hope when they bloomed in November. Now I have my own supply!

What we buy in the store comes from Abruzzi and is terribly expensive because picking the stigmas is so labor intensive. Some villagers substitute food coloring to brighten dull dishes with the tint of saffron. They might put it in *Patate allo Zafferano* (Braised Potatoes with Saffron, page 199), for example, a bland stew my mother used to give us as children when we fussed about our food.

I was curious to see what this bastard saffron was like. It was new to us—some employees from the north had brought the seeds with them. We planted them and soon had tall green plants with an orange and yellow thistlelike flower. We picked the petals in July and dried them, first in baskets in the sun for a few days, then in a very low oven for about ten minutes. (You have to be careful when drying things in the oven—the first year we burned the petals while gossiping!) Once they were completely dry, we crushed the petals to powder. We tried

RIGHT: *Wild dill finds a corner to grow near fields tall with wheat.*

this bastard saffron in several dishes calling for saffron, but we found that although the color was right, when it came to flavor, there was no comparison with true saffron.

Beware when someone tries to sell you a big bag of saffron; it's probably bastard saffron. Look closely: If the bits look more like rust-colored tea leaves than threads and if they have almost no aroma at all, it's surely counterfeit. It's easy to be fooled, especially in a country where they produce saffron, because you think you're getting a big bargain. You'll be thousands of miles away when you learn the truth!

There's no substitute for lavender, either. When you open the doors of a linen closet that has dried lavender in it, the smell is heavenly, and when you sleep between lavender-scented sheets, you can't help but have pleasant dreams. In Sicily, women still pride themselves on their hand-embroidered linens—and they use them. My daughter, Fabrizia, is pressing me to start making the trousseau for her daughter, Virginia. That way she can always say, "My grandmother made this." Those who don't have the time or the skill for this kind of handiwork often buy household linens embroidered by others.

Shrubs of lavender grow in my garden and in the courtyard of Case Vecchie. We cut the plants back in August and dry the lavender for a couple of days. Then it's ready to strip for sachets. Rather than make new bags every year, I empty and refill the old ones, tie them with ribbon, and put the sachets back between the sheets and other household linens in the cupboard. Sometimes I put a quince in the closet too; it absorbs stale odors and imparts its own special fragrance.

Pears are in season at this time of year. With masses of them ripening at the same time, you have to invent as many ways as you can to eat and to preserve them. Besides putting them in the fruit basket to eat, with or without aged pecorino cheese, for dessert, I make *Pere in Insalata* (Pear Salad, page 209), with grappa. Now that Regaleali has its own grappa, I put it on fruit all of the time. It tastes good and helps the fruit keep a little longer.

Gelatina di Pere (Pear Gelatin, page 210), a ring mold filled with pieces of freshly cut pears, is perfect after a heavy meal. If there's time, I filter the juice overnight so the gelatin is clear; it's more elegant that way. The same can be made with apples and citrus in season. *Granita di Pere* (Pear Granita, page 166) is yet another good pear dessert, very refreshing on a hot day.

Some of the pears are boiled down with sugar for jam to eat on bread. My sister Costanza used to buy pear jam imported from Switzerland, and she begged me to make it for her from our own Regaleali pears. It took a few tries, but we finally got it right.

Much as I like being in the summer kitchen at Case Vecchie, I am easily tempted to get away from the heat of the sun and the stove. Usually I retreat to my house in Mondello. One year, though, I made a voyage of rediscovery to the Eolian Islands, where Costanza, Lucio, and I spent summers when we were children. (Rosemarie, who is younger, was sent to Switzerland with our nanny, Louise Feuillet.)

THE EOLIAN ISLANDS
∞

The Eolians lie off the northeastern coast of Sicily, a chain of seven vol-canic islands, flat-topped black cones rising out of a deep blue, almost purple sea. A wine-dark sea, as Homer said. It was there that Odysseus's men opened the bag given to them by Aeolus and unleashed the unfa-vorable winds. Storms at sea are not infrequent, and even in good weather there is a breeze blowing all day long, so you seldom feel hot.

The houses are built to keep out the wind—thick-walled rectangu-lar buildings. Some have domed roofs, like the *dammusi* of Pantelleria, but most have slanted roofs with a downspout in a corner to channel the rainwater into a cistern. The houses have two or three rooms with a big portico or veranda that serves as an open-air living and dining room. Thick pillars, called *polieri* in dialect, support a wooden canopy. Bougainvillea grows wild on top, and braids of garlic and onions and bunches of *pomodorini*, the tiny local tomatoes, hang down under-neath. The view of the sea and the other islands from one of these large terraces in spectacular.

Houses are painted white, peach, or sometimes white with peach and blue trim—colors that make them stand out against the black and violet rock. It's a dramatic landscape, softened by the lush green of grasses and sedums and the vibrant colors of wildflowers. The first time I returned to the Eolians after an absence of many years, I felt my heart beat faster as Alicudi, the island closest to Palermo and one of the smallest, came into view.

Unlike some of the other islands, Alicudi is still untouched by modernization. It must have been like this ever since Odysseus sailed past. No roads, no motorbikes, just shank's mare—that is, one's own feet— and donkeys. *Gli asinelli delle isole*, as they are called, are so small your feet almost sweep the ground when you ride them. They are nearly extinct now, though the environmentalists have mounted an effort to save the species.

Only about a hundred people live on Alicudi. A few buildings surround the fishing quay, which is shaded by two big trees that have somehow survived the onslaughts of wind and saltwater. The rest of the houses are built on the slope of the volcano, facing east. The only way to get to them is by donkey or on foot, yet people continue to live on the mountain, including one old man—they told me he was a hundred years old—who used to come down to the harbor every day to gossip and play cards and then go back at night, his way lit by a lantern.

A ship supplying provisions stops five times a week in summer, less often in winter—unless the sea is too rough. The people live out of their gardens. Of they have more than they need, they barter or sell it to their neighbors. High up on the mountain, there are apple orchards, where old varieties still grow. One is the *limoncella*, which seems to be making a comeback; I see it from time to time in the better fruit shops in Palermo. The other is the *smerza*, a kind of crab apple, quite rare now. Like the *pesca tabacchiera* that grows around Etna, these heirloom apples thrive on volcanic soil.

When my *aliscafo*, or hydrofoil, docked, the fishermen were on shore cleaning and mending their nets. They had just returned from the sea with all kinds of fish and a load of squid. People there make a wonderful dish with them, *Calamaretti alla Malvasia* (Squid Sautéed in Malvasia, page 204). Each bite tastes both sweet and salty at the same time—all of the fashionable flavors yet far from civilization.

Of all the Eolians, Alicudi reminds me most of how the islands were in my childhood, in the days before they were discovered by the film directors Roberto Rossellini and William Dieterle, who made *Stromboli* with Ingrid Bergman and *Vulcano* with Anna Magnani. Two bad movies, but they—and especially the scandal of the Bergman–Rossellini love affair—brought notoriety and a certain measure of prosperity to the islands.

When I was a child, we spent the summer months in Rinella, a small village on Salina. Life was very hard for the islanders. Most of the young had gone to seek a better life in Australia or America. Old people still had their gardens, but the cultivation of grapes, capers, and other seasonal crops had been virtually abandoned. Meat was hare or rabbit or fish from the sea. Until ten years ago, barley was grown instead of wheat because it needed less hand work at harvest time. Bread was made from barley. There was no electricity; the only water was rainwater collected in cisterns. There were no docks, no streets. Just one automobile, won in a lottery, was parked at the dock with no place to go.

For us, though, it was paradise. My father had founded a club for scuba diving and we lived in the big square clubhouse on the bay. The original owner had ordered concrete heads of "warrior priests" to be put up on three sides of the house. They look at the sea from dawn to dusk, protecting the house from pirates. The villages were all built up on the mountain, also to protect them from pirates, but my brother and I didn't know that. We swam or went out in a rowboat and fished all day long. The sea was clean and full of fish then.

Limpets stuck to the rocks in quantities. You had to be fast to stick a blade between the shell and the stone to detach them. Now only the local people know where to find the limpets. When I went back recently, I asked for them and the next day got a big bucketful, which we ate as an appetizer.

When there was a storm, we watched from the terrace. Sometimes you could see a whirlwind coming nearer and nearer. It was terrifying. The local people murmured a prayer, a secret prayer they passed on from generation to generation. We wondered why we couldn't pray too—we felt so helpless.

Years later, the forester took me up to look into the extraordinary crater called *Fossa delle Felci* (Fern Crater). The trail is lined with wildflowers and rarely seen herbs, like calamint and wild savory. When we got to the top and looked into the crater, we saw centuries-old chestnut trees.

In the old days, we had our own cook, Gina, who cooked for everyone. A big icebox stood on the terrace, and blocks of ice were brought in by boat almost every day. When I returned to Salina, I stayed in Santa Marina, the capital, on the other side of the island from Rinella. Teodoro and Marilena Cataffo of the Porto Bello restaurant cooked for

OVERLEAF: *The fishing quay at Alicudi, today as it was centuries ago.*

me. They invited me into their far more up-to-date kitchen, and they shared lots of local recipes and secrets with me.

Some mornings Marilena made *sfince d'ova*, which are similar to the fried *sfince* of western Sicily (pages 31 and 35). These *sfince* are rolled in cinnamon and sugar. Served with a good cappuccino, they make a delicious breakfast, though I wouldn't want to have it every day. In fact, everything Marilena cooked was delicious, whether it was *sfince*, or pasta, or fish. I especially liked her very rich and tasty *Spaghetti con Salsa Bianca* (Spaghetti with Eggplant, Tuna, and Olives, page 193). Every little restaurant in the islands makes this dish and names it after the chef; Peppino would call it *Pasta alla Peppino*, and so on.

EOLIAN CUISINE

The cooking of the islands is based on a very few ingredients that are chopped, stirred, and mixed together—combined and recombined in as many different ways as tradition and the fantasy of the cook will allow. Besides fish, the roster of local ingredients includes wild fennel, olives, capers, herbs, eggplant, tomatoes, figs, dried currants, almonds, and pine nuts. Plus bread and pasta, wine and vinegar, and citrus and other fruits, of course.

For *Pasta con Mandorle* (Pasta with Wild Fennel, Tuna, and Almonds, page 194), for example, the sauce is made with anchovies, capers, and *pomodorini*, the local tomatoes, to add layers of flavor. The almonds are ground and sprinkled on top, like breadcrumbs. In *Pasta con Acciuga e Mollica* (Pasta with Breadcrumbs, Anchovies, and Tomatoes, page 195), breadcrumbs are sprinkled on top, and the sauce is enhanced with parsley, capers, and, again, *pomodorini*.

This *pomodorino*, called *pennula* in dialect, is different from any other tomato I have ever seen—and I consider myself an expert on the tomato. It's small, no bigger than a fat olive, more bright orange than red, and the skin is so thin you don't feel it between your teeth at all. These mini tomatoes are mainly eaten raw or cooked very briefly—it would be a pity to make a sauce with them—or mixed with other local ingredients. Quartered *pomodorini* go on pasta and halved ones are in salads, which is typically seasoned with lots of garlic, ground hot pepper, oregano, and olive oil.

The owners of the Bellavista hotel in Santa Marina combine them with limpets they gather from the rocks. He is from Salina, and he taught his German wife many native dishes. For *spaghetti con patelle*, she puts a few of those little tomatoes cut in four, some chopped garlic, capers, a drop of olive oil, and a little water in a large sauté pan and adds the limpets. Then she cooks them over low heat until they part from their shells. She takes most of them out of their shells (leaving a few attached for decoration), and flavors the sauce with chopped parsley. When the pasta is ready, the limpets go on top.

Everywhere you go in the Eolians, you eat seafood. Sometimes fish is cooked in water, as in *Spigole all'Acqua Pazza* (Poached Sea Bass, page 206), and served hot or cold with mayonnaise or vinaigrette. *Acqua pazza* is seawater, and fish used to be poached in it. But now it's done in salted water because the seas are so polluted. Not quite the same thing, but almost as good.

Otherwise, the fish is grilled, both fish steaks and individual small fish. Every little restaurant offers *Cavagnole alla Griglia* (Grilled Amberjack or Rudderfish, page 205). *Cavagnole* are young *arriciole*, or amberjack (also known as rudderfish), a member of the bluefish family. In August and September, they are so small that two whole ones make a serving. Later in the year they grow to the size of a small tuna and are cut into steaks.

Squid is often on the menu. *Calamaretti alla Malvasia* (page 204) is served as a first or as a second course. The sauce is made with *Malvasia delle Lipari*.

MALVASIA DELLE LIPARI

A *passito* wine, for which the grapes are partly dried in the sun to concentrate their flavor, *Malvasia delle Lipari* is made with the Malvasia grape combined with a small quantity of the tiny black one called Corinto Nero, the same grape as for dried currants. Malvasia is very flavorful and almost syrupy, an orange-amber in color. It is often used in the kitchen the way Marsala is used in western Sicily.

Malvasia has a long history—in Shakespeare's *Richard III*, the Duke of Clarence was drowned in a barrel of Malmsey, as it was called then. By the 1950s and 1960s, the islanders had gradually stopped producing Malvasia for sale, though they continued to make it for home consumption. Fortunately, Carlo Hauner came on the scene and revived the tradition by giving a boost to those small producers.

Hauner, an architect from northern Italy whose peregrinations ended almost thirty years ago when he was captivated by the beauty of Salina, now exports his Malvasia all over the world, including the United States. He also cans or bottles such local products as capers and *zuccotti* (as caperberries are called in the Eolians), olives, honey, and—my eyes nearly fell out of my head when I saw this—*estratto di pomodoro*. He does it with a machine; it's not at all like my *estratto*.

MORE BAROQUE BISCUITS

After spending the morning at Hauner's place, I joined a few people for lunch and had a chance to taste some of the dishes I'd missed before. Best of all was an antipasto of onions called *Cipolle all'Agrodolce* (Sweet-and-Sour Onions, page 211) with typical Sicilian flavors—sweet-and-sour sauce, pine nuts, and currants.

For dessert, we decided to go for a granita. We'd been told the best granitas in the world were to be had at Alfredo's in Lingua, a village a few kilometers from Santa Marina. His granitas are made like any other from fruit juice and sugar, but Alfredo's are incredibly satiny. He makes them with any fruit in season—watermelon, cantaloupe, strawberry, peach, kiwi, fig—and serves the granita in a tumbler.

Leaving Alfredo's, we began a search for the local *biscotti pizzicati* (pinched biscuits). On Salina they call them *vastidduzzi* or *spicchiteddi*; they are like *Mustazzuoli Panteschi* of Pantelleria (page 128). We finally found some at the Hotel Signum in Malfa.

These pastries—they make them in Lipari, too, where they are called *nacatole*—are all very similar. The elements are simple: a pastry dough made with lard or butter and a filling based on almonds and figs with honey or wine must. It is the baroque forms that make the pastries distinctive—and that virtually guarantee their disappearance. It takes skill and enormous patience to fashion them, a labor of love in an era of haste and commerce.

BEAUTIFUL ISLANDS, BOUNTIFUL SEA

Lipari is the biggest of the islands and the only one with a proper harbor where boats can find safe haven in a bad storm. There is a little bit of everything—government offices and an archaeological museum, which is constantly being updated. The latest amphorae were fished out of the sea and installed in the museum in 1995. There are many fine restaurants. At one, La Conchiglia, the owner gave me several good recipes, including *Fettuccine al Pesce Spada* (Fettuccine with Swordfish, page 197), made with marinated raw fish. People claim that fish carpaccio was invented in the Eolians; I don't know if that's true, but it seems like the right place: a chain of beautiful islands in a bountiful sea.

Salina is the most beautiful of the islands for me because of my childhood memories, but Panarea is the most fashionable. Stromboli is nearby. It's the only one of the volcanoes that still erupts, belching smoke and spitting lava and fire, quite something to watch from the deck of a ship at night!

Vulcano is active inside—you can see it breathing smoke through its fumaroles—and said to be ready to erupt at any moment. The people who live there always talk about moving away, but being fatalists, like all Sicilians, they know in their hearts they will stay there and live there until they die there.

THE RECIPES

SPAGHETTI CON I RICCI
Spaghetti with Sea Urchins

Several species of sea urchins live in U.S. coastal waters, but none that I have tasted is as exquisite as those from the Mediterranean. Pacific and Atlantic sea urchins are in season from fall through spring. Whole urchins, seldom seen in retail markets in the United States, are sold at wholesale fish markets.

THIS MAKES ENOUGH FOR 6 PEOPLE.

½ pound (225 g) sea urchin roe, cut into pieces if large (see Note)
3 medium tomatoes (1 lb/450 g), peeled, seeded, and cubed
½ cup olive oil
Salt
Ground hot pepper
1 pound (450 g) spaghetti
1 tablespoon chopped flat-leaf parsley
3 lemons, cut in half

Combine half of the roe, two of the tomatoes, ⅓ cup of the olive oil, and salt and hot pepper to taste in a large serving bowl.

Cook the spaghetti in boiling salted water until al dente. Drain; toss quickly with the roe mixture. Drizzle with the remaining oil if the pasta seems dry. Top with the remaining roe and the remaining tomato. Sprinkle with the parsley and garnish with the lemon halves. Serve immediately.

NOTE. *Sea urchin roe is sold by the half-pound tray in Japanese food stores. Call ahead to check that it is available.*

FUSILLI MEDITERRANEI
Fusilli with Tomatoes, Basil, and Black Olives

Sprinkling tomatoes with sugar and salt draws out the juice and keeps them firm, an important consideration for a pasta salad, which must stand for at least one hour. This way, it can be left out on a buffet for a long time without getting watery. This dish is also good made with spaghettini.

THIS MAKES ENOUGH FOR 4 TO 6 PEOPLE.

2¼ pounds (1 kg) ripe tomatoes, peeled, seeded, and cubed
Salt
Sugar
Ground hot pepper
2 cloves garlic, minced
4 salted anchovies, rinsed, filleted, and chopped, or 6 canned
    anchovy fillets, drained and chopped
1½ cups (90 g) basil leaves, torn
1 cup (200 g) black olives, pitted and cut in half
½ cup (80 g) capers, rinsed and coarsely chopped
⅔ cup (170 ml) olive oil
1 pound (450 g) fusilli or rotelle
½ cup (60 g) dry breadcrumbs (optional)

Put the tomatoes in a colander, sprinkle with salt, sugar, and hot pepper, and turn to coat. Add the garlic, anchovies, basil, olives, and capers and toss to mix. Let stand for 1 hour.

Transfer to a serving bowl; stir in ½ cup (125 ml) of the olive oil.

Meanwhile, bring a large pot of salted water to a boil. Add the pasta and cook until slightly more than al dente but not quite tender. Drain and dip the colander in a bowl of salted ice water for 1 minute. Drain again. Pour the pasta into the serving bowl. Toss with the tomato mixture. Let stand at room temperature for at least 1 hour.

If desired, combine the remaining olive oil, the breadcrumbs, and a pinch of salt in a small skillet and toast the crumbs until lightly browned. Set aside to cool.

Serve the pasta salad at room temperature with the toasted breadcrumbs for sprinkling, if using.

INSALATA DI PASTA ARRABBIATA
Penne Salad with Herbs and Hot Pepper

This salad is a cold version of *pasta arrabbiata* (literally, angry pasta), which can be made very angry indeed with hot pepper. Add as much or as little as you like. In this recipe, plum tomatoes, which tend to be drier than other varieties, are seeded rather than salted to keep the salad from getting watery.

THIS MAKES ENOUGH FOR 6 PEOPLE.

½ cup (30 g) basil leaves, shredded
1 sprig of fresh rosemary, leaves stripped off and chopped
¼ cup (15 g) mint leaves, chopped
1 tablespoon dried oregano
2 cloves garlic, minced
¼ cup (40 g) capers, rinsed and drained
½ cup (125 ml) olive oil
6 ripe plum tomatoes (1 lb/450 g), peeled, seeded, and chopped
1 teaspoon ground hot pepper (see Note)
¼ cup (30 g) grated pecorino
1 pound (450 g) penne
Salt

Combine the basil, rosemary, mint, oregano, garlic, and capers in a small bowl. Pour on enough of the olive oil to cover generously. Combine the tomatoes, hot pepper, and pecorino in a large serving bowl.

Cook the penne in boiling salted water until slightly more than al dente but not quite tender. Drain in a colander and dip into salted ice water to chill and stop the cooking. Drain again.

Transfer the pasta to the serving bowl and mix well with the tomatoes. Add the herb mixture and toss again. Let stand for at least 1 hour or for up to 4 hours.

Taste before serving and add additional oil, if necessary, and salt to taste. Serve at room temperature.

NOTE. *Use 1 small red chili, seeded and minced, in season. It will make the dish redder as well as hotter.*

SPAGHETTI CON SALSA BIANCA

Spaghetti with Eggplant, Tuna, and Olives

This sauce is called white not because it is white but to distinguish it from red sauce. *Pomodorini,* the local tomatoes that are used to garnish the pasta, are orange, very small, and hardly juicy at all. The best substitute I can think of is tiny teardrop-shape yellow cherry tomatoes.

THIS MAKES ENOUGH FOR 6 PEOPLE.

1 medium eggplant (1 lb/450 g), peeled and very finely chopped
½ cup (125 ml) olive oil
12 green Sicilian olives, pitted and chopped
4 salted anchovies, rinsed, filleted, and chopped, or 8 canned
  anchovy fillets, drained and chopped
1 small can (3 oz/90 g) solid white tuna, rinsed, drained,
  and flaked
2 red tomatoes (10 oz/300 g), peeled, seeded, and chopped
1 tablespoon capers, rinsed and drained
4 scallions, finely chopped
½ cup (30 g) basil leaves, chopped
3 tablespoons chopped flat-leaf parsley
1 pound (450 g) spaghetti
12 pomodorini or small cherry tomatoes, preferably yellow
  teardrops, quartered lengthwise

Fry the eggplant in the olive oil in a large sauté pan, until the pieces lose their raw look and just begin to turn golden, about 5 minutes. Add the olives, anchovies, tuna, red tomatoes, capers, scallions, basil, and parsley and leave on the heat just long enough for the tuna to warm through, about 1 minute. Remove from the heat.

Bring a large pot of salted water to a boil. Add the spaghetti and cook until al dente. Drain the spaghetti; gently toss with half of the sauce. Spoon the rest on top, garnish with the tomatoes, and serve immediately.

PASTA CON MANDORLE
Pasta with Wild Fennel, Tuna, and Almonds

This pasta dish combines several classic Sicilian flavors: wild fennel, tuna, saffron, capers, and almonds. The almonds are chopped to the consistency of dry breadcrumbs for a topping. Toast them if they lack good flavor.

THIS MAKES ENOUGH FOR 4 TO 6 PEOPLE.

½ pound (225 g) wild fennel (see Note)
Pinch of saffron threads or ground saffron
¼ cup (60 ml) warm water
1 can (6⅛ oz/173 g) solid white tuna
1 small red onion, finely chopped
1 clove garlic, minced
¼ cup (60 ml) olive oil
4 salted anchovies, rinsed and filleted, or 8 canned anchovy
  fillets, drained
2 tablespoons capers, rinsed and drained
6 pomodorini or small cherry tomatoes, preferably yellow
  teardrops, quartered lengthwise
2 tablespoons chopped flat-leaf parsley
Salt
1 pound (450 g) spaghetti
½ cup (75 g) blanched almonds, toasted, if necessary, and
  finely chopped

Bring a large pot of water to a boil. Add the wild fennel and boil for 20 minutes. Drain, reserving the water for the pasta. Finely chop the fennel and set aside.

Meanwhile, soak the saffron in the warm water. Empty the tuna into a strainer and rinse. Drain well, flake with a fork, and set aside.

Fry the onion and garlic in the olive oil in a large sauté pan until soft, about 5 minutes. Add the anchovies and capers and crush them with a wooden spoon. Add the wild fennel, tomatoes, parsley, and the saffron water. Cover and cook for 5 minutes.

Stir in the tuna and remove from the heat. Let stand while you cook the pasta. Taste before serving and add salt if needed.

Add salt to the fennel water and bring it back to a boil. Add the spaghetti and cook until al dente. Drain the spaghetti and transfer to a serving bowl. Gently toss the spaghetti with half of the sauce. Spoon the rest on top. Sprinkle with the almonds and serve immediately.

NOTE. *Wild fennel is sometimes available in California and in Italian-American neighborhoods. For this dish, you could substitute 2 cups of bronze fennel or dill leaves (about 100 g with stems). Use bronze fennel or dill raw.*

PASTA CON ACCIUGA E MOLLICA
Pasta with Breadcrumbs, Anchovies, and Tomatoes

When Sicilians are not eating from their gardens, they are eating from the pantry. Here is a dish you can make from ingredients you have on hand. As is often the case with fish and pasta dishes, the topping is toasted breadcrumbs.

THIS MAKES ENOUGH FOR 4 TO 6 PEOPLE.

1 clove garlic, minced
⅓ cup (85 ml) olive oil
4 salted anchovies, rinsed and filleted, or 8 canned anchovy
  fillets, drained
2 tablespoons capers, rinsed
2 tablespoons chopped flat-leaf parsley
¼ cup (30 g) dry breadcrumbs
Salt
1 pound (450 g) penne
½ cup (125 ml) white wine (optional)
12 pomorodini or small cherry tomatoes, preferably yellow
  teardrops, quartered lengthwise

Fry the garlic in ¼ cup of the olive oil in a skillet, just until the aroma rises. Add the anchovies and capers and crush them with a wooden spoon. Stir in the parsley and cook just until the anchovies melt, about 1 minute. Remove from the heat.

Combine the remaining olive oil, the breadcrumbs, and a pinch of salt in a small frying pan and toast the crumbs until lightly browned, about 3 minutes. Spoon into a small bowl.

Bring a large pot of salted water to a boil. Add the penne and cook until slightly more than al dente but not quite tender. Drain the penne, reserving some of the cooking water; toss the penne with half of the sauce. If the pasta seems too dry, add a little of the reserved water or white wine. Spoon the rest of the sauce on top and sprinkle with some of the toasted breadcrumbs. Surround the platter with the cherry tomatoes. Serve immediately with the remaining breadcrumbs for passing at the table.

ABOVE: *Trees are so precious in Sicily that the fields are often plowed around them.*

FETTUCCINE AL PESCE SPADA
Fettuccine with Swordfish

This unusual dish includes both raw and cooked swordfish. Remember not to marinate the swordfish for more than 30 minutes. It is a delicate fish, unlike tuna.

THIS MAKES ENOUGH FOR 4 PEOPLE AS A FIRST COURSE.

6 ounces (180 g) swordfish
Fresh lemon juice
1 small red onion, minced
1 clove garlic, minced
3 tablespoons olive oil
Ground hot pepper
Salt
4 cherry tomatoes, cut lengthwise in quarters
12 ounces (350 g) fettuccine or linguine
1 tablespoon chopped flat-leaf parsley

Thinly slice half of the swordfish, cutting with the grain. Marinate in lemon juice to cover for 30 minutes.

Remove from the juice, letting the excess drip off. Do not rinse. Cut the slices of fish into ribbons. Cut the remaining swordfish into ⅜-inch (1-cm) cubes.

Combine the onion, garlic, and olive oil in a sauté pan large enough to hold the pasta later. Sauté until the onion is golden. Add the cubed fish and hot pepper and salt to taste. Remove from the heat as soon as the fish is opaque, about 3 minutes. Add the cherry tomatoes and set aside.

Bring a large pot of salted water to a boil. Add the pasta and cook until al dente. Drain and dip the colander full of pasta into ice water for 1 minute. Drain again and turn into the sauté pan. Mix well.

Transfer to a serving dish and decorate with the ribbons of swordfish in a lattice pattern. Sprinkle with the parsley and serve.

RISO CON MELANZANE, MENTA, E CAPPERI

Cold Rice with Eggplant, Mint, and Capers

Eggplant and mint are a very popular Sicilian flavor combination. Capers give it a sharp edge in this amazing rice salad.

THIS MAKES ENOUGH FOR 4 TO 6 PEOPLE.

1 large eggplant (1 to 1½ lb/450 to 675 g)
Salt
Olive oil and vegetable oil, for frying
½ cup (30 g) mint leaves, torn in half if large
1 tablespoon capers, rinsed and drained
1 cup (225 g) long-grain rice, cooked, drained, and slightly
  cooled (page 113)
Freshly ground black pepper

Peel the eggplant and cut it into ¾-inch (2-cm) cubes. Sprinkle with salt and let stand in a colander for at least 30 minutes.

Combine the oils and pour about ½ inch (1,5 cm) into a large skillet. Heat until nearly smoking. Blot the eggplant dry and fry until lightly browned. Using a slotted spoon, transfer directly to a serving bowl, without draining on paper towels. You may have to do this in batches, adding more oil and heating it as needed.

Add the mint leaves and capers to the eggplant. Add the rice and stir to mix. If the salad seems too dry, add a little of the oil left in the pan. Season to taste with additional salt and pepper. Serve the salad at room temperature.

PATATE ALLO ZAFFERANO
Braised Potatoes with Saffron

This tasty potato side dish doesn't really need lemon, though I like it that way. Put a bowl of lemon wedges on the table and let each person season the dish to his or her liking.

THIS MAKES ENOUGH FOR 4 PEOPLE AS A SIDE DISH.

4 to 5 saffron threads
3 cups (750 ml) warm water
1 small red onion, chopped
¼ cup (60 ml) olive oil
4 cups peeled and quartered small potatoes (about 2 lb/1 kg)
½ cup (60 g) chopped flat-leaf parsley
2 teaspoons dried oregano
2 tablespoons grated pecorino or parmesan
Salt and freshly ground black pepper
Lemon wedges (optional)

Soak the saffron in 1 cup of the water for 10 minutes.

Meanwhile, sauté the onion in the olive oil in a large sauté pan until limp, about 5 minutes. Add the potatoes, the saffron water, and the remaining 2 cups warm water. Cover and simmer until the potatoes are tender, 20 to 25 minutes.

Add the parsley, oregano, and pecorino and stir until the potatoes are partially mashed, about 5 minutes. Season to taste with salt and pepper. Serve warm with lemon, if desired.

SFORMATO DI PATATE AL RAGÙ
Potato Timbale with Meat Sauce and Peas

Although this dish calls for many ingredients, they are all readily available and the dish is easy to make; yet, somehow, it seems elaborate. In the time of the *monzù* chefs, it was called *gatto di patate*, from *gâteau*, or cake in French. Normally we eat it hot, then have the leftovers—if any—cold the next day. It tastes even better!

THIS MAKES ENOUGH FOR 10 PEOPLE.

RAGÙ FILLING

1 onion, finely chopped
¼ cup (60 ml) olive oil
½ cup (60 g) fresh or frozen small peas
1 pound (450 g) ground beef
1 stalk celery, chopped
½ cup (125 ml) dry white wine
⅓ cup (85 g) tomato paste, preferably sun-dried
1 cup (250 ml) water
½ cup (60 g) diced boiled ham
1 cup (140 g) finely diced young caciocavallo or a combination
  of gouda, fontina, and mozzarella
¼ cup (30 g) chopped flat-leaf parsley
Salt

4½ pounds (2 kg) russet (baking) or all-purpose potatoes,
  scrubbed
7 tablespoons (100 g) butter
2 large eggs
¾ cup (90 g) grated caciocavallo or parmesan
½ teaspoon freshly grated nutmeg
⅓ cup (50 g) dry breadcrumbs

Sauté the onion in the olive oil in a large sauté pan until soft. Add the peas and beef and sauté until the meat is browned. Add the celery and wine and cook until the wine evaporates. Mix in the tomato paste and water and cook, uncovered, for about 30 minutes. The mixture should be dry, not watery.

Stir in the ham, the cheeses, and the parsley and remove from heat.

Taste and add salt if necessary. The filling can be made a day in advance and refrigerated.

Boil the potatoes in boiling salted water until done. Drain and set aside until cool enough to handle. Peel the potatoes and rice them into a bowl. Add 4 tablespoons of the butter, the eggs, grated cheese, nutmeg, and salt to taste. Combine thoroughly using your hands.

Preheat the oven to 400° F. (200° C). Butter the bottom and sides of a 10-inch (25-cm) springform or other round pan and sprinkle generously with the breadcrumbs. (You will not use all the butter or breadcrumbs.) Spread about three fourths of the potato mixture about ½ inch (1,5 cm) thick on the bottom and sides of the pan, smoothing the layer with your hands to form a shell.

Spoon the filling into the potato shell, pushing the filling to the sides and smoothing the top. Cover with the remaining potato mixture, spreading it to the edges. Sprinkle with the remaining breadcrumbs and dot with the remaining butter. Bake for 15 minutes.

Reduce the oven temperature to 325° F. (160° C.) and continue baking until golden brown, about 30 minutes more.

Remove from the oven and set on a cooling rack. Let stand for 25 minutes. Unmold and serve at room temperature or cold the next day.

ABOVE: *The Messina herd, which supplies Regaleali with milk, butter, and caciocavallo cheese.*

COTOLETTE ALLA TEDESCA
Breaded Beef Cutlets

These cutlets, literally "German cutlets" in Italian, are a Sicilian version of *Wiener Schnitzel*. The vinegar soak is unique, to my knowledge. Always served at room temperature, the cutlets are good for a picnic. THIS MAKES ENOUGH FOR 4 PEOPLE.

1¼ pounds (550 g) flank steak
1 cup (250 ml) red wine vinegar
1 large egg
½ cup (75 g) all-purpose flour
½ cup (125 ml) water
Salt and freshly ground black pepper
1 cup (120 g) dried breadcrumbs
Olive oil and vegetable oil, for frying

Cut the meat on the diagonal against the grain into thin slices. Pound the slices until very thin. Soak them in the vinegar for 20 to 30 minutes. Most of the vinegar will be absorbed.

Meanwhile, whisk together the egg and flour. Whisk in as much of the water as you need to make a batter the consistency of heavy cream. Whisk in salt and pepper to taste. Remove the meat from the vinegar, letting the excess drip off. Dip in the batter, turning to coat all sides. Let the excess drip off. Dredge the meat in the breadcrumbs. Let stand for 20 to 30 minutes to firm the coating.

Heat 2 inches (5 cm) of oil, half olive oil and half vegetable oil, in a deep-fat fryer or large saucepan until very hot. Dip an end of a cutlet in; the oil should sizzle. Add the cutlets without crowding. You will have to do this in batches. Be sure to bring the oil back to very hot and test it before doing the next batch. Fry the cutlets until golden brown on both sides, 2 to 3 minutes per side. The crust will swell and detach itself from the meat. Drain on paper towels. Serve at room temperature.

PESCE DEL CONTADINO
Fish Mousse, Peasant Style

Though not a native Sicilian ingredient, green peppercorns add a very pleasant twist to this mousse. If you don't have any green peppercorns, or if you want to stay authentic, use ground hot pepper.
THIS MAKES ENOUGH FOR 10 TO 12 PEOPLE.

1½ pounds (675 g) all-purpose or baking potatoes,
*   peeled and quartered*
3 cans (6⅛ oz/173 g each) albacore or solid white tuna
*   fish, rinsed and drained*
3 salted anchovies, filleted and rinsed, or 6 canned anchovy
*   fillets, drained*
3 tablespoons capers, rinsed and drained
1 tablespoon brined green peppercorns, rinsed, or ½ teaspoon
*   ground hot pepper*
1 cup (120 g) minced flat-leaf parsley
1 cup (250 ml) Mayonnaise (page 160)
Salt
1 caper, 2 cornichons, sliced, and additional mayonnaise,
*   for garnish*

Boil the potatoes in lightly salted water until soft, about 30 minutes. Drain and rice the potatoes.

Put the tuna, anchovies, capers, green peppercorns, and parsley in a food processor and process to very fine crumbs. Transfer to a bowl and add the potatoes, mayonnaise, and salt to taste. Mix with your hands until the mixture is well blended.

Shape the mixture into a ball, put it in an oval serving dish, and mold it into a fish, with a tail and a head. Insert a caper as an eye and arrange cornichon slices on the back like fins. Refrigerate for several hours to allow the flavors to blend. Serve at room temperature garnished with mayonnaise.

NOTE. *Another way to garnish the mousse is with thinly sliced peeled, or partly peeled, cucumbers. Salt the slices and let stand for 20 minutes to draw out the juice. Blot dry and arrange like fish scales on the mousse. If all of the mousse is not eaten the first day, remove the cucumber slices before refrigerating; they will give it too much of a cucumber flavor if left on.*

CALAMARETTI ALLA MALVASIA

Squid Sautéed in Malvasia

Get the smallest squid you can find and have the fishmonger clean them for you.

THIS MAKES ENOUGH FOR 4 PEOPLE.

¼ cup (30 g) dry breadcrumbs
1 tablespoon chopped flat-leaf parsley
2 cloves garlic, minced
2 tablespoons grated pecorino or parmesan
Salt and freshly ground black pepper
½ cup (125 ml) olive oil
8 small squid (4 lb/1,8 kg total weight), cleaned, with bodies
  intact and tentacles very finely chopped
1 large red onion, sliced
1 cup (250 ml) Malvasia wine
6 pomorodini or cherry tomatoes, quartered lengthwise

Mix together the breadcrumbs, parsley, garlic, and pecorino. Season with salt and pepper to taste; add 5 tablespoons (80 ml) of the olive oil and the chopped tentacles. Mix the stuffing mixture thoroughly.

Stuff the bodies about three quarters full and close by weaving a toothpick through the edges.

Fry the onion in the remaining 3 tablespoons olive oil in a large sauté pan over low heat until caramelized, about 10 minutes.

Push the onion to the side and add the stuffed squid along with 2 to 3 tablespoons water. Cook, turning, until golden brown, 3 to 4 minutes. Add the Malvasia and scrape the bottom of the pan. In the time it takes to do this, the squid will be done.

Arrange the squid on a platter with the onion surrounding them. Garnish with the tomatoes and serve.

CAVAGNOLE ALLA GRIGLIA
Grilled Amberjack or Rudderfish

Any small fish can be grilled in this manner. Amberjack, also called rudderfish (*Seriola dumerili*), is a member of the bluefish family. Little "snapper blues" or the slightly larger "harbor blues" are a good substitute. The salted breadcrumb coating keeps the fish from drying out.

THIS MAKES ENOUGH FOR 4 PEOPLE.

½ teaspoon salt
1 cup (120 g) dry breadcrumbs
4 small amberjack or other saltwater fish, with head and tail
    (about 1 lb/450 g each), cleaned and scaled

Prepare the grill.

When the fire is ready, mix the salt into the breadcrumbs. Dredge the fish in the breadcrumbs and place in an oiled fish basket. Place on the grill and cook, turning once, until the eyes turn white, about 20 minutes.

Or, preheat the broiler or a heavy grill pan and broil or panbroil the fish. Serve immediately.

SPIGOLE ALL'ACQUA PAZZA
Poached Sea Bass

Fish used to be poached in seawater—that's the *acqua pazza*—but because of pollution, it's now just salted water.

THIS MAKES ENOUGH FOR 1 PERSON.

1 whole ocean fish, such as bass or sea trout, cleaned (about
  1 lb/450 g)
1 small carrot, cut up
1 stalk celery, cut up
1 clove garlic, slivered
1 sprig of flat-leaf parsley
1 tablespoon olive oil
1 tablespoon salt
¼ cup (60 ml) white wine

Put the fish in a pan and add enough water to come halfway up the sides of the fish. Scatter the carrot, celery, garlic, parsley, oil, and salt around the fish. Cover and simmer for 15 minutes.

Remove the fish and place on a serving platter. Remove the vegetables with a slotted spoon and puree in a blender or food processor.

Add the wine to the cooking liquid and cook for 5 minutes. Gradually add to the vegetable puree to make a sauce. Pour over the fish and serve.

CAPONATA
Caponata

Caponata is a close second to *Pasta con le Sarde* (page 42) as the national dish of Sicily. We put up vast quantities of it in the late summer and fall when eggplants are in season, but no matter how much we make, there is never enough to see us through the year. Because it goes equally well with meat and fish, caponata is a good dish to include in a buffet.

THIS MAKES ENOUGH FOR 8 PEOPLE.

2¼ pound (1 kg) eggplant, preferably the long purple kind
Salt
6 stalks (300 g) celery
Vegetable oil and olive oil
1 onion, chopped
3 cloves garlic, minced
2 cups (500 ml) tomato sauce, preferably homemade (page 228)
½ cup (30 g) basil leaves, shredded
1¼ cups (225 g) green olives, pitted and halved
½ cup (80 g) capers, rinsed and drained
Freshly ground black pepper
1 cup (250 ml) wine vinegar
2 tablespoons sugar

GARNISHES (OPTIONAL)
3 hard-boiled eggs, cut lengthwise in half
1 small orange, peeled, quartered, and thinly sliced
Fresh basil sprigs
Canned whole small octopuses (see Note)

Peel the eggplant and cut it into 1-inch (2,5-cm) pieces. Put in a colander, sprinkle with salt, and let drain for at least 30 minutes.

Meanwhile, peel the celery and cut it into pieces about the same size as the eggplant. Drop the celery into boiling water and cook for 6 to 7 minutes to soften it. Drain and set aside.

Pour ¾ inch (2 cm) oil into a large skillet. (I use half vegetable and half olive oil.) Blot the eggplant dry and fry, stirring from time to time, until browned on all sides. Drain on paper towels and set aside.

Put the onion and garlic in a medium saucepan and pour on enough olive oil to cover. Cook slowly until the onion is golden, 8 to 10 minutes.

Stir in the tomato sauce, basil, celery, olives, capers, and salt and pepper to taste. Stir together and bring the mixture to a boil. Stir in the vinegar and sugar. Simmer over low heat for 10 to 15 minutes. Remove from the heat and carefully stir in the eggplant. Taste and adjust the seasoning.

Draining off as much of the liquid as possible, transfer the mixture to a flat serving dish, forming a pyramid. Pat it with a wooden spoon so it holds together, keeping in mind that as it gets cold it will thicken. Let stand until cool.

Just before serving, garnish around the bottom with the eggs, orange, and basil or all over the pyramid with the octopuses.

NOTE. *Canned octopus is sometimes available in Asian grocery stores.*

SALSA VERDE PER IL PESCE
Green Sauce for Fish

Made in these proportions, the sauce is rather thick. If you prefer it thinner, use more olive oil and lemon juice.

THIS MAKES ABOUT 1 CUP OF SAUCE.

2 cups (120 g) flat-leaf parsley
1 clove garlic
2 salted anchovies, rinsed and filleted, or 4 canned anchovy fillets
1 cup (250 ml) olive oil
2 hard-boiled eggs, finely chopped
¼ cup (60 ml) fresh lemon juice
Salt

Remove the tough stems of the parsley. Coarsely chop the leaves in a food processor or blender. Add the garlic and anchovies and process until finely chopped. With the machine running, slowly add the olive oil. Stir in the eggs and lemon juice. Season to taste with salt.

CIPOLLE ALL'AGRODOLCE
Sweet-and-Sour Onions

Serve these onions as an appetizer, fishing them out of the jar and leaving as much of the liquid as possible behind.

THIS MAKES ENOUGH TO FILL 8 1-QUART (OR 1-LITER) JARS.

4 cups (1 l) white wine vinegar
4 cups (1 l) water
1 tablespoon salt
4½ pounds (2 kg) sweet onions, preferably red, thinly sliced
3 to 4 tablespoons sugar
1 cup (180 g) pine nuts
1 cup (120 g) dried currants
Coarsely ground black pepper

Bring the vinegar, water, and salt to a boil in a large saucepan. Add the onions and cook until limp but still crunchy, about 5 minutes.

Remove the pan from the heat and stir in the sugar until it dissolves. Add the pine nuts, currants, and pepper to taste and mix to distribute evenly.

Ladle into hot sterilized jars and cover. Process in a hot-water bath (see Note). Let stand for at least 40 days before eating.

NOTE. *For a hot-water bath, place the jars, without touching, on a rack in a canning kettle and add enough water to cover by 1 inch. Cover the pot, bring to a boil, and boil for 20 minutes. Remove the jars and place them on a rack or towel and let cool. To test, press the center of the lid. If it stays down, the seal is good. If not, refrigerate and eat the peppers soon or reseal with a new lid and repeat the hot-water bath. Store in a cool dry place.*

GELATINA DI PERE
Pear Gelatin

This is a spectacular dessert. The gelatin is a light golden color and the flavor of the pears is heavenly. If you make the gelatin with apples, it will be pink.

THIS MAKES ENOUGH FOR 6 PEOPLE.

PEAR GELATIN
2¼ pounds (1 kg) pears
4⅓ cups (1 l) water
Juice of 2 lemons
1 cup (200 g) sugar
2 envelopes (7 g each) unflavored gelatin

PEAR GARNISH
¼ cup (50 g) sugar
2 cups (500 ml) water
4 medium pears (500 g)
Juice of 1 lemon
2 tablespoons grappa or pear brandy or eau-de-vie

Sprigs of mint, for garnish

To make the gelatin, cut up the pears, removing the blossom and stem ends. Do not core or peel. Place in a saucepan, add the water and lemon juice, and cook, stirring occasionally, until very soft, about 25 minutes. Pass through a food mill or mash with a potato masher.

Transfer the crushed fruit to a jelly bag or a strainer lined with several layers of rinsed cheesecloth. Let the juice drip for several hours, without squeezing the bag. Measure the juice: You should have 4⅓ cups (1 l). If not, add water to the pulp and let it drip longer.

Pour 2 cups of the pear juice into a medium saucepan. Stir in the sugar and heat just until dissolved. Sprinkle on the gelatin and let soften for about 5 minutes. Add the remaining 2⅓ cups juice and bring to a boil over high heat, whisking to dissolve the gelatin. Remove from the heat. Pour the mixture through a fine-mesh strainer, pushing down with a spoon in case any of the gelatin is not dissolved. Pour into a 10-inch (25-cm) ring mold. Refrigerate overnight.

To prepare the pear garnish, combine the sugar and water in a saucepan and cook to make a light syrup, about 10 minutes. Peel the pears, cut them in four, and core and slice them. Add the pears, lemon juice, and grappa to the syrup. Remove from the heat. Let cool, then refrigerate until ready to assemble the dessert.

When ready to serve, invert the mold on a serving dish. Put the sliced pears in the center and decorate the edges of the dish with the sprigs of mint.

N O T E . *Apples can be substituted for the pears. Use the same amount and follow the same procedure as for the pears.*

PERE IN INSALATA
Pear Salad

This fruit salad can stand for several days; in fact, it gets better and better. The grappa preserves the fruit and enhances the flavor.

THIS MAKES ENOUGH FOR 4 PEOPLE.

2¼ pounds (1 kg) ripe pears
¼ cup (60 ml) grappa
Juice of 1 lemon
Juice of 1 orange
2 tablespoons sugar
2 tablespoons orange or grapefruit marmalade

Pour the grappa into a serving bowl. Peel the pears and cut them into quarters. Remove and discard the cores. Cut large pears into eighths. Drop the slices into the serving bowl, add the remaining ingredients, and turn the pears in the sauce, being sure to coat all surfaces. Let stand for at least 1 hour to marinate.

SETTEMBRE

The landscape of the Sicilian countryside begins to change in September. In the vineyards, big clusters of Inzolia grapes, about to burst with the juice man will soon transform into wine, hang heavy on the vine, golden as they catch the rays of the early autumn sun. From a distance, the ravines are specked with gold as the wild quince begins to ripen and poke out from under its ruffled leaves.

White clouds scud across the blue, blue skies, harbingers of the rains that will inundate the countryside in October and cover it with a blanket of green. Then we will be glad to see the heavens open and fill the ravines and gullies with rivers of mud. But for now, in the time of the vendemmia, or grape harvest, we wish the clouds Godspeed. Everyone is working feverishly under the relentless sun to bring in the harvest and preserve it for the future—the grapes, the tomatoes and other vegetables, the fruits, the nuts.

LEFT: *The pale green, yard-long zucca lunga comes to market.*

TOMATOES
∞

Sicilian cooking is unimaginable without tomatoes, peppers, eggplant, and zucchini. Tomatoes are preserved in every conceivable way—whole, both sun-dried and in jars; bottled in *sugo* or *Salsa di Pomodoro Passata* (Classic Tomato Sauce, page 228), the smooth sauce Sicilians put on their pasta almost every day of the year; and in *estratto di pomodoro*, or sun-dried tomato paste.

Tomatoes just off the vine are made into a fresh tomato sauce for pasta or are cooked in *Salsa di Pomodoro Piccante* (Spicy Tomato Sauce, page 229). It tastes very fresh with lots of everything in it. Though it's a bit spicy, it can be used like any other tomato sauce. It's very good for *Formaggio al Pomodoro* (page 230), a baked cheese dish.

Eggs always make a good light dish for summer. Crack two eggs on top of *Formaggio al Pomodoro* and you have *uova in tegamino al pomodoro* (baked cheese with eggs). *Frittata di Pomodoro, Cipolla, e Basilico* (Tomato, Onion, and Basil Frittata, page 231), made with ultra-fresh ingredients, is especially nice for a picnic or casual lunch.

PEPPERS
∞

Although in some parts of the world people eat peppers raw, the taste of uncooked peppers is not appreciated by Sicilians. We prefer them fried or roasted, as in *Peperoni Arrosto con Olio e Aceto* (page 232), in which they are roasted, peeled, and dressed with vinegar and oregano. Peppers are also stuffed and baked in Sicily.

Once I had some excellent *Peperoncini Rossi Ripieni* (page 233), pickled stuffed cherry peppers, which Faith Willinger had brought to a conference in Rome. At first I was suspicious—they looked too big and too spicy. On the other hand, they were obviously handmade and very pretty. My next encounter with these pickled peppers was on Salina in the Eolian Islands. I took a picture, with the idea in mind that I might someday make them myself.

About a month later, I was working in my kitchen at Case Vecchie with Graziella when she said, "We really should make those stuffed peppers so-and-so makes."

"Go ask her," I said.

"No!" she replied. "Never! I hate her! She said bad things about me."

I knew it was useless to insist. Then, like a miracle, Pinuzzo Ognibene, the beekeeper at Regaleali, appeared on the scene. We asked him what he knew about these peppers. Well, he said, he had eaten so many the year before that he wouldn't touch another one for a long, long time. But he did have a recipe, which he gave me.

At first I couldn't find the peppers. They were not being grown at Regaleali, and they were not in the shops in Palermo nor in Valledolmo. But they were all the rage in Vallelunga, the village on the other side of the hill. Such are the vagaries of fashion.

I had to wait in a long line in front of the only stall that was selling the peppers, one I usually bypass because it has such ugly vegetables. The people in line started telling me their recipes. This one made them with vinegar and wine, another with vinegar and water, and so on—a typical Sicilian food conversation. I decided to make them with half vinegar and half water, but you can substitute vinegar for some or all of the water if you are a vinegar fan like Pinuzzo.

After finishing the stuffed peppers, we roasted the seeds and ground them for hot pepper. If you do that, be careful not to do it on a windy day or in a drafty kitchen.

Whole hot peppers are also dried and ground for *peperoncino*, the ground hot pepper that is called for in many recipes in this book. Another use for hot peppers is in *Fuoco* (page 234), a hot pepper sauce I call "fire," which I first tasted in Salina in the Eolian Islands. It has a fresher taste than condiments made from dried peppers, and a little goes a very long way.

EGGPLANT

∞

Sicilians prepare eggplant, which the French and English call "aubergine," in so many different ways that you might say it's the national vegetable. Pity the poor Sicilian who doesn't like it, like my brother-in-law Gio, who likes to shock people by referring to "those

---

OVERLEAF: *An essential flavor of Sicily, the lemon grows in profusion; its perfume follows you everywhere.*

disgusting aubergines." But for those who do like eggplant, there's nothing better than a piece of grilled eggplant dripping with seasoned olive oil, eaten on a slice of bread cut to about the same size to absorb the oil. Sometimes the grilled slices are dressed with garlic and mint— mint has an affinity for eggplant; this dish is called *Melanzane Arrosto con Aglio e Menta* (page 235). Mint is also used to enhance eggplant in *Riso con Melanzane, Menta, e Capperi* (Cold Rice with Eggplant, Mint, and Capers, page 198).

ZUCCHINI
∽

Italy has many different kinds of green summer squash, all called *zucchina*. Fratelli Ingegnoli, the Burpee's of Italy, alone lists seventeen in its seed catalog. Some are short and fat, others long and skinny, or round, some smooth, others ridged; and they come in dark green, gray-green, and light green, striped or mottled.

One, *zucca lunga*, can grow up to six feet long as the vine climbs a tree or a trellis. This zucchini is now being marketed in the United States as "cucuzza squash"; you might see it in fancier supermarkets or food shops. (Seeds are also available.) Several good soups are made with it; *Minestra di Riso e Zucchine* (Rice and Zucchini Soup, page 236) is served at room temperature. If you don't find the cucuzza squash, substitute ordinary zucchini.

Another unusual zucchini is the *zucchina centenaria*. It's the shape of a pear or a quince but a little bigger; pale, pale green like the *zucca lunga*; and covered with shaggy green fuzz. The plant is usually found only in large old gardens because it takes up a lot of room. These are particularly good when fried. Peel the zucchini, cut it into *bâtonnets*, like french fries, and dredge them in flour, turning them so they are completely coated. When you are ready, deep-fry the zucchini. Even Alberto, my godson, who at twenty-three is the most fussy family member when it comes to food, loves these *zucchine fritte!* You can, of course, do this with other kinds of zucchini.

With the zucchini that are more like American ones, the blossoms are fried and slices of zucchini are fried too as a topping for pasta. The squash can also be stuffed in the manner of *Zucchine Pantesche Ripiene* (page 116) or layered with other vegetables as in *Pasticcio di*

Verdure Pantesco (page 121). It's also good raw in salad, *Insalata di Zucchine Verdi* (Zucchini Salad, page 237); for this the best way to cut the zucchini is into *bâtonnets*.

GREEN CAULIFLOWER
∽

I remember the first time Susan Derecskey and Ann Yonkers came to Regaleali to get to know Sicily and Sicilian flavors before starting work on *The Heart of Sicily*. The harvest was at its peak, both in the vineyard—Inzolia and the other grapes for Regaleali Bianco were being picked—and in the gardens. Green cauliflower, the first they had ever seen, was being harvested.

This green cauliflower doesn't taste the same as the white; it is grassier and not at all bland; it is better suited than the white to a dish like *Insalata di Cavolfiore* (page 238), a salad dressed with lemon juice and olive oil. The salad is very good served with hot or cold *Polpettone* (Sicilian Meat Loaf, page 241). Another good accompaniment to *Polpettone* is *Insalata Cotta Classica* (Potato Salad with Green Beans and Onions, page 239).

APPLES, QUINCES, AND POMEGRANATES
∽

The choice of fall fruit in Sicily includes late nectarines and peaches, pears and plums, prickly pears, pomegranates, persimmons, early apples, quinces (toward the end of the month), and, of course, grapes. The first citrus is a long way off, and we have only a few oranges and lemons from storage.

Fruit always presents a dilemma: It ripens faster than you can eat it. In Sicily, fruit is always served at the end of the meal, either whole or as fruit salad, *Insalata di Frutta* (page 242). Apples and pears are often combined in a *Granita di Mele e Pere* (page 166) on a hot day.

Sometimes it happens that the worms make a meal of the apples, but even so, there's usually a side they don't touch. Those parts, combined with a few good apples and a couple of unripe ones for their pectin, are perfect for canned apples to have in winter. One year as an experiment I added some tangerine marmalade that had failed to jell;

it gave the apples an unusual taste and color. Another good way to use a windfall of less than perfect apples is *Gelatina di Mele* (page 166).

I have seen several lost apple varieties in Sicily in recent years. Usually the orchards were abandoned because the fruit didn't ship well or were too ugly for fussy people to put in their fruit baskets, not because it didn't taste good. Among the lost fruits of Sicily is the sorb (*Sorbus terminalis*), a distant relative of the apple. Sorbs look like oval plums about one and a half inches (three centimeters) long; they are yellow with pink cheeks and grow in clusters. There is a saying in Italian, *"col tempo e con la paglia si maturano le sorbe"* (*"*sorbs ripen with time and straw"*), which means that sorbs never ripen on the tree.

The people who still have trees or know where to find abandoned ones pick the sorbs while still unripe and tie them in bunches. Then they put them under straw or hang them like cherry tomatoes—or *pomodorini* in the Eolians—until they turn rust colored and soft. At that point the sorb is ready to eat. The idea is to pick one off and squeeze it into your mouth.

The quince, which some believe to be the Golden Apple of mythology, is a close relative of the apple, botanically speaking, but since it cannot be eaten raw, it is nowhere near as versatile. Every fall we

ABOVE: *Sheaves of cut wheat. The harvest has just begun.*

gather huge quantities of it at Regaleali to make *Cotognata* (page 246), a thick, very sweet paste, which is a deep reddish jewel-like color, carnelian. We make *gelatina di cotogne* (quince jelly) from the quince cooking liquid. It's very nice to eat on buttered semolina bread for breakfast.

The tree in my garden at Regaleali does not bear enough fruit to make quince paste in the quantities we want, so we use wild quince; it looks as if it's been through a war, but it's fine for the paste. Quince turns coral-pink when poached in sugar syrup and a deep, almost garnet red when baked in wine. The sauce, sweetened and seasoned with cinnamon and clove, tastes like mulled wine.

The pomegranate or *melograno* in Italian—the word means seeded apple in both English and Italian—is another fruit of beautiful hue, in this case ruby red. Each tiny seed is surrounded by translucent, deep-red flesh. The pomegranate has a particular significance in Sicily since by eating one of those seeds, Persephone condemned herself to spend half the year in the underworld. Nothing so drastic is likely to happen to mere mortals who can't resist the temptation.

The hardest part of eating a pomegranate is getting it open. Each person has his or her own way. Mine is to cut a circle around the blossom end, score the skin several times from top to bottom, and gently break the fruit apart. Then I bend back the rind and pull out the seeds, being careful not break them and stain my hands or clothes.

The tart flavor and crunch of pomegranate seeds add immeasurably to a tossed green salad, and they are decorative as well. The way to get the most out of a pomegranate, though, is to juice it. At the Hotel Cipriani in Venice, they make a wonderful drink called *Tintoretto;* it's pomegranate juice and *prosecco*, a light sparkling wine from the Veneto region. To get it right, the seeds have to be freshly squeezed by hand in a potato ricer. Then, pour about three tablespoons of the juice into each of two champagne flutes, stir a bit of sugar into each, fill the flutes with bubbly wine, clink glasses, and look into each other's eyes as you sip.

CAROB

∞

The carob tree is a common sight in the countryside in Sicily. A large
evergreen with glossy leaves, it provides shade—a precious commod-
ity—in summer. The seed pods, also called Saint John's bread since
they supposedly nourished San Giovanni in the wilderness, ripen in
September. They contain a sweet pulp that resembles chocolate enough
to serve as a substitute for people who can't digest the real thing. In
fact, *budino di carrubbe* (carob pudding), was one of the specialties of
a macrobiotic health club that tried, unsuccessfully, to convert the
Palermitani a few years back. The pudding was made with carob powder, milk, and cornstarch and decorated with coconut. Dried carob
beans are also used for *caramelle di carruba*, little hard candies that
soothe a cough.

NUTS

∞

Starting in late August or early September, all of the different nuts that
are so much a part of the Sicilian flavor are picked and spread out on
blankets on the ground to dry in the sun. First are the almonds and bitter almonds. As soon as the new crop of almonds comes in, I make a
Semifreddo di Mandorle (Cold Almond Soufflé, page 244). It's still hot
in September, and a cold sweet dessert like this ends the meal on a festive note.

After the almonds come the hazelnuts and then the walnuts. The
green outer casing of the walnut falls off and you can get at the shell
and crack the nut open. Kernels of those first-of-the-season fresh walnuts are a treat you can have only if you or a friend has a walnut tree.

LA VENDEMMIA

∞

Summer in the country in Sicily is hot, dry, and dusty, but we stop
wishing for rain as soon as we start the wine harvest, the *vendemmia*.
In my grandfather's day, it was always started on the Monday after the
first Sunday in October. Always. No matter what. Now, it seems, every
year there's a new rule.

The grapes for sparkling wines are picked in mid-August. Then there's a pause while we wait for the enologist, who tests the grapes every day in the laboratory, to give the signal to start picking. Sometimes there is a storm, a break in the weather called *la rottura del tempo*, between the two *vendemmie*—that too used to be always!—but as long as it doesn't come when the grapes are ready to pick, the rain isn't likely to harm them. Last to be picked are the native varietals, in October, as in grandfather's time.

The *vendemmia* coincides with *l'apertura di caccia*, the opening of the hunt. In the early morning hours in the countryside, you can hear the sounds of gunshot as the men go about looking for rabbits and birds to shoot. Hunting is not such great sport as it once was, but we do get an occasional hare or two.

Hare is another one of those foods that you have to live in the country to enjoy, though it is available frozen by mail order in the United States (page 252). Even in Europe, you see it less and less often in the market. *Insalata di Lepre* (Hare Salad, page 240) is one of many good ways to prepare it.

VINO COTTO

∞

For a long time I'd wanted to make my own *vino cotto*, boiled-down must or grape juice. (*Vino cotto* is called *sapa* in mainland Italy.) I wanted to do this partly out of curiosity and partly to record the method before it got lost forever. At Regaleali and other places in the countryside, the women who used to make it either stopped doing it or moved away.

A concentrated fruit sugar, *vino cotto* has been used as a sweetener for thousands of years. It's the sweetener for *cuccìa* (page 140), the wheat berry pudding served on Santa Lucìa's Day in December. And it's an essential ingredient in certain confections, like *mostaccioli*, biscuits traditionally served on All Souls' Day. Vincenzo Curcio, who manages the land at Regaleali, remembers that as a child growing up in the country, he got a snack of toasted bread with *vino cotto* poured over it like honey. A drop of it in a glass of wine or grappa is something quite special. Now that I've made it, I find more and more uses for it: in *Mandarinetto* (Tangerine Cordial, page 70), in dessert fillings, in fruit salads, in herb-flavored vinegar—wherever a touch of sweetness is needed.

The main use of *vino cotto* in the not-so-distant past, though, was to combine it with fresh grape must to make a stronger wine, *vino incottato*, which could be sold at a higher price than ordinary wine. This practice has not entirely vanished, but it is nowhere near as widespread as it was when my father was a boy. He remembers the must boiling for hours over a roaring fire in tubs so huge you had to climb up on a ladder to look inside!

Vino cotto is also an old folk remedy. It's taken as a cough syrup, and Carmelo Di Martino, who is a great expert in such matters, says it's the best thing for flu, better than "those pills the Marchesa gives me" (Tylenol). His prescription: Warm up half a glass, as hot as you can bear it, drink it, and get into bed. Better bring a change of clothes, he says, because in fifteen minutes you'll be perspiring so much that whatever you're wearing will be soaked through.

When I finally got around to making *vino cotto* in the fall of 1994, the winery sent over forty liters (ten and one-half gallons) of white must, twenty percent *grado babo* (sugar degree). It arrived in the afternoon, too late to start cooking it, so we boiled it for ten minutes just to keep it from fermenting. The next morning we put it on the fire at nine o'clock. It started boiling properly by ten and went on and on until five in the afternoon.

When the must was reduced by half, we strained it to get rid of impurities and filled one bottle for my father, who wanted must reduced by half for one of his experiments. We then reduced the rest to a third of its original volume. Reduce to a third—that's what everyone and all the old books say—until the drop doesn't slip from the spoon. My father took a bottle of that, too, for his experiment.

About half an hour before I thought the remaining portion would be ready, I added a cheesecloth bundle containing cinnamon sticks, cloves, bay leaves, dried orange peel, fresh lemon peel, and jasmine flowers. When the *vino cotto* was done, we let it stand for twenty-four hours to settle and to cool; then, we bottled it. *Vino cotto* can be used right away, but it keeps for a long time.

If you want to make a small quantity of *vino cotto*, crush washed and stemmed green or red (not black) table grapes in a food mill and filter the juice through a coffee filter or double layer of rinsed cheesecloth. Boil the strained juice until it is reduced to one third. For one cup of *vino cotto*, you will need about two pounds of grapes.

Another grape product that goes back more than a thousand years, at least to the Middle Ages, is verjus, or *agresto* as it is called in Italian. This is the unfermented juice of unripe green grapes, a tart golden liquid that can be used much as vinegar and wine are used in cooking. The result, though, is much more delicate. Verjus is to be my next experiment with the fruits of the vine.

MOSTARDA DI MOSTO

One thing I don't think you can make unless you have your own winery—or one nearby that is willing to part with some of its must—is *mostarda di mosto*. For this confection, the must is boiled with white ash from *sarmenti* (vine runners) to clarify it, then cooked with flour to thicken it. The result is a slightly chewy, raisiny paste that is very intense in flavor.

Mostarda di mosto used to be made at Regaleali every year until the 1980s, and I was afraid the recipe had been or would be lost. Fortunately, Vincenzo's wife, Mary, had saved it. She came to Case Vecchio to help me and Graziella make the *mostarda*.

On the first try, some of the ashes were black and the *mostarda* turned out too dark and tasted like licorice—though we ate it all. On the second try, it was perfect. We wrapped the pieces in plastic and put them away in a tin box until December, for Christmas presents—not because the *mostarda* has to be stored, rather because it's a unique gift. Here's how we made the *mostarda*:

First we got the must; it has to be freshly squeezed from green grapes. We figured ten liters (about ten and one-half quarts) would be a good amount to work with. For that much must we needed about 150 grams (five ounces) of white ash. Graziella burned a huge amount of *sarmenti* until the ash was absolutely white with no black or unburned pieces. We had found out the hard way how important that is.

We boiled the must with the ashes, at a full boil, stirring often, until it reduced by about one fourth; this took about four hours. We left the must to stand overnight to allow the ashes to settle. Then we strained and filtered it. We had about seven and one-half liters.

Next, we poured the must back into a clean pot. For each liter (quart) of must, we sifted in one hundred grams (two-thirds sifted cup) of flour. We added about one hundred grams (one cup) each of walnuts and almonds cut into big pieces and the dried zest of three oranges (cut into small pieces). If you don't have dried zest, you can grate the zest of three oranges. We brought this mixture to a boil.

While we were waiting, we wet about thirty small molds or dessert dishes. When the must started to get warm, we began stirring constantly until it came back to a boil. We boiled it for about a minute until it had the consistency of a thick béchamel. We removed it from the heat and ladled it into the molds, which were left to stand in a cool place overnight.

The next morning, we lined trays with cloth, sprinkled the cloth with flour, unmolded the *mostarda,* and covered it with cheesecloth to keep the flies off it. We took the trays outdoors and left the *mostarda* to dry in the sun all day, turning the pieces over once and bringing the trays back inside at night. This continued for ten days, until the pieces no longer stuck to the cloth and could be cut easily with a knife. After one more week, we wrapped each piece in plastic and stored it all in airtight tins. If you want to have some left for Christmas presents, my advice is to lock the box and hide the key!

LA SAGRA DELL'UVA

On the last weekend in September, a big celebration is held in Vallelunga to honor the Madonna di Loreto, a mysterious black Madonna. One week later, a similar celebration is held to honor the Madonna del Rosario in Valledolmo on the other side of the hill. Both celebrations are called *la sagra dell'uva,* or the festival of the grape. Because of the modernization of wine making, however, the festival, which used to take place before the *vendemmia* began, now takes place in the middle.

An agricultural fair is held in connection with each festival. The booths that line the streets of the two villages are decorated with colorful pennants and banners. It's very festive and gay. All kinds of implements and equipment are sold—copper containers, wooden barrels and casks, ladders, lots of wooden utensils such as long spatulas for stirring ricotta. They lie in a jumble on folding tables, casually lean against the buildings, and cover the sidewalk so you have to tiptoe around them.

On the food side, honey and nut confections are the theme—not surprising since by the end of September all of the nuts have been dried and are ready to store and the bees have done their work. All sorts of honey are sold—some from flowers one has never heard of anywhere else—both plain and in the comb. An enormous variety of *torroni*, or brittles and nougats, and *cubbaite*, made only with sugar—mainly the diamond-shaped sesame seed ones—is sold.

The *torroni* are delicious—light golden brittle with blanched almonds, dark brittle with unblanched nuts, sticky nougat made with sugar and honey like *Torrone di Mandorle* (Almond Nougat, page 247). There is even white, green, and red *gelato di campagne*, a kind of fondant made in the colors of the Italian flag! Even though I make my own brittle, I always buy some at the fair, usually hazelnut, which I like very much but don't make because we don't have hazelnuts at Regaleali.

For years I was in charge of decorations for the *sagre*, for both the booth at Vallelunga and the parade of tractors at Valledolmo. For that event, each tractor pulls a cart carrying wine barrels and other paraphernalia behind it; the carts, like the booths, are adorned with sturdy vine branches and bunches of grapes. The participants try to make their carts and stalls the prettiest. Normally I enjoy this kind of challenge. Still, I was not unhappy to pass the task on to the younger generation so I could devote myself to my researches, particularly at this season when there is so much to do and learn.

THE RECIPES

SALSA DI POMODORO PASSATA

Classic Tomato Sauce

At Regaleali we always put a little sugar in tomato sauce; it seems to intensify the flavor of the tomatoes. I suggest you prepare a large quantity of sauce at a time. Use as much as you need and freeze the rest in one- or two-cup containers to have it always on hand.

THIS MAKES ABOUT 6 CUPS OF SAUCE.

4½ pounds (2 kg) ripe tomatoes
1 large onion, finely chopped
4 cloves garlic, minced
½ cup (125 ml) olive oil
½ cup (30 g) basil leaves, shredded
1 tablespoon dried oregano
2 teaspoons sugar
Salt and freshly ground black pepper

Wash the tomatoes and cut them up but do not peel or seed them. Put them in a large saucepan, cover, and cook over low heat, stirring occasionally, until soft, 20 to 30 minutes. Pass the tomatoes through a food mill. Set the puree aside.

Sauté the onion and garlic in the olive oil in a medium saucepan until golden. Stir in the puree, the basil leaves, oregano, sugar, and salt and pepper to taste.

Cover and cook, stirring occasionally, until thickened, about 20 minutes.

NOTE. *If you want to puree the tomatoes in a food processor, you will have to peel them before cooking.*

SALSA DI POMODORO PICCANTE

Spicy Tomato Sauce

This sauce has to be cooked until it is very thick and does not separate. At Regaleali, we make it in batches of 100 kilos (225 pounds) of tomatoes. The huge cauldron usually used for ricotta is set up over a fire in the courtyard and the tomatoes are washed and thrown in whole. (For smaller quantities, the cooking goes faster if they are cut up.) Amounts in this recipe are more manageable; still, they make more sauce than usually needed at one time for pasta or any other dish. Use some, refrigerate some—the sauce will keep for up to one week in the refrigerator—and freeze the rest for later.

THIS MAKES ABOUT 6 CUPS OF SAUCE.

4¹/₂ pounds (2 kg) ripe tomatoes
1 large onion, quartered
6 cloves garlic
2 bay leaves
2 teaspoons sugar
2 tablespoons salt
¹/₂ cup (30 g) basil leaves
1 small red chili, seeded and cut up, or 1 teaspoon
  ground hot pepper
¹/₂ cup (125 ml) olive oil

Wash the tomatoes and cut them up, but do not peel or seed them. Put them in a large saucepan with the onion, 2 cloves of the garlic, and bay leaves. Cover and cook over low heat, stirring occasionally, until soft, 20 to 30 minutes.

Remove and discard the bay leaves; pass the rest through a food mill. Pour back into the saucepan and bring to a boil. Stir in the sugar and salt. Cover and cook over low heat, stirring from time to time, more and more often as the sauce thickens, until very thick, 30 to 45 minutes, depending on how juicy the tomatoes were.

Puree the basil leaves, chili, and the remaining 4 cloves of garlic with some of the olive oil in a food processor. Stir into the sauce and cook for 5 minutes more. Check the seasoning: The sauce should be very tasty. Stir in the remaining olive oil.

FORMAGGIO AL POMODORO
Baked Cheese with Tomato Sauce
This makes a very satisfying appetizer or snack. Eat it immediately, being careful not to burn your tongue. Serve the baked cheese with plenty of bread for mopping up the sauce.

THIS MAKES ENOUGH FOR 4 PEOPLE AS AN APPETIZER.

¾ pound (350 g) cheese, such as caciocavallo, fontina, goat's milk gouda, or mozzarella, sliced ⅜ inch (1 cm) thick
1 cup (250 ml) Salsa di Pomodoro Piccante (page 229)

Preheat the oven to 250° F. (120° C.). Oil a 9 × 13-inch (23 × 33-cm) baking dish.

Pour some of the sauce over the bottom of the dish and put the cheese slices, touching each other or slightly overlapping, on top. Spread the rest of the sauce to cover all of the cheese. Bake until the cheese begins to melt, about 10 minutes. Serve hot.

VARIATIONS. *Formaggio con Acciuga al Forno* (Baked Cheese with Anchovies). Top the cheese with 6 anchovy fillets, torn into pieces and placed here and there, instead of the tomato sauce. Drizzle with oil and bake until the cheese melts.

Uova in Tegamino al Pomodoro (Baked Cheese with Eggs). Heat the tomato sauce and cover the bottom of a single-portion gratin dish with it. Top with slices of melting cheese—mozzarella is good—and put the dish in the oven for 6 to 7 minutes. When the cheese just starts to melt, break 2 eggs on top, sprinkle lightly with salt, and cover with a lid. Bake for 3 minutes, or until the eggs are set to your liking.

FRITTATA DI POMODORO, CIPOLLA, E BASILICO
Tomato, Onion, and Basil Frittata

Sicilian onions are extraordinarily sweet and our basil is very perfumed. Make this frittata with sweet red, white, or yellow onions, such as Vidalias, Mauis, or Walla Wallas, in season.

THIS MAKE ENOUGH FOR 4 PEOPLE.

1 small red onion, thinly sliced
4 tablespoons (60 ml) olive oil
3 medium-size ripe tomatoes (400 g), juiced, seeded, and
  roughly chopped
6 large eggs
Salt
Ground hot pepper
1 cup (60 g) basil, roughly chopped or torn

Sauté the onion in 3 tablespoons of the oil in a nonstick or well-seasoned heavy 8-inch (20-cm) skillet over medium-low heat until limp. Add the tomatoes and stir until some of the juice evaporates.

Lightly beat the eggs in a bowl and season with salt and hot pepper to taste. Stir in the basil. Pour on top of the tomato mixture, spreading the eggs to the edges of the pan. Let cook until lightly browned on the bottom, 6 to 8 minutes. Lift the edge with a spatula to peek.

Slip the frittata onto a pan lid or plate, lightly grease the pan with the remaining 1 tablespoon olive oil, put the pan on the lid, and invert. Cook until brown.

Slide the frittata onto a serving plate. Serve at room temperature, cut into wedges.

PEPERONI ARROSTO CON OLIO E ACETO

Sliced Roasted Peppers with Oil and Vinegar

Covered with oil, these peppers will keep for several days at room temperature. They make a good snack.

THIS MAKES ENOUGH FOR 8 TO 10 PEOPLE AS AN APPETIZER.

1½ pounds (675 g) peppers (10 cubanellas or 6 bell peppers)
1 teaspoon dried oregano
1 tablespoon red wine vinegar
Salt
Olive oil

Roast the peppers in a hot oven, under the broiler, or on the grill until charred all over. Let stand until cool enough to handle. Peel away the skin with a small knife or rub it off.

Cut the peppers lengthwise into pieces, 2 or 3 pieces per cubanella, 4 pieces per bell pepper. Remove and discard the seeds, ribs, and stems. Place in a serving dish and sprinkle with the oregano, vinegar, and salt to taste. Pour on enough olive oil to cover. Let stand for at least 1 hour before serving.

ABOVE: *Fresh hot peppers, both the long twisted ones and the round cherry peppers, liven up Sicilian food.*

PEPERONCINI ROSSI RIPIENI
Stuffed Cherry Peppers

The hardest part of making these stuffed peppers is getting them into the jars without dropping the stuffing. You may want to put up smaller jars for gifts.

THIS MAKES ABOUT 8 1-PINT (500-ML) JARS OF PEPPERS.

6½ pounds (3 kg) cherry peppers, mostly red with some green
4 cups (1 l) white wine vinegar
4 cups (1 l) water
¼ cup (40 g) coarse salt
1 pound (450 g) pepper-stuffed olives
1 pound (450 g) salted anchovies, rinsed and filleted
1½ cups (250 g) capers, rinsed
Olive oil

Using a small pointed knife, neatly core the peppers and remove the seeds and ribs. Discard the cores; set the seeds and ribs aside.

Combine the vinegar, water, and salt in a saucepan and bring to a boil. Add the peppers. When the liquid comes back to a boil, remove the peppers and place upside down on paper towels to drain.

Chop the olives, anchovies, and capers. Stuff the peppers with this mixture.

Put the peppers in a wide-mouthed jar, alternating red and green peppers. Fill the jars with olive oil and let stand for several hours. Add more oil if needed to cover the peppers. Close the jars and process in a hot-water bath (page 211). The peppers can be eaten immediately, but they improve with age.

Preheat the oven to 150° F. (70° C.).

Spread out the reserved seeds and ribs on a baking sheet and roast until golden brown, about 2 hours. Let cool.

Grind the seeds and ribs to a powder in a spice mill. Transfer to jars to store. Be sure there are no drafts or wind when you remove the powder. You should have about 1 cup of ground hot pepper.

NOTE. *For smaller quantities, just divide the ingredients proportionately.*

FUOCO
Hot Pepper Sauce

Use this sauce wherever you would use hot pepper sauce. It has a nice fresh flavor. This recipe makes a large batch. Since it's processed, it will keep for at least a year. Put a jar in your Christmas baskets.

THIS MAKES 10 TO 12 HALF-PINT (500-ML) JARS.

6 pounds (275 kg) ripe tomatoes, peeled
Sugar
Salt
1 pound (450 g) hot chili peppers, preferably the long twisted
  ones, washed and stemmed
1 pound (450 g) capers, rinsed
4 cloves garlic
1 cup (60 g) basil leaves, torn if large
3 cups (750 ml) olive oil

If the tomatoes are very juicy, cut them across and squeeze out some of the juice and seeds. Coarsely chop the tomatoes and put them in a colander. Sprinkle generously with sugar and salt and toss. Let stand for at least 2 hours to drain thoroughly.

Combine the hot peppers, capers, garlic, basil, and 2 tablespoons salt in a bowl. Working in 3 batches, chop the mixture in a food processor with ¼ cup of the olive oil per batch until coarsely chopped. Mix in one third of the tomatoes and process, stopping from time to time to scrape down the sides of the bowl, to a finer consistency. Transfer to a clean bowl. Continue until all is processed. Slowly stir in the remaining olive oil. Be careful not to overprocess.

Spoon the sauce into hot sterilized jars, cover, and process in a hot-water bath (page 211). Store in a cool dry place for at least 2 weeks before eating.

MELANZANE ARROSTO CON AGLIO E MENTA
Roasted Eggplant Slices with Garlic and Mint

The best way to eat these eggplant slices is on a big piece of bread, but you can use a knife and fork if the situation demands. Use as much or as little oil as you want; I think it's best when the slices are completely covered with oil. Proportions are for one eggplant, but you should make more; the dish keeps well at room temperature.

THIS MAKES ENOUGH FOR 4 PEOPLE AS AN APPETIZER.

1 medium eggplant (10 oz/300 g)
Salt
Olive oil
Juice of ½ lemon
½ teaspoon dried oregano
½ clove garlic, minced
6 mint leaves, torn

Peel the eggplant, entirely if the skin is tough or in strips if not, and cut into ⅜-inch (1-cm) slices. Sprinkle with salt, place in a colander, and let stand for 20 minutes.

Blot the slices dry. Pour some of the olive oil in a dish and dip the slices, lightly coating both sides, or paint them using a pastry brush. Broil or grill the slices until lightly browned, about 5 minutes per side.

Make a layer of eggplant slices in the bottom of a serving dish. Sprinkle with salt, olive oil, lemon juice, and oregano. Sprinkle with some of the garlic and mint. Continue layering until all the eggplant is used. Pour on enough olive oil to cover. Let stand for 1 hour before serving. Serve at room temperature.

NOTE. *You can also grill the eggplant dry, then layer it with the oil and other ingredients.*

MINESTRA DI RISO E ZUCCHINE
Rice and Zucchini Soup

This soup is made in Sicily with *zucca lunga*, which is being marketed in the United States as cucuzza squash. Ordinary zucchini can be substituted. As is often the case in Sicily, this soup, which Sicilians like thick, is served at room temperature.

THIS MAKES ENOUGH FOR 6 PEOPLE.

1 cucuzza squash, 40 inches (1 m) long, or 1½ pounds (675 g)
  zucchini, peeled and cut into ¾-inch (2-cm) cubes
1 onion, sliced
3 medium-size ripe tomatoes (1 lb/450 g), peeled and coarsely
  chopped
1 cup (60 g) basil leaves, shredded
½ cup (125 ml) olive oil
Salt and freshly ground black pepper
2 cups (500 ml) water
1 beef bouillon cube
1 cup (75 g) cooked rice
2 tablespoons grated pecorino or parmesan

Combine the squash, onion, tomatoes, basil, ¼ cup of the olive oil, and salt and pepper to taste in a medium saucepan over medium heat. (We call this *tutto dentro*, or all in together.) Cover and cook for 15 minutes.

Stir in the water and the bouillon cube; bring back to a boil. Reduce the heat, cover, and simmer until tender, 15 to 20 minutes.

Turn off the heat and stir in the rice and additional water if the soup seems too thick. Stir in the pecorino and remaining olive oil. Serve at room temperature.

INSALATA DI ZUCCHINE VERDI
Zucchini Salad

I like to serve this salad soon after making is since I like the zucchini crunchy. Others prefer to let the salad sit for a while so the flavors of the sauce penetrate the little zucchini sticks.

THIS MAKES ENOUGH FOR 6 PEOPLE.

1 pound (450 g) small green zucchini
1 tablespoon red or white wine vinegar
¼ cup (60 ml) olive oil
Salt
Ground hot pepper
3 tablespoons chopped flat-leaf parsley

Peel the zucchini, entirely if it's been waxed or sprayed, partially if not, and cut it into ⅜-inch (1-cm) sticks, each about 2 inches (5 cm) long.

In the bottom of a serving bowl, mix together the vinegar, oil, and salt and ground hot pepper to taste. Add the zucchini and toss to coat. Sprinkle with the chopped parsley and serve.

INSALATA DI CAVOLFIORE

Cauliflower Salad

You can make this salad with white cauliflower if green cauliflower, marketed in the United States as broccoflower, is not available. You could also use purple cauliflower, which turns light green when cooked.

THIS MAKES ENOUGH FOR 6 PEOPLE.

1 large head broccoflower (1 lb/45 g)
½ cup (125 ml) olive oil
1 lemon, cut in half (optional)
1 tablespoon chopped flat-leaf parsley
1 lemon, cut into wedges

Core the cauliflower and cut it into large pieces; clean and wash them.

Bring a large pot of salted water to a boil. Cook the cauliflower for about 7 minutes, or until the stalk can be pierced easily with a fork but the florets are still intact. Remove with a slotted spoon and place on a serving platter.

Pour the olive oil over the cauliflower. If desired, squeeze the lemon halves over all. Sprinkle with the parsley and garnish with the lemon wedges. Serve at room temperature.

INSALATA COTTA CLASSICA
Potato Salad with Green Beans and Onions

As the Italian name of the dish says, this is the classic salad of cooked vegetables. It's a pleasant change from plain potato salad.

THIS MAKES ENOUGH FOR 4 TO 6 PEOPLE.

½ pound (225 g) green beans
Salt
2¼ pounds (1 kg) waxy new potatoes, scrubbed
1 medium-size red onion, washed but unpeeled
Freshly ground black pepper
¼ cup (30 g) chopped mixed fresh herbs, such as flat-leaf
  parsley, mint, basil, or thyme, plus dried oregano
Pinch of ground hot pepper
3 tablespoons red wine vinegar
¼ cup (125 ml) olive oil

Tip the beans and if they are thick, "French" them, that is, cut them lengthwise in half.

Bring a large pot of salted water to a boil. Gradually slip the beans into the water without letting it stop boiling. Boil, uncovered, until tender, about 7 minutes. Drain and rinse with cold water. Spread out to hasten cooling. Set aside.

Meanwhile, put the potatoes in a medium saucepan, cover with cold water, and bring to a boil. Add 2 teaspoons salt. Reduce the heat, cover, and simmer until barely tender, 25 to 35 minutes depending on size. After 15 minutes, add the onion. Drain and let stand until cool enough to handle.

Peel the potatoes while still warm and cut them into chunks. Peel the onion and cut into wedges. Place the potatoes and onion in a large serving bowl and add the green beans; sprinkle generously with salt and pepper. Sprinkle with the herbs and hot pepper.

Combine the vinegar and olive oil in a cup, pour over the vegetables, and toss to coat everything. Serve the salad at room temperature soon after it is made.

INSALATA DI LEPRE
Hare Salad

When the men come back from the hunt, we have enough hare to make several different dishes. Hare is available by mail order (page 252); rabbit is sold in specialty butcher shops and some supermarkets.

THIS MAKES ENOUGH FOR 4 PEOPLE.

2 rabbit legs (1 lb/450 g total weight)
3 stalks celery
1 small carrot
3 sprigs of flat-leaf parsley
1 small red onion
1 clove garlic
1 beef bouillon cube
3 tablespoons fresh lemon juice
¼ cup (60 ml) olive oil
2 tablespoons minced red onion
Salt and freshly ground black pepper
2 tablespoons minced flat-leaf parsley

Put the rabbit legs in a saucepan, cover with water, and bring to a boil. Drain.

Put the legs back in the pot and cover with water. Make a bouquet garni with 1 celery stalk, the carrot, and the parsley sprigs. Add to the pot, along with the onion, garlic, and bouillon cube. Simmer over low heat until the meat is tender, 30 minutes. Remove the legs from the broth and let cool. (Save the broth for another purpose.)

While the legs are cooling, cut the remaining 2 celery stalks into julienne. When the legs are cool enough to handle, strip the meat from the bones. Put the meat in a salad bowl and add the celery julienne. Add the lemon juice, olive oil, and minced onion; toss well. Season to taste with salt and pepper; sprinkle with the minced parsley. Serve at room temperature.

VARIATION. *Insalata di Lingua* (Tongue Salad). Cook veal tongue for 45 to 50 minutes, or until tender. Continue as for rabbit salad.

POLPETTONE
Sicilian Meat Loaf
This meat loaf is baked in an unusual way—it is braised in the oven so it cooks by both dry and wet heat—which keeps it very moist.
THIS MAKES ENOUGH FOR 8 PEOPLE.

2¼ pounds (1 kg) ground beef or a combination of beef, pork,
* and veal*
½ cup (60 g) finely chopped mint and flat-leaf parsley
½ cup (60 g) grated parmesan
3 large eggs
½ cup (60 g) dry breadcrumbs
Salt and freshly ground black pepper
1 cup (30 g) torn pieces of stale bread, soaked in water to cover
1 small onion, chopped
2 tablespoons olive oil
1 beef bouillon cube, dissolved in 1 cup (250 ml) hot water
2 sprigs of fresh rosemary
2 sprigs of fresh sage

Put the meat in a large bowl, and add the mint and parsley, parmesan, eggs, breadcrumbs, and salt and pepper to taste. Squeeze the water from the bread and add. Knead thoroughly with one hand until the ingredients are well blended and the mixture is like a paste. Form into a big salami shape about 12 × 3 inches (30 × 8 cm). Set aside for at least 30 minutes.

Meanwhile, preheat the oven to 350° F. (180° C.).

Sauté the onion in the oil in a baking pan. Stir in the dissolved bouillon. Place the meat loaf in the pan, and put a sprig of rosemary and a sprig of sage on each side of the loaf.

Bake for about 45 minutes, or until well browned.

Let stand for at least 20 minutes before slicing. Serve warm or at room temperature.

INSALATA DI FRUTTA

Fresh Fruit Salad

Few simple desserts are nicer than a salad made with fresh fruits in season. It is also a good way to dress up dull, out-of-season fruit. Use grappa or match a fruit brandy to the fruit you are using; Grand Marnier goes with everything.

THIS MAKES ENOUGH FOR 4 TO 6 PEOPLE.

¼ cup (60 ml) grappa or fruit brandy, such as Poire William,
   Calvados, or Grand Marnier
2 bananas, cut into rounds
2 pears, cored and cut into bite-size pieces
2 apples, cored and cut into bite-size pieces
Juice of ½ lemon
Juice of ½ orange
3 tablespoons Marmellata di Fragole (page 96) or citrus
   marmalade
Sugar

Pour the grappa into a serving bowl.

Put the bananas, pears, and apples into the bowl as you cut them. Add the lemon and orange juices, marmalade, and sugar to taste and turn the fruit in the sauce, being sure to coat all surfaces. Let stand for at least 1 hour to marinate. Stir again before serving.

ABOVE: *The fruit of the walnut ripens through the summer and drops to the ground in the fall.*

SEMIFREDDO DI MANDORLE
Cold Almond Soufflé

Ever since I first tasted this *semifreddo* at the Monte San Giuliano restaurant in Erice, I have kept it in my repertoire. It is best when made with the new crop of almonds in September. My sister Costanza makes it with hazelnuts, which grow on her property, and I have made it with walnuts also. This recipe makes two cold soufflés; it hardly seems worthwhile to do only one since you have to make a quantity of praline, and the soufflé keeps well in the freezer.

THIS MAKES 2 SOUFFLÉS, EACH SERVING 8 TO 10 PEOPLE.

PRALINE

1 cup (200 g) sugar
Grated zest of 1 orange
1½ cups (170 g) blanched almonds

10 eggs, separated
1½ cups (300 g) sugar
2 teaspoons vanilla extract
½ teaspoon almond extract (optional)
4 cups (1 l) heavy cream
Pinch of salt
¼ cup (60 ml) rum

To make the praline, oil a heat-resistant surface (the back of a jelly-roll pan is good) and a spatula and place it near the stove.

Combine the sugar and orange zest in a large sauté pan and cook over low heat, without stirring, but shaking the pan from time to time, until the sugar is almost melted. Add the almonds and stir with 2 wooden spoons until the sugar turns brown and the almonds are coated. Pour the mixture out onto the oiled surface and spread it out, using the spatula. Score it with the spatula or a knife. Let cool.

Meanwhile, for the *semifreddo*, use an electric beater to beat the egg yolks with 1 cup of the sugar and the vanilla and almond extract, if using. Beat until a ribbon forms, 20 to 25 minutes. The mixture should be thick enough to write your name with it. Refrigerate until ready to assemble the soufflé. Whip the cream with the remaining ½ cup sugar until soft peaks form. Refrigerate until ready to use.

Break the praline apart and crush it to a medium-fine powder. Use on/off pulses if doing this in the food processor.

Prepare two 8-cup (2-liter) soufflé dishes, metal molds, or small springform pans by lightly buttering them and lining them with foil to make the soufflés easier to remove later. Make the foil come up higher than the rim, like a soufflé collar. Sprinkle the foil with some of the praline powder.

Beat the egg whites with a pinch of salt until stiff but not dry.

Fold the egg yolk mixture into the whipped cream. Fold in the whites, slowly adding the remaining praline a little at a time. Stir in the rum. Divide evenly between the soufflé dishes; smooth the tops. Cover and put in the freezer overnight.

To serve, remove from the freezer 30 minutes before serving. (If you are not serving both soufflés, wrap one well in aluminum foil and freeze it. Remove it from the freezer several hours before serving.) Caress the dish with your warm hands or a warm napkin or towel. Gently unmold the dessert by pulling up the foil.

Place on a pretty plate and remove all of the foil. Let stand to soften, about 15 minutes, depending on the weather. Using a knife dipped into hot water, cut the soufflé into thin wedges to serve.

ABOVE: *Flavorful wild quince makes the best Cotognata (page 246), though we also make it with cultivated fruit.*

COTOGNATA

Quince Paste

Wild quinces are small compared to the giant cultivated ones I have seen in stores in the United States, and there is more waste. But there is no difference in the method or results. What's important is to cook the puree with sugar until it is very thick, almost impossible to stir.

THIS MAKES 5 TO 6 CUPS (1,25 TO 1,5 L) OF PASTE.

4½ pounds (2 kg) quinces
3 lemons, scrubbed and sliced
About 2¼ pounds (1 kg) sugar (about 5 cups)
Juice of 4 lemons

Wash the quinces and put them in a large pot. Add the lemon slices and water to cover. Cook, uncovered, until tender enough to be pierced with a fork, about 30 minutes. Drain, discarding the lemon slices.

Quarter and core the quinces and pass them through a food mill. Weigh the puree and put it back in the pot. Weigh out about three quarters as much sugar and stir it into the puree. Add the lemon juice.

Bring the mixture to a boil. Reduce the heat and simmer, stirring constantly. Protect your hand and arm, as the puree is very hot and will spatter. Cook until the puree is very stiff and shiny, about 1 hour.

Oil a pan or several dessert dishes or small molds. Spoon the puree into the pan or molds, cover with cheesecloth, and put it out in the sun to dry for 4 to 5 days, bringing it inside at night.

When the paste begins to pull away from the sides of the mold, unmold it and invert to dry the other side. Leave, uncovered, in a cool, dry place for up to 1 month. Wrap in wax paper after that.

NOTE. *If it's not possible to dry the paste in the sun, leave it in a warm dry place (a breezy spot, like a sunporch, would be good) for as long as it takes to dry. When the paste loses its tackiness on top, unmold it to dry the bottom.*

TORRONE DI MANDORLE
Almond Nougat

Once you start eating this very sweet and very sticky confection, you can't stop. It should be sandwiched between *ostie*, thin flour wafers, the same as are used for the Host of Holy Communion. Imported from Germany, where they are called *Oblaten*, they are available by mail order. If you can't find them, make the nougat without them.

THIS MAKES 3 ½ POUNDS (1,5 KG) OF NOUGAT.

1 pound (450 g) honey
1 cup (200 g) sugar
3 egg whites
2¼ pounds (1 kg) blanched almonds
1 package edible wafer paper (optional)

Wet a heat-resistant surface (the back of a jelly-roll pan is good) and set it near the stove.

Combine the honey, sugar, and egg whites in the bowl of an electric mixer and beat until the mixture becomes white and very shiny, about 15 minutes.

Transfer the mixture to a small saucepan over low heat. Add the almonds, stirring constantly, until the syrup turns pale gold, 10 to 15 minutes. Drop some on a small dish and feel it with your fingers; it should be tacky.

Transfer to the wet surface. Wet your hands thoroughly and mold the mixture into two 10½-inch (26-cm) squares, each about ¾ inch (2 cm) thick. Cut them to fit the wafer paper, if using. Place 2 sheets of paper on the work surface, top with a piece of nougat, and cover with 2 more sheets of the paper. Press down with a pan. Cut into pieces the size of 2 bites and wrap in plastic. Store in a cool dry place.

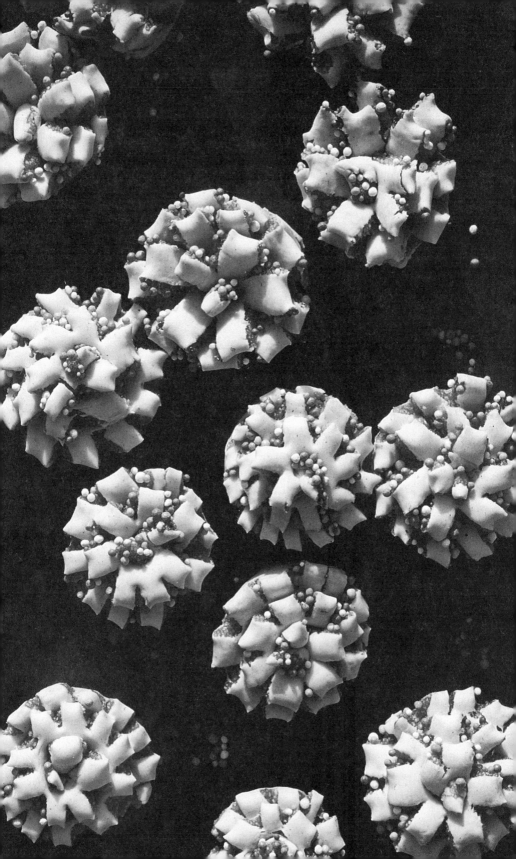

NELLA NOSTRA DISPENSA

Certain ingredients in the recipes in this book may be unusual or hard to find, although many are more widely available now than when I wrote *The Heart of Sicily*. Mail-order sources are listed on page 252, but look in a large supermarket or specialty food store first.

ANCHOVIES. Sicilians use salted anchovies, which are available from Dean & Deluca and from many Italian grocery stores. They have to be rinsed and filleted before using. You can substitute canned anchovies, the flat fillets.

BOUILLON CUBES. We use bouillon cubes that have no additives. They give good strong flavor to soups and stews. If you don't want to use the cubes, substitute homemade meat stock or canned broth.

BREAD. Our bread is made from semolina flour, usually with a sourdough starter, although the one in this book is made with yeast. It is never wasted or thrown away. Make crostini, croutons, or bread-crumbs with stale bread.

CAPERS. We use salted capers, mostly from the island of Pantelleria. They are big and juicy. Salted capers are available from Dean & Deluca and many Italian grocery stores. You may want to rinse them before using. You can substitute brined capers.

CHEESE. Caciocavallo, a cow's milk cheese, and pecorino, sheep's milk cheese, both in slices or chunks and grated, are used extensively in Sicily. Parmesan from northern Italy is an acceptable substitute for pecorino, but it won't give the same sharp flavor.

CORNSTARCH. We use cornstarch (or wheat starch) in desserts like *Gelo di Melone* and *Biancomangiare*.

LEFT: *Colored sugar sprinkles offset the whiteness of the dough of Mustazzuoli (page 128).*

CURRANTS. These are dried tiny grapes, a very Sicilian flavor.

FLOUR. We use both semolina flour and 00 flour. You can buy semolina flour in the United States, but it is rather coarse. Grind it in the food processor for about five minutes, or until it feels silky. The 00 flour is similar to American *bleached* all-purpose flour, and we use it for cakes, pastries, and sauce thickening. King Arthur Flour Baker's Catalogue advertises a 00-type flour if you would like to experiment.

GARLIC. Not so vital a flavor as in other parts of Italy. We almost never use it raw.

GELATIN. European gelatin comes in sheets. I have adapted my recipes to American granular gelatin.

HERBS. Herbs are extensively used in Sicilian cooking. Many kinds thrive in the dry, sunny climate. Among the most commonly used are basil, bay, mint, flat-leaf parsley, rosemary, sage, thyme, and wild fennel. Oregano is *always* used dried. Recently I started using dill in my herb mixtures and cilantro in my flavored vinegars.

HONEY. The oldest sweetener known to man. I sometimes put a drop in my salad dressing if the lemon juice is very sour.

LEGUMES AND DRIED BEANS. Lentils, fava beans, and chick peas have been known since antiquity. Dried chick peas and favas are ground for flour as well as cooked whole. Many varieties of New World beans are grown as well.

LEMONS. Lemons of all sizes, from the small *Verdello* to the huge citron, grow everywhere in Sicily and are used to flavor just about everything.

OILS AND FATS. Olive oil is used extensively in Sicily, but in recent years, people have started to use vegetable oil for frying. Always use the best quality you can afford. Other fats include butter, margarine, and lard, though lard is used less now than it was in the past.

OLIVES. Olives are plentiful in Sicily, and both black and green ones are used in cooking and on the table. In recent years, many fine European olives have been turning up in specialty food stores in the United States. For a treat, try the Sicilian Cerignola olive.

ONIONS. Sicilian onions are quite sweet. Use red onions or one of the sweet varieties like Vidalia, Maui, or Walla Walla.

PASTA. Mostly, we use dried pasta. We always cook the long strand or ribbon shapes al dente.

PINE NUTS. Especially when combined with currants, a basic Sicilian flavor.

PORK PRODUCTS. Sicilians love pork, but I tend not to cook much with it, except for prosciutto and cooked ham.

RICE. Dishes in this book call for long-grain rice, though Sicilians do use short-grain rice for risotto. White rice is preferred.

SPICES AND OTHER SEASONINGS. Saffron is an ancient Sicilian flavoring. Many households still season food only with salt and black pepper, but I like to add a touch of ground hot pepper.

SUGAR. Almost an addiction for Sicilians. In addition to sweets, it is used for sweet-and-sour sauces. Many Sicilians—but not all—use sugar with tomatoes to bring out their flavor.

TOMATOES. The Sicilian sun gives tomatoes a rich, deep flavor. We eat tomatoes fresh as long as they are in season and preserve them in sauce, in *estratto*, a tomato paste, and by drying them in the sun to have the rest of the year.

TUNA (CANNED). Canned tuna is one of the handiest things to have in the cupboard. You can always make a pasta sauce, a salad, a mousse, or a pâté with it.

VINEGAR. In the land of the grape, there is always vinegar, wine vinegar. Most people use red wine vinegar.

WINE. I use wine everywhere in cooking.

MAIL-ORDER SOURCES

BALDUCCI'S
424 Avenue of the Americas
New York, NY 10011
800/225-3822
Large variety of foodstuffs.

D'ARTAGNAN, INC.
399-419 St. Paul Avenue
Jersey City, NJ 07306
800/327-8246
Game meats, including hare.

DEAN & DELUCA
560 Broadway
New York, NY 10012
800/221-7714
Salted capers, salted anchovies, cheeses, olives, olive oil, vinegar, imported pasta, dried beans, almond flour, sea salt, spices, and dried herbs.

HADLEY FRUIT ORCHARDS
P.O. Box 495
Cabazon, CA 92230
800/854-5655
Excellent quality dried fruits and nuts.

KING ARTHUR FLOUR BAKER'S CATALOGUE
P.O. Box 876
Norwich, VT 05055
800/827-6836
Kamut wheat berries; baking ingredients, including semolina flour, 00-type flour (called American "Italian" flour), and baker's ammonia; and baking equipment.

LA CUISINE
323 Cameron Street
Alexandria, VA 22314-3219
800/521-1176
Baking equipment, including cannoli molds, and ingredients, including baker's ammonia and *Oblaten.*

MAID OF SCANDINAVIA. *SEE* **SWEET CELEBRATIONS.**

MOZZARELLA COMPANY
2944 Elm Street
Dallas, TX 75226
800/798-2954
Italian-style cheeses, including fresh mozzarella and sheep's milk ricotta.

SWEET CELEBRATIONS
7009 Washington Avenue South
Edina, MN 55439
800/328-6722
Large selection of baking equipment, including cannoli molds, and ingredients, including baker's ammonia.

VIVANDE PORTA VIA
2125 Fillmore Street
San Francisco, CA 94115
415/346-4430
Italian pantry specialties include imported olive oils, vinegars, flours, beans, cheeses, Sicilian sea salt, Pantelleria capers, and many other hard to find items.

WILLIAMS-SONOMA
100 North Point Street
San Francisco, CA 94133
800/541-2233
Kitchen equipment and ingredients.

ZINGERMAN'S
422 Detroit Street
Ann Arbor, MI 48104
313/663-3400
Foodstuffs, including olives, olive oil, vinegar, sea salt, spices, and dried herbs.

INDEX